D1292121

FOR DATE DUE
SEE CARD IN BOOK POCKET

mcCherg
707250

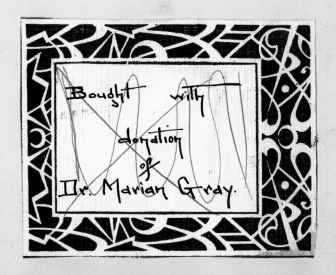
Bought with
donation
of
Dr. Marian Gray.

LITTLE ROCK PUBLIC LIBRARY

MARLBOROUGH
HIS LIFE AND TIMES

VOLUME I
1650–1688

BY WINSTON S. CHURCHILL

JOHN, DUKE OF MARLBOROUGH
By permission of Earl Spencer

MARLBOROUGH

HIS LIFE AND TIMES

By

THE RIGHT HONOURABLE

WINSTON S. CHURCHILL, C.H.

LITTLE ROCK PUBLIC LIBRARY

VOLUME I

LITTLE ROCK PUBLIC LIBRARY

1650-1688

NEW YORK

CHARLES SCRIBNER'S SONS

MCMXXXIII

COPYRIGHT, 1933, BY
CHARLES SCRIBNER'S SONS

Printed in the United States of America

*All rights reserved. No part of this book
may be reproduced in any form without
the permission of Charles Scribner's Sons*

A

LITTLE ROCK PUBLIC LIBRARY

TO
THE GRENADIER GUARDS
FORMERLY "THE 1ST GUARDS,"
IN WHICH JOHN CHURCHILL,
AFTERWARDS DUKE OF MARLBOROUGH,
RECEIVED HIS FIRST COMMISSION ON SEPTEMBER 14, 1667,
OF WHICH HE WAS COLONEL FROM THE YEAR 1704 TO 1711
AND FROM 1714 TILL HIS DEATH,
AND WHICH SERVED UNDER HIM AT THE BATTLES OF
THE SCHELLENBERG, BLENHEIM, RAMILLIES, OUDENARDE,
AND MALPLAQUET,
AND IN ALL THE PRINCIPAL SIEGES AND OTHER
GREAT OPERATIONS
DURING TEN VICTORIOUS CAMPAIGNS,
THIS WORK IS DEDICATED BY THE AUTHOR
IN MEMORY OF
THE COURTESIES AND KINDNESS
SHOWN TO HIM BY THE REGIMENT IN
THE GREAT WAR

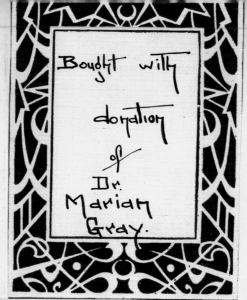

Bought with donation of Dr. Marian Gray.

**CHURCHILL, WINSTON LEONARD SPEN-
CER.** Marlborough, his life and times. 2v
$6 Scribner [25s Harrap]

 B or 92 Marlborough, John Churchill, 1st
duke of

"Winston Churchill, direct descendant of
John Churchill, first Duke of Marlborough, here
writes the story of his famous ancestor. The
first volume describes 'handsome Jack Churchill's' boyhood, youth, and early manhood. It
describes the early campaigns in France in
which he won his spurs and his part in the
exciting court intrigues in the days of Charles
the Second and James the Second. [The second
volume takes him only to the eve of his great
campaigns. The work] is based on a long
and exhaustive study of documents, state and
personal, referring to the first Duke." Publish-
er's note

Booklist 30:118 D '33

"This book is like its subject: huge, ambitious, many-sided, often dazzling, compounded
of extraordinary faults and virtues, but with
the virtues tra scending the faults. . . Mr.
Churchill sees his great ancestor clearly and
steadily as one of the founders of the imperial
domain of the British ruling class. And it is
as so much dependable history." Edmund Noble
 + Boston Transcript p1 N 11 '33 1500w

"Marlborough excited, for different reasons,
the antagonism of three great men of letters.
Swift, Macaulay and Thackeray have all libeled
him, and they have kept the ear of mankind,
while his defenders have been listened to by
the few. Those few have long known that the
charges were false; but they have not been
able to make their voices heard above the roar
of calumny. It is therefore a matter of rejoic-
ing that one who can make his voice heard has
at last appeared. Mr. Winston Churchill's book
will, we hope, kill the slanders forever. It is
written, as might be expected, in a brilliant
style: sometimes, perhaps, too brilliant. There
is an excess of interjections and of notes of
exclamation. But that is a small matter; here
is the truth." E. E. Kellett
 + Christian Science Monitor p6 O 7 '33
700w

Reviewed by P. W. Wilson
 Current Hist 39:vi D '33 60w

heim papers. But this is not the
phy, because it is not a work of art. His continual bursts of weighty humour at the expense
of the present day may be justified in intention
as they undoubtedly are by fact; but these
things should be done with a sharp point, and
not with a bludgeon." Bonamy Dobrée
 + — Spec 151:448 O 6 '33 1100w
tain documents, and excellent maps and plans.
 + Times [London] Lit Sup p679 O 12 '33
2750w

LITTLE ROCK PUBLIC LIBRARY

B
M vol.1

PREFACE

"THERE are few successful commanders," says Creasy, "on whom Fame has shone so unwillingly as upon John Churchill, Duke of Marlborough." I believe this is true; and it is an interesting historical study to examine the causes which have made so great a contrast between the glory and importance of his deeds and the small regard of his countrymen for his memory. He commanded the armies of Europe against France for ten campaigns. He fought four great battles and many important actions. It is the common boast of his champions that he never fought a battle that he did not win, nor besieged a fortress he did not take. Amid all the chances and baffling accidents of war he produced victory with almost mechanical certainty. Even when fighting in fetters and hobbles, swayed and oppressed by influences which were wholly outside the military situation, he was able to produce the same result, varying only in degree. Nothing like this can be seen in military annals. His smaller campaigns were equally crowned by fortune. He never rode off any field except as a victor. He quitted war invincible: and no sooner was his guiding hand withdrawn than disaster overtook the armies he had led. Successive generations have not ceased to name him with Hannibal and Cæsar.

Until the advent of Napoleon no commander wielded such widespread power in Europe. Upon his person centred the union of nearly twenty confederate states. He held the Grand Alliance together no less by his diplomacy than by his victories. He rode into action with the combinations of three-quarters of Europe in his hand. His comprehension of the war extended to all theatres, and his authority alone secured design and concerted action. He animated the war at sea no less than on land, and established till the present time the British naval supremacy in the Mediterranean. His

70750

eye ranged far across the oceans, and the foundations of British dominion in the New World and in Asia were laid or strengthened as the result of his Continental policy. He was for six years not only the Commander-in-Chief of the Allies, but, though a subject, virtually master of England. He was the head of the most glorious Administration in her history, when he led Europe, saved the Austrian Empire, and broke irretrievably the exorbitant power of France. The union with Scotland was but a feature of a period in which our country made its greatest advances in world rank and fame.

In 1688 Europe drew swords in a quarrel which, with one uneasy interlude, was to last for a quarter of a century. Since the duel between Rome and Carthage there had been no such world war. It involved all the civilized peoples; it extended to every part of the accessible globe; it settled for some time or permanently the relative wealth and power, and the frontiers of almost every European state. It outlined their various inheritances to the new domains beyond the ocean. In its course it drew out, matched, and exhausted the life energies of the nations in the same way—though not, of course, with the same scientific thoroughness—as did the Great War through which we ourselves have passed. Indeed, there are other remarkable similarities between this period and the beginning of the twentieth century. There was the same peril that the supremacy of one race and culture would be imposed by military force upon all others. There was the impotence of Europe without British aid; the slow but sure acceptance by England of the challenge and the call; and the same tremendous, increasing development of British effort during the struggle.

The wars of William and Anne were no mere effort of national ambition or territorial gain. They were in essentials a struggle for the life and liberty not only of England, but of Protestant Europe. Marlborough's victorious sword established upon sure foundations the constitutional and Parliamentary structure of our country almost as it has come down to us to-day. He carried all that was best in the life-work of Oliver Cromwell and William III to an abiding conclusion.

4

LITTLE ROCK PUBLIC LIBRARY

PREFACE

In no world conflict have the issues, according to modern standards, been more real and vital. In none has the duty to defend a righteous cause been more compulsive upon the British nation. In none have the results been more solid, more precious, more lasting. The triumph of the France of Louis XIV would have warped and restricted the development of the freedom we now enjoy, even more than the domination of Napoleon or of the German Kaiser.

It is usually pretended that Marlborough's personal affections followed his worldly interests and changed sides and agents with them. He certainly abandoned King James, and quarrelled with King William. But apart from these two sovereigns, around whom ranged some of the supreme constitutional and religious struggles of our history, and in whose circle business of State overrode private attachments, his character shows an astonishing constancy. His romantic love for his wife Sarah during nearly fifty years of wedlock, his fidelity to the Princess and Queen he served without a break for the thirty years from 1682 to 1712, were the keynotes of his life. His main friendships and political connexions were proof against all the stresses and surprises of violent times when nothing was sure or safe. He worked in steady and mutual confidence with Halifax, Shrewsbury, Russell, and Legge for a generation. Godolphin was his close friend and ally for forty years. Death alone severed these ties. The same elements of stability and continuity marked his great period. The ten years of war, with their hazards, their puzzles, their ordeals, their temptations, only strengthened a brotherhood in arms with Prince Eugene, unmatched between captains of equal fame. Not all the wear and tear of the Grand Alliance, nor the ceaseless friction between England and Holland, disturbed his similar association with the Pensionary Heinsius. Cadogan was his Chief Staff Officer, and Cardonell his secretary through all his campaigns, and both shared his fortunes and misfortunes to the end.

Yet fame shines unwillingly upon the statesman and warrior whose exertions brought our island and all Europe safely through its perils and produced glorious results for

5

Christendom. A long succession of the most famous writers of the English language have exhausted their resources of reproach and insult upon his name. Swift, Pope, Thackeray, and Macaulay in their different styles have vied with one another in presenting an odious portrait to posterity. Macpherson and Dalrymple have fed them with misleading or mendacious facts.

Neither of the two historic British parties has been concerned to defend Marlborough's national action. Every taunt, however bitter; every tale, however petty; every charge, however shameful, for which the incidents of a long career could afford a pretext, has been levelled against him. He in his lifetime remained silent, offering or leaving behind him no explanation or excuse, except his deeds. Yet these have sufficed to gather around him a literature more extensive than belongs to any military commander who was not also a sovereign. Hundreds of histories and biographies have been written about him and his wife Sarah. Many have been maliciously hostile, and others have destroyed their effect through undiscriminating praise. Many more have been meritorious but unread. It is only within recent times that the new school of writers who are reconciling scientific history with literary style and popular comprehension have begun to make headway against the prejudice of two hundred years.

It is with a sense of deep responsibility that I have attempted the task of making John Churchill intelligible to the present generation. Many of his defenders have shown the highest ability and immense learning; but their voices have not prevailed against the prestige and art of his assailants. When in the closing months of his life Macaulay was challenged in his facts, in his methods, and in his bias by the brilliant but unknown Paget, he felt strong enough to treat the most searching correction and analysis with contempt. Posterity, he reflected, would read what he himself had written. His critics, if he but ignored them, would soon be forgotten. It may perhaps be so. But time is a long thing.

I hesitated about undertaking this work. But two of the most gifted men I have known urged me to it strongly.

LITTLE ROCK PUBLIC LIBRARY

PREFACE

Lord Balfour, with all the rare refinement of his spacious mind, cool, questioning, critical, pressed it upon me with compelling enthusiasm. Lord Rosebery said, "Surely you must write *Duke John* [as he always called him]: he was a tremendous fellow." I said that I had from my childhood read everything I came across about him, but that Macaulay's story of the betrayal of the expedition against Brest was an obstacle I could not face. The aged and crippled statesman arose from the luncheon table, and, with great difficulty but sure knowledge, made his way along the passages of The Durdans to the exact nook in his capacious working library where "Paget's Examen" reposed. "There," he said, taking down this unknown, out-of-print masterpiece, "is the answer to Macaulay."

Paget's defence of the 'Camaret Bay Letter' has been judged valid by modern opinion. As these pages will show, I could not be satisfied with it. Paget, in fact, proved that Marlborough's alleged letter betraying to the Jacobite Court the Brest expedition, could only have been written after he knew that it had been betrayed already and could do no harm. My researches have convinced me that the document purporting to be a letter is a fabrication, and that no such letter exists or ever existed. The argument upon this point occupies about four chapters of this volume. Upon this issue I join battle. I believe that the Jacobite records preserved in the Scots Jesuit College in Paris are one of the greatest frauds of history. They are nothing more than the secret service reports of Jacobite agents and spies in England. It is astounding that so many famous writers should have accepted them to traduce not merely Marlborough, but the entire generation of statesmen and warriors of William and Anne, who bore England forward in the world as she has never been borne before or since. It is an aberration of historical technique.

In a portrait or impression the human figure is best shown by its true relation to the objects and scenes against which it is thrown, and by which it is defined. I have tried to unroll a riband of English history which stretches along the reigns

7

of Charles II, James II, William and Mary, William III, and Anne. The riband is always of equal width. Through it runs the scarlet thread of John Churchill's life. In this volume we trace that thread often with difficulty and interruption. It slowly broadens until for a goodly lap it covers the entire history of our country and frays out extensively into the history of Europe. Then it will narrow again as time and age impose their decrees upon the human thrust. But the riband is meant to continue at its even spread.

I feel that, for one reason or another, an opportunity will be accorded to me to state in a manner which will receive consideration Marlborough's claim to a more just and a more generous judgment from his fellow-countrymen. In this work I am compelled before reaching the great period of his life to plough through years of struggle and to meet a whole host of sneers, calumnies, and grave accusations. The court is attentive, and I shall not be denied audience. It is my hope to recall this great shade from the past, and not only invest him with his panoply, but make him living and intimate to modern eyes. I hope to show that he was not only the foremost of English soldiers, but in the first rank among the statesmen of our history; not only that he was a Titan, for that is not disputed, but that he was a virtuous and benevolent being, eminently serviceable to his age and country, capable of drawing harmony and design from chaos, and one who only needed an earlier and still wider authority to have made a more ordered and a more tolerant civilization for his own time, and to help the future.

My cousin the present Duke of Marlborough has placed the Blenheim papers at my disposal. Earl Spencer and many other custodians of the treasures of the bygone years have shown me the utmost consideration. To them all I express my gratitude; also to Professor Trevelyan, who may think some sentences I have written about Macaulay a poor return for his own historical reparations. But I can faithfully declare I have sought the truth. I have profited greatly from my conversations with Mr Keith Feiling, whose authority on this period stands so high. I am much indebted to Mr M. P.

LITTLE ROCK PUBLIC LIBRARY

Ashley, who for the last four years has conducted my researches into the original manuscripts at Blenheim and Althorp, as well as in Paris, Vienna, and London, and has constantly aided me in reading and revising the text. His industry, judgment, and knowledge have led to the discovery of various errors, and also of some new facts which are not included in the current versions of Marlborough's life. We have tried to test all documents and authorities at the source; nevertheless we await with meekness every correction or contradiction which the multiplicate knowledge of students and critics will supply.

WINSTON SPENCER CHURCHILL

CHARTWELL
WESTERHAM
August 13, 1933

CONTENTS

VOLUME I

CONTENTS

VOLUME I

ILLUSTRATIONS

Volume I

PLATES

FACSIMILES OF DOCUMENTS

MAPS AND PLANS

ABBREVIATIONS

C. = Chancery Records in the London Record Office.
C.J. = *House of Commons Journals.*
C.S.P. = *Calendar of State Papers.*
C.S.P. (Dom.) = *Calendar of State Papers, Domestic Series.*
D.N.B. = *Dictionary of National Biography.*
H.M.C. = *Report of the Royal Historical Manuscripts Commission.*
R.O. = The Public Record Office, London.
S.P. = State Papers.

For further details as to footnote references see the Bibliography (Vol. II, p. 273).

In quoting from old documents and letters the original text has been preserved wherever it is significant. Letters of Marlborough and Sarah which enter directly into the narrative have been modernized in spelling, grammar, and the use of capitals.

Documents never before made public are distinguished with an asterisk (*).

METHOD OF DATING

Until 1752 dates in England and on the Continent differed owing to our delay in adopting the Reformed Calendar of Gregory XIII. The dates which prevailed in England were known as Old Style, those abroad as New Style. In the seventeenth century the difference was ten days, in the eighteenth century eleven days. For example, January 1, 1601 (O.S.), was January 11, 1601 (N.S.), and January 1, 1701 (O.S.), was January 12, 1701 (N.S.).

The method I have used is to give all dates of events that occurred in England in the Old Style, and of events that occurred abroad in New Style. In sea battles and a few other convenient cases the dates are given in both styles.

It was also customary at this time—at any rate, in English official documents— to date the year as beginning on Lady Day, March 25. What we should call January 1, 1700, was then called January 1, 1699, and so on for all days up to March 25, when 1700 began. This has been a fertile source of confusion. In this book all dates between January 1 and March 25 have been made to conform to the modern practice.

LITTLE ROCK PUBLIC LIBRARY

CHAPTER I

ASHE HOUSE

(1644–61)

IN January 1644 a Devonshire lady, Eleanor (or Ellen), widow of Sir John Drake, alarmed by the Royalist activities in the West Country, had asked for a Roundhead garrison to protect her house at Ashe, near Axminster.[1] She was "of good affection" to the Parliament, had aided them with money and provisions, and had "animated her tenants in seven adjoining parishes" to adhere to their cause. The troops were sent ; but before they could fortify the place Lord Poulett, a neighbour who commanded for the King, marched upon it with his Irish soldiers, drove out the Parliamentarians, burned the house, and "stripped the good lady, who, almost naked and without shoe to her foot but what she afterwards begged, fled to Lyme for safety."

Here she encountered fresh hardships. The Roundhead seaport of Lyme Regis was soon attacked by the Royal forces. Early in April Prince Maurice, with six thousand men and "an excellent artillery," laid siege to the town. The story of its resolute defence is a cameo of the Civil War. For nearly three months a primitive, fitful, fierce combat was waged along and across the meagre ramparts and ditches which protected the townsfolk. Women aided the garrison in their stubborn resistance, relieving them in their watch by night and handing up the powder and ball in action. Colonel Blake, afterwards the famous Admiral of the Commonwealth, commanded the town. He several times offered the Royalists to open a breach in his breastworks and fight out the issue face to face on a front of twenty or on a front of ten men. His leadership, and twenty-six sermons by an eloquent Puritan

[1] For this chapter see the map facing p. 214.

17

divine, sustained the courage of the defenders. They depended for their supplies upon the sea. From time to time ships came in sight and aroused hopes and fears in both camps. Lady Drake was for a while in extreme distress. She must have watched the coming of ships with mingled feelings. The Royalist navy, such as it was, was commanded by her sister's grandson, James Ley, third Earl of Marlborough.[1] Every week it was rumoured that her dreaded relation would arrive from the Channel Islands with reinforcements for the enemy. But he never came. The Parliament held the seas. Only Roundhead ships appeared. Eleanor endured privations, bombardments, and burnings for nearly three months. She was for her livelihood " reduced to the spinning and knitting of stockings, in which miserable condition she continued until the siege of Lyme was raised " by the arrival of a relieving Puritan army from London under the Earl of Essex, " whereof she got away and came to Parliament."[2]

Her son John was no help to her in her misfortunes. We have been assured that he was " loyal to the King and on bad terms with his Puritan mother."[3] But this seems incorrect. He was, on the contrary, at this time himself a prisoner of war in Prince Maurice's hands, and it was his mother who exerted herself on his behalf. Her sister, the Countess of Marlborough, stood high with the Royalists and appealed for the release of the captive. But the Parliamentary forces were now moving towards Axminster, and as the young Drake had said imprudently that he would get Lord Poulett's house burned in revenge for the burning of Ashe, his liberation was not unnaturally refused.

Lady Drake, though a resolute Puritan, continued to address herself to both sides, invoking with the Royalists her sister's, and with the Roundheads her own political merit.

---

1 Wolseley calls James Ley wrongly (*Life of Marlborough*, i, 8) the second Earl of Marlborough, and rightly (ii, 64) the third Earl of Marlborough.

2 This account of the activities of Eleanor, Lady Drake, is based on *C.S.P.* (*Compounding*), pp. 65–66, 1051–53, 1317; her petition of March 22, 1648, to the House of Lords in *H.M.C.*, vii, 16b; and A. R. Bayley, *The Great Civil War in Dorset,* p. 129. Bayley, chapter vi, gives a good description of the siege of Lyme Regis.

3 Wolseley (ii, 8) describes John Drake as a Royalist, but *C.S.P.* (*Compounding*), 866, disproves this.

On September 28, 1644, Parliament ordered " that being wholly ruined by the enemy forces, she should have a furnished house in London rent free, £100 at once and £5 a week." The Westminster Commissioners accordingly four days later selected for her the house of a Royalist gentleman then still in arms—Sir Thomas Reynell ; and she remained in these quarters for nearly four years, pursuing her claims for compensation through the slowly working mills of Westminster. Sir Thomas made his peace with Parliament and 'compounded for'—that is, ransomed—his house in 1646. He demanded reinstatement, as was his right ; and he complained that Lady Drake during her tenancy " had digged up the ground and pulled up the floors in search of treasure." Nevertheless she continued to reside there in his despite, and perseveringly pursued her case against Lord Poulett for the burning of Ashe ; and she had sufficient credit with the now irresistible Parliamentarians to carry it at last to a conclusion in the spring of 1648, when she was awarded £1500 compensation, to be paid out of Lord Poulett's estate.

It had taken Eleanor four years to secure the award. Two years more were required to extract the money from the delinquent, upon whose rents meanwhile she had a virtual receivership. In July 1650 she complained to Parliament that Lord Poulett still owed her £600. A further laborious investigation was set on foot. Six years passed after the burning of Ashe, which she claimed had lost her £6000, before Lady Drake recovered her £1500 compensation. She had need of it—and, indeed, of every penny. Hers was a family divided against itself by the wars. Her son fought for the Parliament; her son-in-law, Winston Churchill, fought for the King. Both he and his father had taken arms in the Royal cause from the early days. Both in turn—the father first [1]—were drawn into the clutches of the Parliament. The Dorsetshire Standing Committee which dealt with the cases of the local Royalists reports in its minutes that in April 1646 John Churchill, a lawyer of some eminence, of Wootton Glanville, near Sherborne, had stated before them that he had formerly

[1] For the composition paid by the first Duke of Marlborough's grandfather see Bayley, p. 405 (local records) ; *C.S.P.* (*Compounding*), pp. 1176–77 (central records).

been nominated a Commissioner for the King ; but he pleaded that in November 1645 he had taken the National Covenant and the Negative Oath. He had paid £300 for the Parliamentary garrison at Weymouth, and £100 on account of his personal estate. Moreover, reported the Committee, he was sixty years of age and unable to travel. In these circumstances in August 1646 he was fined £440, and a month later the sequestration of his estates was suspended.

The reckoning with his son Winston was delayed.[1] Joining the King's army at twenty-two, he had made some mark upon the battlefields. He had become a captain of horse, and his bearing had been noted in the fights at Lansdowne Hill and Roundway Down. He was a youthful, staunch, and bigoted adherent of the King. Towards the end of 1645 he was wounded, and his plight amid the Roundheads now victorious throughout Dorset and Devon was most awkward. However, he had a refuge among the enemy. His father's house at Wootton Glanville was only a day's ride from Ashe. He was married to Lady Drake's third daughter, Elizabeth.

No one has hitherto been able to fix the date of the marriage, or whether it took place before or during the Civil Wars. The Chancery Records, however, state that in October 1649 Winston and his wife Elizabeth sued Sir Henry Rosewell, one of the executors of Sir John Drake, for part of her inheritance, due to her when she was twenty-one. From this case it appears that Sir John died in October 1636, that Elizabeth was twenty-one in February 1643, and that she married in May of that same year.[2] We know that a formal settlement was made between Winston's father and Lady Drake giving Elizabeth a dowry of £1500. As John Drake had at least four daughters, all of whom were left a similar capital in land, besides the estates left to his widow and son, the Drakes were evidently a substantial family.

1 For the composition paid by the first Duke of Marlborough's father see *C.S.P.* (*Compounding*), pp. 299, 1177; *C.S.P.* (*Advance of Money*), pp. 1092–93; vol. ccxxi of the Royalist composition papers in the R.O.

2 C.6/145, No. 51. Only the interrogatories of the Chancery case exist, and they are so badly damaged that the year of the lawsuit does not appear. From the evidence of the Committee on Compounding, however, it would seem to have taken place not later than 1649.

It is remarkable that such contracts should have been effected between persons so sharply divided by the actual fighting of the Civil Wars. We can see the stresses of the times from the fact that Winston's first child, Arabella, of whom more later, was not born till 1648, or more than five years after the date of the marriage, although thereafter children were born almost every year. No doubt the couple were parted by the severities of the war, and did not live regularly together till the struggle in the Western counties was ended. It is probable that Elizabeth lived with her mother during the whole of the fighting, and that from about the beginning of 1646 Winston joined her there. At any rate, from that time forward the two young people, wedded across the lines of civil war, lay low in the ruins of Ashe, and hoped to remain unnoticed or unpersecuted until the times should mend.

For a while all went well. But a regular system of informers had been set on foot, and, despite Winston's Roundhead connexions and Lady Drake's influence and record, the case against him was not allowed to lapse. At the end of 1649 he was charged with having been a captain in the King's army. According to the Dorsetshire records, witnesses, greedy, interested, but none the less credible, certified that as late as December 1645 Winston was still in the field against the Parliament, that he had been shot through the arm by the forces under Colonel Starr, and that he had resisted to the end with the royal garrison at Bristol. None of these facts could be rebutted.

However, the processes of law continued to work obstinately in spite of war and revolution. Beaten foes had rights which, unless specifically abolished by statute, they could assert. The delinquent captain fell back upon the law. He sought to collect debts owing to him from others. He claimed that a thousand marks given to his wife by her father, the late Sir John Drake, could not be sequestered. He laboured to put off the day when the final sentence would be pronounced. Long delays resulted. By August 1650 the Parliamentary authorities had lost patience. " Some cases," say their records, are sued out for no other end but to protract time, as that of Winston Churchill, who, it seems by his order, pretended his father (John Churchill) and Lady Ellen Drake had an interest in his portion, whereas he has still a suit depending against Colonel William Fry and Sir Henry Rosewell in his own name, only for his wife's portion ; had anybody else a title to it, he would not have commenced such a suit. As to his being in arms, he will surely not so far degenerate from his principles as to deny it.

Nevertheless, it was not till April 29, 1651, that the Commissioners for Compounding finally ordered that

*Winston Churchill of Wootton Glanville in the county of Dorset, gent. do pay as a fine for his Delinquence the sum of Four hundred and four score pounds ; whereof four hundred and forty-six pounds eighteen shillings is to be paid into the Treasury at Goldsmith's Hall, and the thirty-three pounds two shillings received already by our Treas. Mr Dawson of Sir Henry Rosewell in part of the money oweing by him to John Churchill, father of the said Winston, is hereby allowed of us in part of the sayd Four hundred and four score pounds.[1]

Once a statement gets into the stream of history it is apt to flow on indefinitely. In Hutchins' *History of Dorset*, published in 1774, this sum of £446 18s. is, by a misprint, recorded as £4446 18s. This would indeed have been a remarkable fine—the equivalent of perhaps nearly £18,000 of our money—to inflict upon a small country gentleman. A long succession of historians—Coxe (1819), Wolseley (1894), Bayley (1910), Atkinson (1921), and Edwards (1926)— have not only repeated the erroneous and absurd figure, but have expatiated in turn upon its astonishing severity. From

---

[1] S.P., 23/221, f. 855 and v. This document is endorsed on the back "The p'ticular of Winston Churchill gent of Glanvills Wooton in the countye of Dorsett.—A rente charge in fee of one hundred sixtye pounds p. Ann. uppon the whole state of John Churchill Esq, of Glanvill Wotton in the Countye of Dorsett excepting onely a leasehold of the Colledge of Winchester which is not liable here too—[signed] W. Churchill." The amount of the fine is further confirmed by a paper headed "Accounts of the Dorset Sequestration Committee, 1652-4," on the back of which is given "The names of the severall psons whoes have payd theis somes followinge into the Treasury att Goldsmiths Hall for theire fines." These include "Winston Churchill," who had paid £446 18s. (S.P., 23/80, f. 282.) The only secondary authority the author has come across which gives this figure correctly is Dale, *History of Glanville's Wootton.*

it they have concluded that Winston must have been most exceptionally obnoxious to the Parliament, whereas actually he was very nearly overlooked in the reckoning. Striking contrasts have been drawn between the treatment of father and son, which was in fact almost identical, and Winston has been credited with a far larger share in the wars than was his due. Thus tales are told.

The penalty was, however, severe for a man whose estate seems to have been worth only £160 a year.[1] Although Winston paid his fine at the end of 1651, he did not attempt to keep an independent home. Nor did he live with his father at Wootton Glanville. There may have been other reasons besides impoverishment for this. His father had married a second time about 1643 ;[2] Winston was apparently on bad terms with his stepmother, and it was to his mother-in-law rather that he turned for aid. When the ultimate judgment and compassion of the Almighty, as the victors would have expressed it, had become fully manifest throughout the West Country, Lady Drake sate indignant on the winning side amid her ruins, and Ashe House continued to be a refuge from poverty, if not from destitution, for the broken Cavalier, his young wife, and growing family. They do not seem to have returned home till Winston's father died in the year before the Restoration. Thus they lived at Ashe for thirteen years, and hard must those years have been. The whole family dwelt upon the hospitality or charity of a mother-in-law of difficult, imperious, and acquisitive temper ; a crowded brood in a lean and war-scarred house, between

---

1 It is clear from the preceding note and other references in vol. ccxxi of the composition papers that this sum settled on him by his father was the income for which Winston Churchill compounded; in addition his wife had at one time 1000 marks (£666 13s. 4d.) of her own ; but there is no indication that Winston Churchill had a further income for which he did not compound. It is true that Wolseley (i, 19) quotes Sarah, Duchess of Marlborough, as saying that Winston, when he married, had £1000 a year given him by his father. But all that the Spencer MSS., from which Wolseley derived his information, state is that Winston Churchill "had about £1000 a year from his father "—i.e., presumably when his father died in 1659. See Appendix, II.

2 In her reply to Winston Churchill's bill in Chancery of July 10, 1660, Mrs Mary Churchill refers to an agreement made when she was about to marry John Churchill " seventeen years ago " (C.6/148, No. 27).

them and whose owner lay the fierce contentions of the times.

No record is in existence of the daily round of the composite Drake household. We must suppose from its long continuance that family affection and sheer necessity triumphed over unspeakable differences of sentiment and conviction. Lady Drake did her duty faithfully to her daughter's family. She fed, clothed, and sheltered them in such portions of her house as their partisans had left her. They, having scarcely any other resources, accepted her bounty. While Lady Drake, vaunting her fidelity, pursued her claims for compensation from the Parliament, Winston, with her aid and collusion, sought to escape its exactions. It may be that in this prolonged double effort to save as much as possible from the wreck of their affairs a comradeship of misfortune was added to family ties. It must, none the less, have been a queer and difficult home. We may judge of their straitened means by the fact that they could not afford to put a fresh roof over the burned-out parts of the house until after the Restoration. They huddled together all these years in the one remaining wing. The war had impoverished the whole West countryside, and to keep up the style of gentlefolk and educate children must have imposed a severe frugality on all at Ashe.

To the procreation of children and the slow excitements of frequent litigation Winston added the relief of writing and the study of heraldry. In a substantial and erudite volume, *Divi Britannici*, still widely extant and universally unread, he explored from " the Year of the World 2855 " downwards those principles of the Divine Right of Kings for which he had fought and suffered. He went so far in doctrine as to shock even Royalist circles by proclaiming the right of the Crown to levy taxation by its mere motion. To quote from this book [1] is to meet its author across the centuries. In his dedication to Charles II he refers earnestly to Cromwell as

A Devil . . . who . . . intended questionless the same Violence to your Sacred Person, as was offer'd to that of your Father, had not your Tutelar Angels, like those which are said to

[1] *Divi Britannici*, pp. 43, 323–324, 355.

24

LITTLE ROCK PUBLIC LIBRARY

have preserv'd Lot from the Sodomites, shut the Door of Government upon him, and baffled his Ambition by the Revolt of those whom himself first taught to Rebell.

Of the origin of the Scottish nation he gives the following account :

The Scots would be thought a Branch of the antique Scythian Stock, . . . and they have this colour above many others, that as their Ancestors are entituled to as ancient Barbarity as those of any other Nation whatever, so like those rude Scythes, they have always been given to prey upon their Neighbours. . . . Some thinking them a By-slip of the Germans ; others of the Scandians ; some affirming them to be the Out-casts of some Mongrel Spaniards that were not permitted to live in Ireland, . . . and some there are that with no small probability take them to be a Miscellany of all these nations.

He cherished the theory that all nations derived their names from their food, dress, appearance, habits, etc. He thinks, therefore, the Britons got their name from a drink which the Greeks called " bruton or bruteion, which Athinæus defined as *ton krithinon oinon*—i.e., *Vinum hordeaceum*, Barley Wine." He expatiates on barley wine :

Cæsar affirms that all other Nations of the known World drink Wine or Water only ; but the Britains, saith he (who yet have Vines enough) make no other use of them, but for Arbours in their Gardens, or to adorn and set forth their houses, drinking a high and mighty liquor, different from that of any other Nation, made of Barley and Water, which being not so subtil in its operation as Wine, did yet warm as much, and nourish more, leaving space enough for the performance of many great Actions before it quite vanquisht the Spirits.

All this seems very sound doctrine so far as it goes.

Winston's account of the execution of the King shows the intensity of his political feelings and the vigour of his vocabulary.

Here seemed to be the *Consummatum est* of all the happiness of this Kingdom, as well as of the Life of this King : For upon his Death the Vail of the Temple rent, and the Church was overthrown. An universal Darkness overspread the State, which

25

lasted not for twelve hours only, but twelve years. The two great Luminaries of Law and Gospel were put out : Such as could not write supply'd the place of Judges, such as could not read of Bishops. Peace was maintain'd by War, Licentiousness by Fasting and Prayer. The Commonalty lost their Propriety, the Gentry their Liberty, the Nobility their Honour, the Clergy their Authority and Reverence. The Stream of Government ran down in new-cut Chanels, whose Waters were alwayes shallow and troubled : And new Engines were invented by the new Statesmen that had the steerage, to catch all sorts of Fish that came to their Nets ; some were undone by Sequestration others by Composition, some by Decimation or Proscription ; In fine, it appear'd (when too late) that the whole Kingdom suffer'd more by his suffering then he himself, who being so humbled as he was, even unto death, falling beneath the scorn, mounted above the Envy of his Adversaries, and had this advantage by their Malice, to gain a better Crown then they took from him.

The preface to *Divi Britannici*, which was not pub-lished till 1675, contains in its dedication a sentence the force and dignity of which may justify the book. It was, wrote the author, " begun when everybody thought that the monarchy had ended and would have been buried in the same grave with your martyred father," and " that none of us that had served that blessed Prince had any other weapons left us but our pens to show the justice of our zeal by that of his title."

Since Arabella had been born on February 23, 1648,[1] births and deaths swiftly succeeded one another with almost annual regularity. Mrs. Winston Churchill had twelve children, of whom seven died in infancy. The third child of these twelve and the eldest son to live is the hero of this account. It is curious that no previous biographer—among so many—should have discovered the entry of his birth. A mystery has been made of it, which Coxe and other writers have used devious methods to solve. It is still often wrongly

---

[1] The parish registers of St Michael's, Musbury, which the present rector, the Rev. J. Ferguson, allowed the author to consult, give Arabella Churchill as having been born on February 23, 1648, and baptized on March 16, 1648. This corrects er-roneous dates in Wolseley (i, 23) and in *D.N.B.*, which says she was born in March.

given.[1] We therefore offer the evidence from the parish register of St. Michael's, Musbury, in facsimile. The infant was baptized in the tiny private chapel of Ashe House seven days later.

[John the sonne of Mr Winston Churchill, born the 26 day of May, 1650.]

The first ten years of his life were lived in the harsh conditions which have been suggested. We are here in the region of surmise. Facts are vague and few ; but it seems easy to believe that the child grew up in a home where wants were often denied, and feelings and opinions had nearly always to be repressed. Public affairs marched forward, and their course was viewed at Ashe from standpoints separated by deep and living antagonisms. Blood and cruel injuries lay between those who gathered around the table. Outraged faith, ruined fortunes, and despairing loyalties were confronted by resolute, triumphant rebellion, and both were bound together by absolute dependence. It would be strange indeed if the children were not conscious of the chasm between their elders ; if they never saw resentment on the one side, or felt patronage from the other ; if they were never reminded that it was to their grandmother's wisdom and faithful championship of the cause of Parliament they owed the bread they ate. It would be strange if the ardent Cavalier then in his prime, poring over his books of history and heraldry, watching with soured eyes the Lord Protector's victories over the Dutch or the Spaniards and the grand position to which England seemed to have been raised by this arch-wrongdoer, and dreaming of a day when the King

[1] E.g., by Sir John Fortescue, Marlborough (1932). Lord Wolseley reproduces the entry of John's baptism from St. Mary's, Axminster, and erroneously implies that there is no record at Musbury of his birth.

27

should enjoy his own again and the debts of Royalist and regicide be faithfully and sternly settled, should not have spoken words to his little son revealing the bitterness of his heart. The boy may well have learned to see things through his father's eyes, to long with him for a casting down of present pride and power, and have learned at the same time— at six, seven, and eight years of age—not to flaunt these opinions before half at least of those with whom he lived.

The two prevailing impressions which such experiences might arouse in the mind of a child would be, first, a hatred of poverty and dependence, and, secondly, the need of hiding thoughts and feelings from those to whom their expression would be repugnant. To have one set of opinions for one part of the family, and to use a different language to the other, may have been inculcated from John's earliest years. To win freedom from material subservience by the sure agency of money must have been planted in his heart's desire. To these was added a third : the importance of having friends and connexions on both sides of a public quarrel. Modern opinion assigns increasing importance to the influences of early years on the formation of character. Certainly the whole life of John Churchill bore the imprint of his youth. That impenetrable reserve under graceful and courteous manners ; those unceasing contacts and correspondences with opponents ; that iron parsimony and personal frugality, never relaxed in the blaze of fortune and abundance ; that hatred of waste and improvidence in all their forms—all these could find their roots in the bleak years at Ashe.

We may also suppose that Winston Churchill concerned himself a good deal with the early education of his children. For this he was not ill qualified. He had gathered, as his writings show, no inconsiderable store of historical knowledge. He presented in these years the curious figure of a cavalry captain, fresh from the wars, turned perforce recluse and bookworm. Time must have hung heavy on his hands. He had no estates to manage, no profession to pursue. He could not afford to travel ; but in the teaching of his children he may well have found alike occupation and solace. Or, again, he may have loafed and brooded, leaving his children to play in the lanes and gardens of that tranquil countryside. The only information we have on John's education is provided by the unknown author of *The Lives of the Two Illustrious Generals* (1713) :

> He was born in the Time of the grand Rebellion, when his Father for Siding with the Royal Party against the Usurpers, who then prevailed, was under many Pressures, which were common to such as adher'd to the King. Yet, notwithstanding the Devastations and Plunderings, and other nefarious Practices and Acts of Cruelty which were daily committed by the licentious Soldiery, no Care was omitted on the Part of his tender Parents for a Liberal and Gentile Education. For he was no sooner out of the hands of the Women but he was given into those of a sequestered Clergyman, who made it his first concern to instil sound Principles of Religion into him, that the Seeds of humane Literature might take the deeper Root, and he from a just Knowledge of the Omnipotence of the Creator, might have a true Sense of the Dependence of the Creature.

Many modern biographers of Marlborough have asserted that Richard Farrant, rector of the neighbouring village of Musbury, was the clergyman here named. It would seem, however, that Farrant was no sequestered Royalist, but, on the contrary, a strong Puritan into whose hands Winston would hardly have let his son fall.[1]

It is said that famous men are usually the product of unhappy childhood. The stern compression of circumstances, the twinges of adversity, the spur of slights and taunts in early years, are needed to evoke that ruthless fixity of purpose and tenacious mother-wit without which great actions are seldom accomplished. Certainly little in the environment of the young John Churchill should have deprived him of this stimulus;

[1] Wolseley (i, 28) was responsible for the assertion that Richard Farrant was Marlborough's "first regular tutor." *The Lives of the Two Illustrious Generals* (p. 5), which is Wolseley's authority, only states that "he was given into [the hands] of a sequestered clergyman." But Farrant was a Puritan divine who became rector of Musbury—probably after the death of Matthew Drake in 1653—and was ejected as a Nonconformist in 1662. This information is based on the parish registers of Musbury and Calamy, *Nonconformist's Memorial, sub* "Musbury."

29

and by various long-descending channels there centred in him martial and dangerous fires.

Besides attending to his son's education Winston in his studious leisure bethought himself often of his pedigree and his arms. His researches into genealogy have produced as good an account of the origin of the Churchills as is likely to be required.[1] He traced his " Lyon Rampant, Argent upon a Sable coat," to Otho de Leon, Castelan of Gisor, " whome we call our common ancestor." The said Otho had two sons, Richard and Wandrill, Lord of Courcelle, " whose youngest son came into England with William the Conqueror." After recounting conscientiously several generations Winston rested with confidence upon " John . . ., Lord of Currichill, or as 'tis in divers records Chirechile, since called Churchill in Somersetshire," whose son, Sir Bartholomew de Churchill, " a man of great note in the tyme of King Steven, . . . defended the castle of Bristow against the Empress Maud and was slaine afterward in that warr." In the time of King Edward I, after the Barons' War, the lordship of Churchill was seized by the Crown and given to some favourite, whose posterity continued in possession till " nere about Henry VIII, his tyme." After passing through the hands of a family of the name of Jennings, of whom more later, it was sold eventually in 1652 to a Sir John Churchill, sometime Master of the Rolls, " and had come to my son in right of his wife, had it not been so unfortunately alianated by her said father."

All this was very fine, but when, descending these chains, we come to John, " ancestor of the present Churchills of Munston, and Roger, who by the daughter of Peverell, relict of Nicholas Meggs, has issue Mathew, father of Jaspar, my grandfather," we enter a rather shady phase. Edward Harley rudely asserts " that John Churchill's great grandfather was a blacksmith who worked in the family of the Meggs,"[2] and certainly, as his great-great-great-grandfather married a Mrs Meggs, this seems very suspicious and even

1 Bath Papers, *H.M.C.*, ii, 173–175.
2 This reference, which is from a commonplace-book in the possession of the Duke of Portland, the author owes to the kindness of the Duke's librarian, Mr F. Needham.

disquieting. In any case, there are strong grounds for believing that John's grandfather solidly improved the fortunes of this branch of the Churchill family. He was a practising lawyer, a deputy registrar of Chancery as well as a member of the Middle Temple, and lawyers were a prosperous class at this date.[1] Not only did he make a marriage himself into an aristocratic family, the Winstones,[2] but he seems to have arranged a step for his eldest son. For all the genealogical table produced by Winston, the Drakes were a more renowned and substantial family than the Churchills, of whom there were numerous branches of various conditions, some quite lowly, in Dorset alone ; whereas John Drake's family descended eight in line from father to son, and all called John, through the Bernard Drakes, who were already in good repute at the Court of Queen Elizabeth, and passed on the properties at Musbury which had been in their hands from the fifteenth century. Bernard Drake had been a man of so robust quality that he had physically assaulted his relation, the renowned Sir Francis Drake, for daring to display upon his coat of arms a wyvern which he deemed

1 There is no doubt that he acquired considerable property. He bought Newton Montacute and lands at Wootton Glanville worth at least £600 a year (multiply by about four for the modern equivalent) ; he leased the neighbouring 'messuage' of Mintern from Winchester College, and he held mortgages on other Devonshire lands. He made a good marriage, and, finally, the fact that he was a man of enterprise and business ability is shown by the proposal made to his tenants at Wootton Glanville in 1639 that he should enclose the common waste in order to improve the agriculture of his property at the public expense. John Churchill *v.* Thomas and Edward Mayo (May 16, 1639, C.8/86, No. 101) mentions the proposal to enclose the common waste. Winston Churchill Knight *v.* Henry Mullett (November 15, 1669; C.5/460, No. 220) shows that at this date the waste was still unenclosed. Polwhele, *History of Devon,* and the various papers relating to the Chancery case of Winston Churchill *v.* Mrs Mary Churchill (1660–61) give details of the property of John Churchill senior and its value.

2 Winston says in his letter to Blue Mantle about his coat of arms (1685), "My father by Sarah one of the daughters and co-heires of Sir Henry Winstone of Standish in the county of Gloster, had issue John my elder brother, who dyed presently after his birth, and myselfe who by my wife Elizabeth, third daughter of Sir John Drake of Ashe, have had a plentifull issue; to wit, eight sons and three daughters, my eldest daughter, and the only daughter now living was Arabella, now wife of Colonel Charles Godfrey; my eldest son is the present Lord Churchill who has marryd Sarah one of the daughters and co-heires of Richard Jennings of St Albans, the unfortunate looser of the mannor of Churchill, which is now to be sold, but my son being disappointed of having it given to him as Sir John Churchill allways did promise him, refuses to buy it."

31

poached from him. Hearing this, Queen Elizabeth conferred upon Sir Francis a wyvern dangling head downward from the yards of a ship, and asked Sir Bernard what he thought of that! He replied, with some temerity, " Madam, though you could give him a *finer*, yet you could not give him an *ancienter* coat than mine."[1] So the marriage arranged for Winston with Lady Drake's daughter Elizabeth was socially satisfactory, and was, as we have seen, a veritable salvation during the Civil Wars.

Another streak of blood, strange and wanton, mingled in the child John's nature. His grandmother, Lady Drake, was herself the daughter of John, Lord Boteler, who had married the sister of George Villiers, Duke of Buckingham, the favourite of James I and Charles I. Some students have amused themselves in tracing all the men—some of the greatest and wickedest in our history—who have descended from George Villiers, father of Buckingham. They are said to have repeatedly produced, across the centuries, the favourites, male and female, of kings and queens ; and Chatham and Pitt, as well as Marlborough, bear the distinction of this taint or genius.

When at length, at the end of her life, Sarah, Duchess of Marlborough, read—tardily, for it had been kept from her— Lediard's history of the Duke, she made the following extremely up-to-date comment upon this part of the subject : * " This History takes a great deal of Pains to make the Duke of Marlborough's Extraction very ancient. That may be true for aught I know ; But it is no matter whether it be true or not in my opinion. For I value nobody for another's merit." [2]

Be this as it may, students of heredity have dilated upon this family tree. Galton cites it as one of the chief examples on which his thesis stands.[3] Winston himself has been accounted one of the most notable and potent of sires. Had he lived the full span, he would have witnessed within the space of twelve months his son gaining the battle of Ramillies

---

[1] Prince, *Worthies of Devon*, p. 245.
[2] Spencer MSS., paper enclosed in a letter from Sarah, Duchess of Marlborough, to David Mallet, October 4, 1744.
[3] Galton, *Hereditary Genius*, pp. 81, 154.

LITTLE ROCK PUBLIC LIBRARY

and his daughter's son that of Almanza ; and would have found himself acknowledged as the progenitor of the two greatest captains of the age at the head of the opposing armies of Britain and of France and Spain. Moreover, his third surviving son, Charles, became a soldier of well-tried distinction, and his naval son virtually managed the Admiralty during the years of war. The military strain flowed strong and clear from the captain of the Civil Wars, student of heraldry and history, and champion of the Divine Right. It was his blood, not his pen, that carried his message.

Although in this opening chapter we have set the reader in these bygone times, eleven years of our hero's life have already been accomplished. Ashe House, still unroofed, passes from the scene. Lord Wolseley was keenly stirred by its remnants and their surroundings. They awoke in this brave and skilful officer " memories of English glory." " Surely," he exclaims,

> the imagination is more fired and national sentiment more roused by a visit to the spot where one of our greatest countrymen was born and passed his childhood than by any written record of his deeds. This untidy farmhouse, with its [now] neglected gardens, and weed-choked fish-ponds, round which the poor, badly clothed boy sported during his early years, seems to recall his memory—aye, even the glory with which he covered England— more vividly than a visit to Blenheim Palace, or a walk over the famous position near the village of Hochstadt on the banks of the Danube. The place, the very air, seems charged with reminiscences of the great man who first drew breath here.[1]

These scenes certainly played a curiously persistent part in John Churchill's life. It was on the very soil of his childhood, in sight almost of his birthplace, that he was in 1685 to lead the Household Cavalry, feeling their way towards Monmouth's army ; and three years later on the hill across the river he was to meet the Prince of Orange after deserting James II. So much for Ashe!

But now the times are changed. Oliver Cromwell is dead. General Monk has declared for a free Parliament. His troops

1 Wolseley, i, 11–12.

have marched from Coldstream to Hounslow. The exiled Charles has issued the Declaration of Breda. The English people, by a gesture spontaneous and almost unanimous, have thrown off the double yoke of military and Puritan rule. Amid bonfires and the rejoicings of tumultuous crowds they welcome back their erstwhile hunted sovereign, and by one of those intense reactions, sometimes as violent in whole nations as in individuals, change in a spasm from oppressive virtue to unbridled indulgence. On April 23, 1661, Charles II was crowned at Westminster, and the restoration of the English monarchy was complete.

These memorable events produced swift repercussions at Ashe House. Winston Churchill passed at a stroke from the frown of an all-powerful Government to the favour of a King he had faithfully served. The frozen years were over, and the Cavaliers, emerging from their retreats, walked abroad in the sun, seeking their lost estates. We need not grudge him these good days. He had acted with unswerving conviction and fidelity. He had drunk to the dregs the cup of defeat and subjugation. Its traces can be seen in his anxious eyes. Now was the time of reward. Instantly he sprang into many forms of activity. In 1661 he entered Parliament for Weymouth. In 1664 he became one of the original members of the Royal Society. Although his fortunes were much depleted, he regained his independence and a hearth of his own. More important than this, he stood in a modest way high in the favour of the new régime. He was received with consideration and even intimacy at Court. The terms under which Charles had returned to his kingdom were not such as to allow him to bestow wealth upon his humbler adherents. His sovereignty rested on a compromise between rebels and Royalists, between Anglicans and Presbyterians, between those who had seized estates and those who had lost them, between the passions of conflicting creeds and the pride of lately hostile regiments. He had no means of meeting even the just claims which faithful subjects might urge, still less could he satisfy the ravenous demands of long-nursed grievances or blatant imposture.

LITTLE ROCK PUBLIC LIBRARY

SIR WINSTON CHURCHILL
Sir Peter Lely
By permission of the Duke of Marlborough   34

LITTLE ROCK PUBLIC LIBRARY

Burnet says, speaking of an earlier time :

The herd of the Cavalier party was now very glorious and full of courage in their cups, though they had been very discreet managers of it in the field and in time of action, but now every one of them boasted he had killed his thousands, and all were full of merit and as full of high pretentions.

It is remarkable, however, that amid the crowds of hungry and often deserving suitors who thronged the antechambers of Whitehall so much attention should have been paid to the merits and services of Winston Churchill. Far more was done for him than for most. There was one cheap, sure way to please him. It was apparently well known. Accordingly an augmentation of arms and a crest unusual in a family of such standing was offered to his heraldic propensities.[1] Nevertheless, this evidence of royal favour and affection was not in itself sufficiently substantial, in Winston's opinion at least, to repair the injuries he had suffered in pocket and skin. He remained cherished but disconsolate, blazoning on his new coat of arms an uprooted oak above the motto *Fiel pero desdichado* (" Faithful but unfortunate "). More practical reliefs, as will be shown in the next chapter, were however in store.

1 The King to Sir Edward Walker, Garter, December 11, 1661; "Orders an augmentation of a St George's cross gules, on a canton argent, to the arms of Winston Churchill, of Miniterne [*sic*], co. Dorset, for service to the late King as captain of horse, and for his present loyalty as a member of the House of Commons." (*C.S.P.* (*Dom.*), 1661–62, p. 176.) For Winston's comment on this grant see Bath Papers, *loc. cit.*

CHAPTER II

THE JOVIAL TIMES

(1661–69)

OUR readers must now brace themselves for what will inevitably be a painful interlude. We must follow the fortunes or misfortunes of a maiden of seventeen and her younger brother as they successively entered a dissolute Court. The King was the fountain not only of honour, but of almost every form of worldly success and pleasure. Access to his presence, intimacy with his family or favourites, were the sole pathway even of modest and lawful ambition. An enormous proportion of the amenities and glories of the realm was engrossed in the narrow family circle of royal personages, friends, dependants, and important Ministers or agents of the Crown. Nearly all chances of distinction and solid professional advancement went by favour. An officer well established at Court was a different kind of officer from one who had nothing but the merits of his sword. The success of jurists and divines was similarly determined. The royal light shone where it listed, and those who caught its rays were above competition and almost beyond envy, except—an important exception—from rivals in their own select sphere.

If those were the conditions which ruled for men, how much more compulsive was the environment of the frailer sex. To sun oneself in the royal favour, to be admitted to the charmed circle, to have access to a royal lady, to be about the person of a queen or princess, was to have all this exclusive, elegant, ambitious, jostling world on one's doorstep and at one's footstool. Aged statesmen and prelates ; eager, ardent, attractive youths ; the old general, the young lieutenant—all produced whatever treasure they had to bestow to win the favour of the sovereign's mistress, or of his relations' mistresses, and

36

LITTLE ROCK PUBLIC LIBRARY

of his important friends or servants. That nothing should be lacking to frame the picture of privilege and indulgence, it must be remembered that all this was dignified by the affairs of a growing state, by the presence of upright and venerable men and formidable matrons, providing the counterpoise of seriousness and respectability. Scientists, philosophers, theologians, scholars ; the mayors of cities, rugged sea-captains, veteran colonels, substantial merchants—all pressed forward on the fringes of the parade in the hope of being gratified by some fleeting glint of the royal radiance.

Such ideas seem remote to the English-speaking nations in these times. Here or in the United States we can scarcely conceive a social life where a royal, or at least a very wealthy person would not be compelled to set an example. Our aristocracy has largely passed from life into history ; but our millionaires—the financiers, the successful pugilists, and the film stars who constitute our modern galaxy and enjoy the same kind of privilege as did the outstanding figures of the seventeenth and eighteenth centuries—are all expected to lead model lives. We must make allowances for the backward conditions which prevailed in England and France, to say nothing of the barbarous countries, when Charles II and Louis XIV sat upon their thrones. There was undoubtedly an easy commerce of the sexes, marked at times by actual immorality. Men and women who had obtained power were often venal, and insolent besides, to those whom they dubbed their inferiors. Even judges were occasionally, and members of the legislature frequently, corrupt. Generals and admirals were usually jealous of each other, and sometimes stooped to intrigue to gain promotion. Even brilliant writers and pamphleteers, the journalists of those primitive times, wrote scurrilous gossip to please their patrons and employers. We in this happy and enlightened age must exercise our imagination to span the gulf which separates us from those lamentable, departed days. Securely established upon the rock of purity and virtue, ceaselessly cleansed by the strong tides of universal suffrage, we can afford to show tolerance and even indulgence towards the weaknesses and vices of those vanished generations without in any way compromising our own integrity.

It is strange indeed that such a system should have produced for many generations a succession of greater captains and abler statesmen than all our widely extended education, competitive examinations, and democratic system have put forth. Apart from the Church and the learned professions, the area of selection was restricted entirely to the circles of rank, wealth, and landed property. But these comprised several thousand families within which and among whom an extremely searching rivalry and appraisement prevailed. In this focus of the nation men were known and judged by their equals with intimate knowledge and a high degree of comprehension. There may be more truth than paradox in Lord Fisher's brutal maxim, " Favouritism is the secret of efficiency." There was, of course, great need to seek out ability. Appointments and promotions went largely by favour : but favour went largely by merit.

The English Court under Charles II was no Oriental scene of complete subservience, where women were secluded and where men approached the supreme figures with bated breath. It had not the super-centralization of the French Court under Louis XIV. The nobility and wealthy gentlefolk could live on their estates, and though excluded from the fame of national employment, had effective rights which they used frequently against the Crown. There were always independent powers in England. This counterpoise enhanced the strength of the central institution. There were degrees, values, and a hierarchy of considerable intrinsic virtue. A great society, sharply criticized, but accepted as supreme, indulging every caprice and vanity, and drawing to itself the chief forms of national excellence, presided at the summit of the realm.

It is important to remember also the differences of feeling and outlook which separate the men and women of these times from ourselves. They gave a very high—indeed, a dominating—place in their minds to religion. It played as large a part in the life of the seventeenth century as sport does now. One of their chief concerns was about the next world and how to be saved. Although ignorant compared with our standards, they were all deeply versed in the Bible and the Prayer Book. If they read few books, they studied them and digested them thoroughly. They had settled opinions on large questions of faith and doctrine, and were often ready to die or suffer on account of them.

Rank and breeding were second only to religion in their esteem. Every one in Court or county society was known, and all about them. Their forbears for many generations were carefully scrutinized. The coat of arms which denoted the family's achievements for hundreds of years was narrowly and jealously compared. It was not easy to get into the great world in those days, if one did not belong to it. A very clear line was drawn between ' gentles ' and ' simples,' and the Church and the Law were almost the only ladders by which new talent could reach the highest positions. Indeed, religion and family pride together absorbed much of the sentiment now given to nationalism. The unity of Christendom had been ruptured at the Reformation, but strong cosmopolitan sympathies prevailed among the educated classes in all the Western countries.

We must not imagine that our ancestors were as careless and ignorant about international politics as are the immense political democracies of the present age. Had they been absorbed or amused as we are by the inexhaustible trivialities of the day, had their sense been dulled by speed, sport, luxury, and money-making, they could never have taken consciously the dire decisions without which England would not have been preserved. There were many solid citizens, secure in their estates, who pondered deeply and resolved valiantly upon the religious and political issues of the times. Although the administration of England had not attained to anything like the refined and ordered efficiency of France, there was already a strong collective view about fundamental dangers. There was already a recognizable if rudimentary Foreign Office opinion. And there were in every capital grave,

39

independent men who gave lifelong thought to doctrine and policy. Their business was transacted by long personal letters, laboriously composed, in which every word was weighed, and conversations, few and far between, the purport of which was memorable. Government was then the business of sovereigns and of a small but serious ruling class, and, for all their crimes, errors, and shortcomings, they gave keen and sustained attention to their task.

In these days society was callous about prisoners and punishments, and frightful forfeits were senselessly exacted. But these were the ages of Pain. Pain, when it came, was accepted as a familiar foe. No anæsthetic robbed the hospital of all the horrors of the torture-chamber. All had to be endured, and hence—strangely enough—all might be inflicted. Yet in some ways our forerunners attached more importance to human life than we do. Although they fought duels about women and other matters of honour, instead of seeking damages from the courts, and although death sentences were more numerous in those days, they would have recoiled in lively horror from the constant wholesale butcheries of scores of thousands of persons every year by motor-cars, at which the modern world gapes unconcernedly. Their faculties for wonder and indignation had not been blunted and worn away by the catalogues of atrocities and disasters which the advantages of the electric telegraph and the newspaper press place at our disposal every morning and evening. Above all, they were not in a hurry. They made fewer speeches, and lived more meditatively and more at leisure, with companionship rather than motion for their solace. They had far fewer facilities than we have for the frittering away of thought, time, and life. Altogether they were primitive folk, and we must make allowances for their limitations. The one trait which they shared in common with the twentieth century was the love of money, and respect and envy for its fortunate possessors. But, then, money in those days was still mainly derived from land, and the possession of land usually denoted ancient lineage.

The Convention Parliament of the Restoration was dis-

LITTLE ROCK PUBLIC LIBRARY

solved in 1660, and the so-called Cavalier, or Pensionary, Parliament met in May 1661. This was " a parliament full of lewd young men, chosen by a furious people in spite to the Puritans, whose severity had distasted them." They were " of loyal families, but young men for the most part, which being told the King, he replied that there was no great fault, for he could keep them till they got beards."[1] So in fact he did; for this Parliament continued to sit for eighteen years. In it Winston Churchill represented the constituency of Weymouth. During its first two sessions he was an active Member; he served on various committees, and as late as May 10, 1662, he was sent by the Commons to request the participation of the Lords in a joint committee to discuss questions arising out of an Army Bill.[2]

Meanwhile the Restoration settlement in Ireland was proceeding very slowly.[3] On November 30, 1660, the King had issued a declaration which had laid it down that lands in the possession of the Cromwellian settlers up to May 1659 were to be retained by them; Royalist Protestants and ' innocent ' Roman Catholics were to receive restitution or compensation; Church lands were to be given back; and certain persons specially named were to be rewarded from this source for their past good services to the Royal cause. Thirty-six commissioners had been appointed to carry out this statute, and had set up an office in Dublin in May 1661. But, whether because of contradictory clauses in the Act or because, as the Irish alleged, of the interested motives of the commissioners, after nearly a year's work only one claim—that of a widow— had been settled. In April 1662 the office was closed pending the introduction into the Irish Parliament of a Bill of Settlement embodying the royal declaration. The King had himself blamed the commissioners for their failure to make progress in their work, and seven new commissioners were now

---

[1] Osmund Airy, *Charles II*, p. 177.

[2] See *Commons Journals*, viii, *passim*, and especially p. 425.

[3] The most recent account of the Restoration settlement in Ireland is to be found in R. Bagwell, *Ireland under the Stuarts*, vol. iii (1916), chapters xli, xlii. See also E. A. Dalton, *History of Ireland* (1906), chapter xx, and J. P. Prendergast, *Ireland from the Restoration to the Revolution* (1887).

41

chosen to go over to Ireland and reopen the Court of Claims. " His Majesty," wrote the Lord Chancellor Clarendon,

> made Choice of seven Gentlemen of very clear Reputations; one of them being an eminent Sergeant-at-Law whom He made a Judge upon his Return from thence; two others, Lawyers of very much Esteem; and the other four Gentlemen of very good Extractions, excellent Understandings, and above all Suspicion for their Integrity, and generally reputed to be superior to any base Temptation.[1]

Among these latter Winston Churchill, who had not been one of the thirty-six and had no interest in Irish lands, was named. He seems to have obtained this honourable post through the influence of Sir Henry Bennet, about to be created Lord Arlington and Secretary of State, under whose patronage he had first been introduced into the Court at Whitehall.[2] Winston probably sailed to Ireland to carry out his new duties in July; for there is a warrant for him to ship horses and goods thither dated July 19, 1662.[3] He took his family with him, his wife being with child. His Irish task was neither lucrative nor inspiring. His own experiences in an earlier decade had made him only too well acquainted with the dismal process of redistributing seques- tered lands. Week after week crowds of tattered nobles and dispossessed landowners who sought to regain their estates from the Commission by proving their past loyalty beset the harassed tribunal. But there was little to share, and less still was bestowed.

Meanwhile the boy John for a time attended the Dublin Free Grammar School. Lord Wolseley suggests that he was frequently a witness of the proceedings of the Court of Claims, and that he learned from this dreary spectacle how scurvily loyalty is often treated, and how brazenly successful rebellion

---

[1] Continuation of his *Life* (ed. 1759), p. 117.

[2] *Cf.* Sir Winston Churchill to the Earl of Arlington, April 28, 1666, Dublin: " And this my Lord I have chosen to deliver by the hands of my son [John?], that by being witness to mine he may learn his own obligations, and make his first entry into the Court (as I did) under the patronage of your Lordship's favour." (S.P. 63/320, f. 226.)

[3] *C.S.P.* (*Treasury Books*), 1660–67, p. 411.

and treachery maintain themselves, even after a restoration. This again is pure surmise. A youth, by all accounts of singular beauty and address, with qualities of force and fire which were already noticeable, was growing to manhood. The grim years at Ashe House had made their mark upon his fibre. The joyous transformation which the return of the King had effected in the family fortunes, the events and spectacle of the Restoration, the Irish squalor, must all have been observed by an intelligence certainly discerning and perhaps already profound. Still, we do not think that external events played after childhood a dominating part in the development of his character. The personality unfolds with remorseless assurance, sometimes in harmony with, but as often in opposition to its environment.

Throughout 1663 Winston Churchill and his fellow-commissioners remained in Ireland. Their task was a difficult one. On March 25 they wrote to Whitehall affirming that

> Since our coming into this Kingdom, we have found so many unexpected discouragements, from those whose security and settlement was and is a powerful part of our care, that we confess we were much dejected. . . . But we have now received new life from his sacred Majesty's most gracious letters to us, by which we understand that neither our sufferings, nor our innocence, were hid from, or unconsidered by his Majesty.[1]

Nevertheless, in December Churchill begged Arlington for leave to return home for just two months,[2] so desirous was he of a rest from his labours. A month later his wish was gratified, for the King summoned him back to England on January 10, 1664,[3] and twelve days later rewarded his services with a knighthood.[4] If Winston brought his eldest son with him from Dublin on this occasion, as there is every reason to suppose, it must have been at this date that John Churchill became one of the 153 scholars of St Paul's School. His father bought a house somewhere in the City, where the

1 S.P., 63/313, f. 78, partly printed in C.S.P. (Ireland), 1663–65, p. 49.
2 S.P., 63/315, f. 42. Cf. C.S.P. (Ireland), 1666–69, p. 281.
3 H.M.C., iv, 247. This is wrongly calendared as January 10, 1662/3, instead of 1663/4, a mistake which confused Lord Wolseley.
4 W. A. Shaw, The Knights of England, ii, 239.

fourteen-year-old boy lived while he attended school;[1] but on September 13, 1664, Winston was appointed Junior Clerk Comptroller to the Board of Green Cloth, a minor post in the royal household, and moved into Whitehall.[2]

There is no contemporary record of John Churchill at St Paul's School.[3] In fact, all the records of the school were destroyed in the Great Fire of 1666. However, the Rev. George North, Rector of Colyton, has inscribed on p. 483 of his copy of Knight's *Life of Colet*, long preserved in the Bodleian Library and now at St Paul's School, the following note against a reference to Vegetius' *De Re Militari*:

> From this very book, John Churchill, scholar of this school, afterwards the celebrated Duke of Marlborough, first learnt the elements of the art of war, as was told to me, George North on Saint Paul's day 1724/5 by an old clergyman who said he was a contemporary scholar, was then well acquainted with him, and frequently saw him read it. This I testify to be true.
>
> G. NORTH[4]

Several of his biographers have weighed the significance of this fact, if it be true. On the one hand, it is contended that John's knowledge of Latin at that time could not have enabled him to derive any profit from the military principles expounded by Vegetius, even in so far as such principles were applicable to the conditions of eighteenth-century warfare. On the other hand, it has often been suggested that by some occult dispensation our hero was able to extract various modern sunbeams from this ancient cucumber.

About 1665 the Duchess of York was graciously pleased to offer Winston's eldest daughter, Arabella, a coveted appointment as maid of honour. Historians have inquired in wonder how a strict and faithful husband, a devoted father, and a

1 The Duchess of Marlborough to David Mallet, October 4, 1744, following the passage about St Paul's School quoted below at p. 46: "And the Duke of Marlborough . . . shewed me the House where he lived." (Spencer MSS.)

2 Wolseley, i, 22, quoting the records of the Board of Green Cloth.

3 There is an article by R. B. Gardiner in *The Pauline* of June 1892 which assembles the printed evidence of Marlborough's presence at St Paul's School. The best evidence of this, however, is that of Marlborough's wife, quoted below at p. 46.

4 Coxe (*Memoirs of Marlborough*, chapter i) wrongly asserts that this note is in a copy of Vegetius. The information that the note is to-day in the Walker Library of St Paul's School is from the present librarian, the Rev. I. Mavor.

God-fearing Anglican Cavalier could have allowed his well-loved daughter to become involved in a society in which so many pitfalls abounded. In fact he was delighted, and so was his wife, and every one whom they knew and respected hastened to congratulate the family upon an auspicious and most hopeful preferment. Who should say what honours might not flow from such propinquity to the King's brother and heir to the throne? The sanction of Divine Right descended not only on all around the sovereign, but upon all within the sacred circle of the blood royal. Power, fame, wealth, social distinction, awaited those who gained the royal favour. The association was honourable and innocent, and should any mishap occur, Church and State stood attentive to conceal or vindicate the damage. Thus it was thought a splendid advantage for a young girl to be established at Court and take her fortune there as it came.

Arabella after some delays prospered in the Duke of York's household. Anthony Hamilton, who is famous for the authorship of Grammont's memoirs, has penned some mischievous pages from which historians diligently fail to avert their eyes.[1] There is a tale of a riding-party to a greyhound-coursing near York, and of Arabella's horse running away in a headlong gallop; of a fall and a prostrate figure on the sward; of the Royal Duke to the rescue, and of a love born of this incident. Hamilton declares that, while Arabella's face presented no more than the ordinary feminine charms, her figure was exceedingly beautiful, and that James was inflamed by the spectacle of beauty in distress and also in disarray. It is, however, certain that some time before 1668 Arabella became the mistress of the Duke of York, and that in the next seven or eight years she bore him four children, of whom the second was James Fitz-James, afterwards Duke of Berwick, Marshal of France and victor of Almanza. There is no disputing these facts, and historians may rest upon them with confidence.

---

[1] This story is to be found in C. H. Hartmann's edition of the *Memoirs*, translated by Peter Quennell (1930), pp. 285–286. Lord Wolseley says the incident took place near York.

Among the many stains with which John Churchill's record has been darkened stands the charge that he lightly and even cheerfully acquiesced in his sister's dishonour—or honour, as it was regarded in the moral obliquity of the age. Why did he not thus early display the qualities of a future conqueror and leader of men? Why did he not arrive hot-foot at Whitehall, challenge or even chastise the high-placed seducer, and rescue the faltering damsel from her sad plight? We must admit that all researches for any active protest upon his part have been fruitless. Nearly sixty years afterwards the old Duchess, Sarah, whose outspoken opinions have already been quoted, made her comments upon this default in terms certainly not beyond the comprehension of our own day. Writing to David Mallet about Lediard's history, she says in the letter already quoted:

* I want to say something more than I have done in the enclosed Paper, to shew how extremely mistaken Mr Lediard was in nam-ing the Duke of Marlborough's Sister and her Train of Bastards. Because they had Titles he seems to think that was an Honour to the Duke of Marlborough. I think it quite the contrary. For it seems to insinuate that his first Introduction was from an infamous Relation, when the whole Truth of that matter was as follows: His sister was a Maid of Honour to the first Duchess of York, Hyde. She had at least two or three Bastards by the Duke of York or others, when her Brother was whipt at St Paul's School for not reading his Book. . . . Now I would fain have any Reasonable Body tell me what the Duke of Marlborough could do when a Boy at School to prevent the Infamy of his Sister, or why Mr Lediard could have any Judgment in mention-ing King James's Favourite.[1]

On September 28, 1665, the King commanded the Board of Green Cloth to " dispense with the attendance of Sir Winston Churchill, one of the comptrollers of my household, he being appointed a commissioner for carrying into effect the bill for the better settlement of Ireland." [2] By the following January Sir Winston was back again in Dublin, but he had left his wife and family behind him in England. By this date his

[1] See above, p. 44 n. 1. [2] C.S.P. (Dom.), 1664–65, p. 575.

ARABELLA CHURCHILL
After Sir Peter Lely
By permission of Earl Spencer

46

eldest son, John, had left school and had been made page to James, Duke of York. The author of *The Lives of the Two Illustrious Generals* relates that James had been struck by the beauty of the boy, whom he had often seen about the Court. It may be, however, that the influence of Sir Winston's patron, the Earl of Arlington, had effected this choice. The father was well content with this: he thought it the best opening he could find for any of his sons. Shortly afterwards Arlington obtained a similar, if not so exalted, position for John's brother George, to accompany the famous Earl of Sandwich, late commander-in-chief of the Navy, to the Court of Madrid. In writing from dismal Ireland to thank the Secretary of State for this attention Sir Winston, now a civil servant, observed, " though (as times go now) it is no great preferment to be a Page, yet I am not ignorant of the benefit of disposing him (in such a Juncture of time as this) into that country where all the Boys seem Men, and all the men seem wise." And he concluded his letter by hoping that " my Sons may with equal gratitude subscribe themselves as I do," his faithful servant.[1]

Sir Winston Churchill remained in Ireland, serving upon his Commission, until 1669. He returned at intervals to London to fulfil his Parliamentary duties, and seems to have acted as a sort of agent at Whitehall for the other commissioners. How competent was Sir Winston in his business? The fact that his father had been a lawyer may have given him some training in adjudicating disputes, and he seems to have waded his way honestly through the stream of petitions and counter-petitions submitted to him. In 1675 one of Ormonde's correspondents informed him that Churchill had left his papers and accounts in great confusion.[2] But a curious fact is that in his administration of his duties he

---

[1] Sir Winston Churchill to the Earl of Arlington, January 13, 1666, Dublin (S.P. 63/320, f. 9). The editor of the *C.S.P.* (*Ireland*) attributes this reference in his index to John, Duke of Marlborough, but the original letter clearly says "my younger son." As John was his eldest surviving son and George his second son it seems probable that this must be George, especially as Charles, Sir Winston's third son, was only ten years old at this date. No reference is made to the appointment in any of the biographies in *D.N.B.*

[2] Ormonde Papers, *H.M.C.*, iv, 90.

got into the bad books of the Duke of York. One of the chief causes that delayed the settlement was the grant which the Duke of York had been given of the Irish estates of the regicides. The Duke's rascally agents, " the worst under-instruments he could well light on," as the Lord-Lieutenant Ormonde described them, made claim after claim on the basis of this grant, and effectively prevented the commissioners from dealing with the cases of the poor and deserving. One summer's morning Sir Winston Churchill lost his temper with the Duke's agents, calling them " a pack of knaves and cheats that daily betrayed their master."

One of these agents, a certain Captain Thornhill, thereupon came to him, hoping to trap him into treason. There is a record of the conversation which throws an intimate and not unpleasing gleam of light on Winston's character.

> Having told him how much he had suffered by what he said in open Court, the Captain desired to know who he meant by " the Duke's agents "? The other hotly replied, " What! Are you come to challenge and Hector me? I meant *you*! " The other replied: " The words were ' the Duke's agents '—that it could not be he only meant me! " " No! " said Sir Winston, " I intended you and Dr Gorges—and the whole pack of you." " Sir! " said Thornhill, " Will you give me under your hand that I am a knave? " " Alas! " replied Churchill, " how long is it since you became so squeasy-stomached that you could not brook being called a knave? You shall have it under my hand," and called his man to fetch paper and ink. But the whilst the Captain took occasion to proceed in temptation, and told him Sir Jerome [?] was the Duke's chief agent. He presumed he durst not call him so. " Yes," in passion replied the Knight, " He's the chief knave, and so I can prove you all," and with that directed the Captain to the stairs, who seeing the necessity of either running down the stairs or being thrown down [beat a retreat] as the least of two evils.[1]

His son John would perhaps already have handled the business with more discretion. The tale was speedily carried to Whitehall. When Sir Winston was in England he found

[1] For this passage see Bagwell, *op. cit.*, and the thirty-second report of the Deputy Keeper of the Public Records (on the Carte Papers), pp. 170–181.

48

LITTLE ROCK PUBLIC LIBRARY

some difficulty in explaining his attitude to the Duke and Duchess of York. Already on March 10, 1668, he had written, " I am quite tired out with the continual duty I am upon here having obtained no other rewards from the Duchess but to be represented to the Duke as the very greatest enemy he hath of all the Commissioners." [1] However, his reckless outspokenness did not kill his favour.

Meanwhile the annals of John are even more scanty than those of his father. Marlborough is, indeed, the last of the great commanders about whose early life practically nothing is recorded. That he was born in 1650, that he lived in his grandmother's house for nine years, that he went with his father to Dublin, that he attended St Paul's School, and that he went to Court as page to the Duke of York at about the age of sixteen and later entered the Army, sums the total of our information. We know as much of the early years of Alexander the Great, Hannibal, and Julius Cæsar as we do of this figure separated from us by scarcely a couple of centuries. Thereafter we enter the periods of voluminous biographies, and Frederick the Great, Wolfe, Clive, Napoleon, Wellington, Lee, Jackson, Grant, Moltke, Marshals Foch and Haig, and General Pershing offer us rich opportunities of studying military genius in its dawn.

1 Stowe MSS., 745, f. 10.

CHAPTER III

BARBARA

(1667–71)

JOHN served the Duke of York as page, and, like his sister, dwelt happily in the royal household. His duties were neither onerous nor unpleasant. He had no money; but he lived in comfort and elegance. He knew all the great people of the English world, and many of its prettiest women. No one was concerned to be disagreeable to this attractive, discreet, engaging youth, who moved gaily about the corridors and anterooms of Whitehall with a deft, decided step, and never slipped or slid on those polished floors where a clumsy fall may so easily be final. He must have met about this time one of the King's pages, a young man five years his senior— Sidney Godolphin. There is a gulf between youths of sixteen and twenty-one. It soon narrowed. The two became friends; and their unbroken association runs through this story.

The Duke of York was a resolute and experienced commander. After religion the art of war claimed the foremost place in his thoughts. As Lord High Admiral he knew the service of the sea. His interest in the land forces was no less keen. It was his custom to spend a part of many days in reviewing and drilling the troops. He would frequently muster two battalions of the Guards in Hyde Park, and have them put through their elaborate exercises in his presence. His page accompanied him on these occasions. The mere operation of loading and firing the musket involved twenty-two distinct motions. The flint-lock was not yet adopted in England, and the priming of the weapon and the lighting of the matches were added to the process of loading the powder and ramming home wad and bullet. The bayonet, though invented, was not yet in use. One pikeman served as protection to two musketeers when the approach of cavalry was

50

BARBARA

apprehended. Very deliberate and stately were the Royal
Guards in their round beaver hats and scarlet uniforms as
they performed their complicated ritual. All the evolutions to
form a front in any direction, or to change into a column, or a
square with the steel-helmeted pikemen at the angles, were of
the same complex order. But by the long usage of drill and
discipline it was hoped that everything would be carried out
faultlessly and nothing slurred over in the heart-shaking
moments before a whirlwind of horsemen might fall with
sabres upon ranks which, their volleys once fired, were for
the time well-nigh defenceless.

At these parades the Duke of York noticed the interest of
his page. He saw the boy following with gleaming eyes the
warlike ceremonial. One day after a review he asked him
what profession he preferred. Whereupon John fell upon
his knees and demanded " a pair of colours in one of these
fine regiments." The request was not denied.[1]

We are, of course, assured that this was a piece of favouritism which he owed to his sister's shame; and—somewhat
inconsistently—that at the same time it made him the lifelong
debtor of the Duke of York. There is no need to use these
strained interpretations of what was a very ordinary transaction. It was natural enough that the son of a loyal, hard-
fighting Cavalier should be received at King Charles's Court.
In these youthful days John gained no office or promotion
that might not have come to any young gentleman accepted
there. To be made a page and afterwards an ensign was not
excessive favour, nor beyond the deserts of a healthy, well-
bred youth from a public school. These small appointments
were suited to his years and station, and were justified on his
own merits not less than on paternal claims. There is surely
no need to ferret for other explanations; nor shall we join
in the meticulous disputings in which some writers have
indulged about whether John received his commission before
or after Arabella became the Duke's mistress. The Guards
gained a good recruit officer in the normal course.

[1] The original authority for this story is *The Lives of the Two Illustrious Generals*. The date of Churchill's first commission as ensign is September 14, 1667.

51

Besides his sister Arabella John had a tie of kinship and
acquaintance with another favourite of high importance.
On the eve of his restoration Charles II met at The Hague
Barbara Villiers, then newly married to Roger Palmer, afterwards Earl of Castlemaine. She became his mistress; she
preceded him to England; she adorned the triumphs and
enhanced for him the joys of the Restoration. She was a
woman of exceeding beauty and charm, vital and passionate
in an extraordinary degree. In the six years that had passed
she had borne the King several children. At twenty-four,
in the heyday of her success, this characteristic flower of the
formidable, errant Villiers stock was the reigning beauty of
the palace. She held Charles in an intense fascination. Her
rages, her extravagances, her infidelities seemed only to bind
him more closely in her mysterious web. She was John
Churchill's second cousin once removed. His mother's
sister, a Mrs Godfrey, was her closest confidante. The
young page, it is said,[1] was often in his aunt's apartments
eating sweets, and there Barbara soon met and made friends
with this good-looking boy. Very likely she had known him
from his childhood. Naturally she was nice to him, and
extended her powerful protection to her young and sprightly
relation. Naturally, too, she aroused his schoolboy's admiration. There is not, as we shall hope to convince the reader,
the slightest ground for suggesting that the beginning of
their affection was not perfectly innocent and such as would
normally subsist between a well-established woman of the
world and her cousin, a boy of sixteen, newly arrived at the
Court where she was dominant.

That Barbara was an elevating influence upon John's life,
even in these early days, it is far from our purpose to contend. Says Burnet:[2]

> The ruine of his [Charles'] reign, and of all his affairs, was
> occasioned chiefly by his delivering himself up at his first coming
> over to a mad range of pleasures. One of the race of Villiers,
> then married to Palmer, a Papist, soon after made Earl of Castle-
> maine, who afterwards being separated from him was advanced

1 *The New Atalantis* (ed. 1720), i, 31. 2 *History of My Own Time*, i, 94.

BARBARA, DUCHESS OF CLEVELAND

By permission of Viscount Dillon

to be Duchess of Cleveland, was his first and longest mistress, by whom he had five children. She was a woman of great beauty, but most enormously vitious and ravenous; foolish but imperious, very uneasy to the King, and always carrying on intrigues with other men, while yet pretending she was jealous of him. His passion for her and her strange behaviour towards him, did so disorder him, that often he was not master of himself, nor capable of minding business, which in so critical a time required great application.

More than forty years later (1709) there was published a book *The New Atalantis*, written by a certain Mrs Manley. She was a woman of disreputable character paid by the Tories to take part in the campaign of detraction which, in the intense political passion of the time, was organized against Marlborough. Swift, who to a large extent directed this vilipending, speaks of her as one of his " under spur-leathers." *The New Atalantis* is a scandalous and indecent chronicle of the Court of Charles II, conceived in the mood of the *Decameron* or the memoirs of Casanova, but without the grace and sparkle which have redeemed these works. In its scurrility and lasciviousness it goes far beyond Grammont. No names of actual persons are mentioned, but the identity of the characters is apparent. A sexual or corrupt motive is assigned for almost every action or transaction. The vilest aspersions are cast upon the morals of William III. Marlborough figures as " Count Fortunatus," and a filthy tale is told of his seduction at sixteen by Lady Castlemaine, and of the lavish bribes with which she kept him in her toils.

The book, which extended to four small volumes, was widely read, and passed through six editions in the ten years following its first publication. It is, apart from its malice, such a jumble of anachronisms and obvious mistakes that it was not taken seriously even by the particular kind of base public for whom such scribes cater in every age. We should not think it worth while to notice it here, but for the fact that Lord Macaulay, in his desire to insult and blacken the memory of the Duke of Marlborough, has transcribed whole passages, or such parts of them as were printable, into his famous history. He of course rejects Mrs Manley as a witness against his hero William, and dismisses her and other low-class pamphleteers in terms of blistering scorn. Yet he accepts this same Mrs Manley as entirely credible and valid where Marlborough is concerned. She is his authority for much that he has written about Marlborough's loves and marriage. He incorporated these forgotten slanders verbatim in his stately pages, and set them rolling round the world.

John was certainly a success at Court, and his favour was not diminished by his smart uniform. Still, adolescence is a trying period both for the victim and his companions. In those days there was a feeling that young men about the Court should take their turn of service with the fleet or Army as gentlemen-volunteers. Still more was this opinion effective upon a young officer. Leave to serve abroad would readily be granted by his regiment, and all his friends and well-wishers would give their cordial approval. John found doctrine and prospect alike congenial.

Some time in 1668 he quitted the Court and sailed for Tangier. The gossip-mongers suggest that the Duchess of York herself had begun to show him undue attention: or, again, that he was getting rather old to be on such privileged terms with Lady Castlemaine. But there is no excuse for looking beyond the reasons which have been set forth. Such evidence as exists shows that his departure and prolonged absence were entirely in accordance with his own inclination. He went to Tangier, or at any rate he stayed there and in the Mediterranean for nearly three years, because he liked the life of adventure, and because the excitement of the petty warfare was refreshing after the endless glittering ceremonial of the Court. Few youths of spirit are content at eighteen with comforts or even caresses. They seek physical fitness, movement, and the comradeship of their equals under hard conditions. They seek distinction, not favour, and exult in manly independence.

Tangier, newly acquired as the dowry of Catharine of Braganza, was the scene, then as now, of constant fighting with the Moors.[1] The House of Commons hated Tangier, and grudged its expense in speeches singularly modern. The King and his military and naval advisers—indeed, the cream of informed opinion—regarded it as far more important to the future strategy of England than had been the possession of the lately sold and lamented Dunkirk. Tangier was not only one of the gate-posts of the Mediterranean, but it was an important base for all the naval operations against the Algerian corsairs. These pirates pursued the policy of not being at peace with more than one or at most two of the European Powers at once. They preyed on the commerce of all the rest, capturing their ships and cargoes and selling the crews as slaves. As many as sixty or seventy galleys rowed by slaves sometimes harried the Mediterranean in a single year; and many were the merciless fights between them and the ships of the slowly rising Royal Navy of England. Tangier itself was a peculiar military proposition. It lived in a state of almost perpetual siege. The town was defended not only by walls, but by several lines of redoubts constructed of earth and palisades, protected by very deep ditches and held by garrisons of sometimes as many as two or three hundred men. On the desert plains between and before these strong points the Royal Dragoons paraded in constant presence of the enemy cavalry, and on occasion sallied out upon them at the charge.

We cannot fix with exactness the period in which John Churchill served at Tangier. There is, indeed, no contemporary evidence of his ever having been there. The episode is ignored in *The Lives of the Two Illustrious Generals*. There is, however, a circumstantial account in Lediard (1733), sixty years after the event had occurred, of his being attached to the Tangier garrison. This has been freely accepted by all Marlborough's biographers, notably by Coxe, and perhaps receives some confirmation from Marlborough's letter to his wife of June 26, 1707,[2] in which he says:

> The weather is so very hot and the dust so very great that I have this hour to myself, the officers not caring to be abroad till

1 *Cf.* E. M. G. Routh, *Tangier* (1912). 2 Printed in Coxe, chapter lviii.

the hour of orders obliges them to it. It is most certain that *when I was in Spain, in the month of August,* I was not more sensible of the heat than I am at this minute.

There is little doubt that Marlborough considered Tangier 'Spain.' If the story of his presence at Tangier is true, when was he there and for how long? It cannot have been earlier than September 1667, when he received his " pair of colours"; nor can it be later than the February of 1671, when he fought a duel in London. We may therefore assume that his service in Tangier covered the years 1668 to 1670.

He seems to have lived from eighteen to twenty the rough, care-free life of a subaltern officer engaged in an endless frontier guerrilla. That the conditions were by no means intolerable is shown by the following letter, written from Madrid in March 1670 to the Earl of Arlington by the Earl of Castlemaine, on his way back from Tangier.

* At my arrival, I was never so surprized than to find so many officers so very well clad and fashioned that though I have been in most of the best garrisons of Europe I do not remember I ever yet saw the like, and which added to my admiration was that though necessaries are a great deal dearer, and all superfluities there four times the value of what they are in England, yet the Generality both of our Commanders and Soldiers lay up something, which argues much industry. . . .

For the Town itself (if the Mole be made) all the world sees it will, as it were, command the Mediterranean, by stopping its mouth; how quick a receipt it is for the Merchants with [in] any War with Spain, what a Bridle it will be of the Pirates of Barbary, as a Constant place of our own, for our men of War, with opportunities also of revictualling and fitting as if we were at home; which bears now no small proportion with the expense of an expedition; neither is it a little honour to the Crown to have a Nursery of its own for soldiers, without being altogether beholding to our Neighbours for their Education and breeding.[1]

On the very day this letter was written there was signed also one of those infrequent contemporary documents which

1 S.P., 94/56, ff. 94–94 v.

BARBARA LITTLE ROCK PUBLIC LIBRARY

give us facts in Marlborough's youthful history. A Signet Office order of Charles II dated March 21, 1670, of which there are three copies in the Record Office,[1] runs as follows:

* Right trustie and Wellbeloved Counsellors, Wee greete you well. Whereas wee are informed that there is due unto Our trustie & Wellbeloved Servant Sr Winston Churchill Knt (late of Our Commissioners for ye Settlement of Our Kingdome of Ireland) an Arreare for his allowance for dyett and lodging whilst he was in Our service there amounting unto ye Summe of One hundred & forty pounds. And it having been represented to Us in favour of John Churchill sonne of ye sd Sr Winston that ye said summe so in arreare hath been bestowed upon him by his father for & towards his equippage & other expenses in ye employment he is now forthwith by our command to undertake on board ye Fleet in ye Mediterranean Seas.

Wee being graciously willing to give all due encouragement to ye forwardness & early affecons of ye sd John Churchill to our Service as also in justification of what is due to ye said Sr Winston Churchill as aforesaid have thought fitt hereby to Signifie Our pleasure to you accordingly. Our Will & pleasure is that immediately after your Receipt of these Our L(ett)ers you issue out & pay unto the said Sr Winston Churchill or his Assignes, Out of any our Treasure now in Yo(ur) hands the said Summe of One hundred & forty pounds in full satisfacon of the said Arrears so due from us aforesaid. (All prohibitions notwithstanding) wherewith Wee are graciously pleased in p̄ticular bounty to the said John Churchill upon this occasion to dispense.

Several conclusions can be drawn from this warrant. The English fleet in the Mediterranean was in 1670 engaged in an intermittent blockade of Algiers. Sir Thomas Allin was setting out with a squadron of fourteen ships to renew his blockade. An Admiralty regiment, or, as we should say, a 'Naval Brigade' or Division, was being recruited and embarked as marines for the operation. It seems certain that John obtained permission to exchange his service of the land for that of the sea, and was attached to the Algiers expedition of 1670. Whether he came home to England beforehand, or whether, as is possible, he joined the squadron when it or

1 S.P., Signet Office, vii, 195, and S.P., 63/327, ff. 54–55.

57

part of it called at Tangier, is uncertain. We know that he required an outfit for the campaign and that his father bought it for him. The warrant clearly shows that both father and son had very little money at this time. If John then had been Lady Castlemaine's lover, and if the tales of his early subornation by her were true, so modest a sum as £140 would surely not have been a difficulty sufficient to be brought to the compassion of the King. It is also obvious from the terms of the warrant that he was not out of favour with the King. Charles II was going bankrupt in 1670, and the phrase " all prohibitions notwithstanding " shows that this sum of £140 was specially exempted from what was no doubt an almost general moratorium of cash payments from the Royal Exchequer.

The conclusions which we base upon this document— hitherto strangely unnoticed by historians—are confirmed by the significant negative evidence of Pepys. His *Diary* contains the fullest accounts of the fashionable scandals of the Court of Charles II. Nothing seems to be missed. He had as good opportunities as anyone else of knowing about such affairs. It is inconceivable that a notorious and outrageous intrigue between the Duke of York's page and the King's mistress, about which all tongues were wagging, should not have been recorded by him. But his voluble, engaging *Diary* is dumb on this subject. It stops short in May 1669, and a few years later Pepys began his great career as manager and virtual master of the Admiralty, about which few have ever troubled to read. Evidently before that date no whisper had reached his attentive ears.

John's experiences with the fleet are unrecorded. All we know is that in August 1670 Admiral Allin defeated a number of Algerian corsairs, and was afterwards relieved of his command. Surveying all the facts we have been able to marshal, we may accept the following conclusions: that Churchill, still penniless and heart-whole, quitted the Court in 1668, that he served at Tangier till 1670, that early in that year he sailed with the fleet against the pirates, and served for some months in the Mediterranean. Eagerly seeking adventure

LITTLE ROCK PUBLIC LIBRARY

by land or sea, he pulled all the strings he could to convey him to the scenes of action, and his zeal was noticed and well regarded in the highest circles.

So far all is well, and the conduct of our hero will command general approbation. We now approach a phase upon which the judgment of individuals and periods will vary. In all his journey Marlborough found two, and only two, love-romances. Two women, both extraordinary beings, both imperious, tempestuous personalities, both well-known historical figures, are woven successively into his life. Here and now the first appears. We have already made her acquaintance.

At the beginning of 1671 John Churchill, grown a man, bronzed by African sunshine, close-knit by active service and tempered by discipline and danger, arrived home from the Mediterranean. He seems to have been welcomed with widespread pleasure by the Court, and by none more than by Barbara, now become Duchess of Cleveland. She was twenty-nine and he twenty. They were already affectionate friends. The distant degree of cousinly kinship which had hitherto united them had sanctioned intimacy, and did not now prohibit passion. Affections, affinities, and attractions were combined. Desire walked with opportunity, and neither was denied. John almost immediately became her lover, and for more than three years this wanton and joyous couple shared pleasures and hazards. The cynical, promiscuous, sagacious-indulgent sovereign was outwitted or outfaced. Churchill was almost certainly the father of Barbara's last child,[1] a daughter, born on July 16, 1672, and the ties between them were not severed until the dawn of his love for Sarah Jennings in 1675.

It is an exaggeration to speak of Churchill as " rivalling the King in his nearest affection." After ten years Charles II was already tiring of the tantrums and divagations of the Duchess of Cleveland, and other attractions made their power

---

1 Cf. G. S. Steinmann, Barbara, Duchess of Cleveland, p. 235, quoting Abel Boyer, Annals. See the plate facing p. 66.

felt. From 1671 onward the bonds which were to bind the King and the Duchess were their children, most of whom were undoubtedly his own. None the less, the intimacy of John and Barbara continued to cause Charles repeated annoyance, and their illicit loves, their adventures and escapades, were among the most eminent scandals of the English Court at this period.

We have two indications of John's whereabouts during this year.[1]

News-letter from London

February 6, 1671

Yesterday was a duel between Mr Fenwick and Mr Churchill esquires who had for their seconds Mr Harpe and Mr Newport, son to my Lord Newport; it ended with some wounds for Mr Churchill, but no danger of life.

And again:

Sir Christopher Lyttelton to Lord Hatton

LANDGUARD
August 21, 1671

I have y^r Lordships of Aug^st 3d, in wch you give mee a worse account of Mr Bruce then by y^r former, and for wch I think you could not be too severe with him. His captaine has not had much better luck at home, for hee has bine lately engaged in a rencounter with young Churchill. I know not ye quarrel; but Herbert rann Churchill twice through the arme, and Churchill him into ye thigh, and, after, Herbert disarmed him. But w^ht is ye worse, I heare y^t Churchill has so spoke of it, that the King and Duke are angry wth Herbert. I know not w^ht he has done to justifie himself.

Two of the adventures of the lovers are well known. The first is that, being surprised by Charles in the Duchess's bedroom, John saved her honour—or what remained of it—by jumping from the window, a considerable height, into the courtyard below. For this feat, delighted at his daring and address, she presented him with £5000.[2]

---

1 *C.S.P.* (*Dom.*), 1671, p. 71. *Hatton Correspondence* (Camden Society), i, 66.
2 Burnet (i, 475) describes this episode, but does not name Churchill. *Cf.* Chesterfield's *Letters*, i, 136, and *The New Atalantis*, i, 21 *seq.*

CHARLES II
Copy of a portrait by Sir Peter Lely
By permission of the Duke of Portland

The second anecdote is attributed to the French Ambassador, Barillon. The Duke of Buckingham, he says, gave a hundred guineas to one of his waiting-women to be well informed of the intrigue. He knew that Churchill would be one evening at a certain hour in Barbara's apartments. He brought the King to the spot. The lover was hidden in the Duchess's cupboard (she was not Duchess till 1670). After having prowled about the chamber the King, much upset, asked for sweets and liqueurs. His mistress declared that the key of the cupboard was lost. The King replied that he would break down the door. On this she opened the door, and fell on her knees on one side while Churchill, discovered, knelt on the other. The King said to Churchill, " Go; you are a rascal, but I forgive you because you do it to get your bread." [1]

It is a good story, and the double-barrelled insult is very characteristic of Charles. But is it true? Barillon, who did not himself arrive in England till September 1677, probably got it from his predecessor, Courtin. He fixes the date as 1667. Burnet's story belongs to 1670. Here is a fine exposure of these gossips. There can be little doubt, as we have shown, that nothing of this kind can have occurred before 1671. It is therefore one of those good stories invented long afterwards and fastened, as so many are, on well-known figures.[2]

We are on much firmer ground when we come to money matters. The famous Lord Halifax in the intervals of statecraft conducted a rudimentary form of life insurance. The rates were attractive, for the lives of young gallants and soldiers—the prey of wars, duels, adventures, and disease—were precarious. At twenty-four John purchased from Lord Halifax for £4500 an annuity of £500 a year for life. It was a profitable investment. He enjoyed its fruits for nearly fifty years. It was the foundation of his immense fortune. Where did the money come from? No one can suggest any other source than Barbara. Was this, then, the £5000 that

1 *Correspondance politique, Angleterre*, t. 137, f. 404.
2 It may well be that these two stories are one, and that untrue.

she had given him when he leaped from the window, and if
so what are we to think of the transaction? Some of Marlborough's defenders have disputed the facts. They point to
the scanty evidence—contemporary gossip and a passing
reference in one of Lord Chesterfield's letters. The Blenheim
papers contain the actual receipt, which, since it has not seen
the light of day for more than two hundred and fifty years,
we present in facsimile on the opposite page.

The code of the seventeenth century did not regard a man's
taking money from a rich mistress as necessarily an offence
against honour. It was no more a bar to social success and
worldly regard than are marriages for money in these modern
times. But every one has been struck by the judicious fore-
sight of the investment. Moralists have been shocked by the
fact that John did not squander Barbara's gift in riotous
living. Cards, wine, and other women would seem to be
regarded by these logicians as more appropriate channels for
the use of such funds. They treat the transaction as the
aggravation of an infamy. It may well be true that no other
man of twenty-four then alive in England would have turned
this money into an income which secured him a modest but
lifelong independence. The dread of poverty inculcated in
his early days at Ashe may be the explanation. It may be that
Barbara, knowing his haunting prepossession, resolved to free
him from it, and that an annuity was the prescribed purpose
of the gift. However this may be, there is the bond.

It is curious to see how the whole episode has been judged
in different generations. Lediard gloated as eagerly as Lord
Macaulay upon *The New Atalantis,* and like him extracted
and adopted the spicy bits. But Lediard had a different
object. Writing in 1733, he dwells with gusto upon these
exploits and evidently thinks that they redound to the credit
of his hero.[1]

To relate all the Atchievements of our young Adventurer in
the Cause of Venus, which were the Amusement of the Beau
Mond, and furnish'd Matter of Discourse for the Gallant Assem-

1 *Life of John, Duke of Marlborough,* i, 28–29.

1674

Know all persons by these presents That I
George Lord Viscount Halifax Have on
and before the day of the Date of these presents
received and had of John Churchill Esq
Sonne and heire apparent of Sir Winston
Churchill of Greate Mintern in the
County of Dorsett Knight the Summe of
foure Thousand and five hundred
pounds of lawfull money of England
being the Consideration money of (and
mentioned to bee paid to mee by the said
John Churchill in and by) one paire of
Indentures bearinge even Date with
these presents and made or mentioned
to bee made betweene mee the said
Viscount Halifax of the one part And
the said John Churchill of the other
part off and from which said Summe of
foure Thousand and five hundred
pounds I the said George Viscount
Halifax Doe hereby release and
discharge the said John Churchill his
heires Executors and Administrators
for ever by these presents In witnes
whereof I the said George Lord Viscount
Halifax have hereunto sett my hand &
Seale the thirtieth day of Aprill one
Thousand six hundred Seaventy and
foure ./.

Sealed and delivered in
the presence of

Wm Cavenny
John Prince
John Bird
Arnold Squibb

Halifax

LORD HALIFAX'S RECEIPT

Blenheim MSS.

blies of those jovial Days, would carry me too far from the main
Design of this Work.

Therewith he yields himself to the temptation with an
appetite which sharpens as it feeds.

It was said, in those Times, that the handsomest of King
Charles's Mistresses, being importuned, by a Gentleman of
more Fortune than Discretion, to bestow the last Favour upon
him; She agreed to let him enjoy what he was sollicitous for,
at the moderate Expence of £10,000 for one Night. This the
enamour'd Fool paid down; But, thinking to heighten the
Pleasures of Venus, by those of Bacchus, took so large a Portion
of the latter's Favour, that when the happy Hour came, he was
not in a Capacity, to take Possession of the Jewel he had so dearly
purchas'd. The Gallant, having met with this Disappointment
thought the Lady would be too conscientious not to admit him,
a second Time, to her Favours, when able to enjoy them, for the
same Fee; But she had the Modesty to insist on a new Bargain,
and the same Sum over again. Surprized at the unreasonable
Demand, Rage took Place of the Passion of Love, and the
Gentleman, in a Fury, left her to satiate her Inclination for a more
amiable Person, then justly call'd the Handsomest and most
Agreable Cavalier at Court. To him she gave the entire Sum
left her by her Cully, as a Token of her future Favour, which he
took better Care to deserve, and is supposed in the Sequel, to have
had so large a Share of, as, in some Measure, laid the Foundation
of his Fortune.

He proceeds to reinforce this scandalous narration by
quoting Pope's imitation of Horace, written thirty years later:

> Not so, who of Ten Thousand gull'd her Knight,
> Then ask'd Ten Thousand for a second Night;
> The Gallant too, to whom she paid it down,
> Liv'd to refuse that Mistress half a Crown.

It must have cost Macaulay a pang to reject, as he does,
this culminating calumny. It fitted so well the scenario he
had set himself to prepare. It was exactly the feature he
required for his villain. But the fact that the Duchess of
Cleveland died a wealthy woman and was never in want of
money, still less of half a crown, was an obstacle which even
his enthusiasm could not surmount. So he put it aside, and

paraded his sacrifice as an evidence of his sense of justice and responsibility.

Archdeacon Coxe, writing in 1819, deals far more decorously with the matter:

> So handsome and accomplished an officer could not fail to be entangled in the gallantries of a dissipated court. But we spare the reader the detail of these irregularities, which are doubtless exaggerated by the licentious pens of that and subsequent times. We shall barely advert to an ancedote which has obtained credit relative to a connexion with the duchess of Cleveland, whom he is accused of treating afterwards with the basest ingratitude. The falsity of this tale will be sufficiently shown by the observation that it is originally drawn from so impure and questionable a source as *The New Atalantis.* Admitting, however, that Colonel Churchill might have experienced the liberality of the duchess, we need not seek for the cause in an intercourse of gallantry, since he had a strong claim to her protection from affinity, being nearly related to her on the side of his mother, who was her cousin.
>
> Whatever may have been the conduct of Colonel Churchill during the fervour of youth, and amidst the temptations of a dissolute court, his irregularities soon yielded to the influence of a purer passion, which recalled him from licentious connexions, and gave a colour to his future life.[1]

It was reserved for Macaulay, writing in 1858 in the pristine vigour of Victorian propriety, to add a lurid colour to this already sharply defined woodcut. "He was," says Macaulay, "thrifty in his very vices, and levied ample contributions on ladies enriched by the spoils of more liberal lovers." "He was kept by the most profuse, imperious, and shameless of harlots." "He subsisted upon the infamous wages bestowed upon him by the Duchess of Cleveland." He was "insatiable of riches." He was "one of the few who have in the bloom of youth loved lucre more than wine or women, and who have, at the height of greatness, loved lucre more than power or fame." "All the precious gifts which nature had lavished upon him he valued chiefly for what they would fetch." "At

1 i, 9–10.

twenty he made money of his beauty and his vigour; at sixty he made money of his genius and glory."[1]

Charles Bradlaugh, another hostile historian, under some provocation from Lord Randolph Churchill, who had described his constituents as "the dregs of the gutter," developed these themes in the eighties with somewhat more restraint.[2]

Macaulay's taunts did not go unanswered. In 1864 a writer of extraordinary power, but hardly ever read, published a book, long out of print, the staple of which is a series of essays particularly challenging not only the accuracy, but the good faith of the famous historian. "Paget's Examen" sums up the story of Churchill's youth with a knowledge, justice, and force which are unsurpassable.

Plunged at a very early age into the dissipations of the Court of Charles II, his remarkably handsome person and his engaging manners soon attracted notice. For the loathsome imputation cast upon him by Lord Macaulay, that he availed himself of these advantages for the purposes which he intimates—that he bore to the wealthy and licentious ladies of the Court the relation which Tom Jones did to Lady Bellaston—we can discover no foundation even in the scandalous chronicles of those scandalous days. That he did not bring to the Court of Charles the virtue which made the overseer of Potiphar's household famous in that of Pharaoh, must be freely admitted. The circumstances of his intrigue with the Duchess of Cleveland are recorded in the pages of Grammont. Never, says Hamilton, were her charms in greater perfection than when she cast her eyes on the young officer of the Guards. That Churchill, in the bloom of youth, should be insensible to the passion which he had awakened in the breast of the most beautiful woman of that voluptuous Court, was hardly to be expected. He incurred, in consequence, the displeasure of the King, who forbade him the Court. Far be it from us to be the advocates of lax morality; but Churchill must be judged by the standard of the day. He corrupted no innocence; he invaded no domestic peace. The Duchess of Cleveland was not only the most beautiful, but she was also the most

1 *History*, i, 460–462; iii, 437–438.
2 C. Bradlaugh, *John Churchill, Duke of Marlborough* (1884).

licentious and the most inconstant of women. From the King down to Jacob Hall she dispensed her favours according to the passion or the fancy of the moment. She was as liberal of her purse as of her person, and Marlborough, a needy and handsome ensign, no doubt shared both. But it is a mere misuse of language to charge Churchill with receiving "infamous wages" or to say that he was "kept by the most profuse, imperious, and shameless of harlots" because he entertained a daring and successful passion for the beautiful mistress of the King.[1]

Between these various accounts the reader must choose according to his temperament and inclination. We have presented the facts, edifying or otherwise, as they are known. They can best be judged in the war-time setting which further chapters afford.

[1] J. Paget, *The New " Examen,"* No. I, " Lord Macaulay and the Duke of Marl-borough " (1861), reprinted in *Paradoxes and Puzzles* (1874).

BARBARA, DUCHESS OF CLEVELAND, AND HER DAUGHTER BARBARA
Henri Gascars
By permission of Viscount Dillon

CHAPTER IV

THE EUROPE OF CHARLES II

(1667–72)

IT is fitting to turn from the scraps and oddities which, pieced together, form our only record of Churchill's youth to survey the vast, stately European scene wherein he now began to move and was one day to shine.

The supreme fact upon the Continent in the latter half of the seventeenth century was the might of France. Her civil wars were over. All internal divisions had been effaced, and Louis XIV reigned over a united nation of eighteen or nineteen million souls possessed of the fairest region on the globe. Feudalism, with its local warriors and their armed retainers, had at length been blown away by gunpowder, and as wars were frequent, standing armies had arisen in all the states of Europe. The possession of organized regular troops, paid, disciplined, trained by the central Government, was the aim of all the rulers, and in the main the measure of their power. This process had in the course of a few generations obliterated or reduced to mere archaic survivals the Parliamentary and municipal institutions of France. In different ways similar effects had followed the same process in other Continental countries. Everywhere sovereignty had advanced with giant strides. The peoples of Europe passed out of a long confusion into an age of autocracies in full panoply against all foes from within or from without.

But for the storm-whipped seas which lapped the British islands, our fortunes would have followed the road upon which our neighbours had started. England had not, however, the same compulsive need for a standing army as the land Powers. She stood aloof, moving slowly and lagging behind the martial throng. In the happy nick of time her

Parliament grew strong enough to curb the royal power and to control the armed forces, and she thus became the cradle, as she is still the citadel, of free institutions throughout the world.

There she lay, small, weak, divided, and almost unarmed. The essence of her domestic struggle forbade a standing army. Scotland and Ireland lay, heavy embarrassments and burdens, on her shoulders or at her flank. Although there was much diffused well-being throughout the country, very little money could be gathered by the State. Here again the conditions of the internal struggle kept the executive weak. The whole population of England—their strength thus latent and depressed, their energies dispersed, their aim unfocused—attained little more than five millions.

Yet upon the other side of the Channel, only twenty-one miles across the dancing waves, rose the magnificent structure of the French monarchy and society. One hundred and forty thousand soldiers in permanent pay, under lifelong professional officers, constituted the peace-time force of France. Brilliant, now famous, captains of war or fortification, Turenne, Condé, Vauban; master organizers like Louvois; trainers like Martinet (his name a household word)—forged or wielded this splendid instrument of power. Adroit, sagacious, experienced Foreign Ministers and diplomatists urged the march of French aggrandisement. Financiers and trade Ministers as wise and instructed as Colbert reached out for colonies bound by exclusive commercial dealings, or consolidated the expanding finances of the most modern, the most civilized, and the strongest society.

Nor were the glories of France confined to the material sphere. The arts flourished in a long summer. In the latter half of the century French was becoming not only the universal language of diplomacy outside the Holy Roman Empire, but also that of polite society and even of literature. The French drama was performed and French poetry read, the names of Molière, Racine, Boileau were honoured, throughout the cultured cities of the world. French styles of architecture, of painting, even of music, were imitated in every

LITTLE ROCK PUBLIC LIBRARY

Court in Germany. Even the Dutch, who were contributing notably to the progress of civilization in the financial, industrial, and domestic arts, accused themselves under William of Orange of being "debauched by French habits and customs."[1] French Court theologians, their wits sharpened first by the Jansenist and secondly by the Gallican controversy, rivalled those of Rome. French Catholicism, adorned by figures like Fénelon or Bossuet, was the most stately, imposing, and persuasive form of the Old Faith which had yet confronted the Reformation. The conquest, planned and largely effected, was not only military and economic, but religious, moral, and intellectual. It was the most magnificent claim to world dominion ever made since the age of the Antonines. And at the summit there reigned in unchallenged splendour for more than half a century a masterful, competent, insatiable, hard-working egoist, born to a throne.

Since the days of Queen Elizabeth and the Spanish Armada Spain had been the bugbear of Protestant England. Many devout families, suffering all things, still adhered to the Catholic faith. But deep in the hearts of the English people from peer to peasant memories of Smithfield burned with a fierce glow which any breeze could rouse into flame. And now Spain was in decrepitude, insolvent, incoherent, tracing her genealogies and telling her beads. Her redoubtable infantry, first conquered nearly thirty years ago by Condé at Rocroi, had vanished. In their place, alike in the Spanish Netherlands, which we now know as Belgium and Luxembourg, and in the New World, stood decaying garrisons, the mockery of soldiers. The Spanish harbours were filled with rotting ships; the Spanish treasury was bare. The once-proud empire of Charles V, irreparably exhausted by over a century of almost continuous war, had fallen a victim to religious mania. Layer upon layer of superstition and ceremonial encrusted the symbols of departed power. Cruelties ever more fantastic enforced a dwindling and crumbling authority. There remained an immense pride, an ancient and secure aristocracy, the title-deeds of half the outer world,

[1] P. Blok, *History of the People of the Netherlands,* vol. iv, chapters xii, xix.

a despotic Church, and a throne occupied by a sickly, sterile child who might die any day, leaving no trace behind.

Gradually the fear of Spain had faded from the English mind. In Oliver Cromwell, a man of conservative temperament, born under Queen Elizabeth, the old prejudice obstinately survived. But when, in 1654, he proposed to join France in war against Spain, his council of Roundhead generals surprised him by their resistance. Left to themselves, they would probably have taken the opposite side. The authority of the Lord Protector prevailed, and his Ironside redcoats stormed the Spanish positions upon the sanddunes by Dunkirk. Wide circles of instructed English opinion regarded these antagonisms as old-fashioned and obsolete. To them the new menace to English faith, freedom, and trade was France. This Battle of the Dunes marked the end of the hundred years' struggle with Spain. Henceforth the dangers and difficulties of England would not arise from Spanish strength, but from Spanish weakness. Henceforth the mounting power of France would be the main preoccupation of Englishmen.

Nearest akin in race, religion, and temperament to the English, the Dutch were their sharpest rivals upon the seas, in trade and colonization. It is said that at this time one-half of the population of Holland gained their livelihood from commerce, industry, and shipping.[1] A tough, substantial race, welded by their struggles against Spanish tyranny, dwelling, robust and acquisitive, under embattled oligarchies, the Dutch clashed with the English at many points. There was the Dutch navy, with its memories of Tromp and his broom "to sweep the English from the seas." There were the dangers of Dutch competition in the colonies and in trade as far as the coasts of India, in the East, and as far as New Amsterdam, since 1664 renamed New York, across the Atlantic. Thus the war which Cromwell had waged against Holland had broken out again in the earlier years of Charles II. Its course was ignominious to England. The sailors of the Royal Navy were in those days paid only at the end of a three

---

[1] De la Court, *Political Maxims of the State of Holland.*

or four years' commission. The crews who came home in 1666 received their pay warrants, called tickets, for three years' hard service. Such was the poverty of the Crown that when these were presented at the Naval Pay Office no payment could be made. Conceiving themselves intolerably defrauded, some of the sailors committed an unpardonable crime. They made their way to Holland and piloted the Dutch fleet through the intricate approaches of the Thames estuary.[1] Several of the laid-up English ships in the Medway and the Thames were burned, and the rumble of the Dutch guns was plainly heard in London. But the lack of money forbade effectual reprisals. Charles and his subjects swallowed the insult, and peace was made in 1667. A great bitterness continued between the countries, and the claim of England to the unquestioned sovereignty of the Narrow Seas, though recognized by the peace treaty, accorded ill with the actual incidents of the naval war. "With the Treaty of Breda," says the historian of the United Netherlands,[2] "began the most glorious period of the Republic."

The relations between England and Holland followed a chequered course, and many years were to pass before their grievous quarrels about trade and naval supremacy were finally thrust into the background before the ever-growing French power. It is easy nowadays to say that Charles "should have marched with the Dutch and fought the French" or "marched with the Protestants and fought the Papists." But the Dutch attitude was oblique and baffling, and many great Catholic states were opposed to France. Holland was then ruled by John de Witt and his brother Cornelius. The De Witts were friendly to France. John de Witt believed that by astute conciliation he could come to terms with Louis XIV. Louis had always a potent bribe for the Dutch in the carrying trade of France, on which they thrived. Had not France been the friend, and even champion, of the Republic during its birth-throes? And what was Belgium, that fief of Spain, but a convenient, useful buffer-

---

1 Callender, *The Naval Side of British History*, pp. 116, 117.
2 P. Blok, *op. cit.*

state whose partition, if inevitable, offered large, immediate gains to both its neighbours? There were, indeed, two Hollands—the pacific, and at times the Francophile, Holland of John de Witt and Amsterdam, and the Holland which adhered to the memory and lineage of William the Silent, and saw in his frail, spirited, already remarkable descendant the prince who would sustain its cause. No Government, French or English, could tell which of these Hollands would be supreme in any given situation.

These uncertainties arose in part from the dubious, balancing attitude of what we now call Prussia. The Great Elector of Brandenburg ruled the main northern mass of Protestant Germany. But upon his western bounds along the whole course of the Rhine, and stretching southward to Bavaria and the Danube, lay a belt of powerful minor states, partly Protestant, partly Catholic in sympathy, whose accession to the one side or the other might be decisive in the balance of power. Beyond Prussia, again, lay Poland, a large, unkempt, slatternly kingdom, ranging from the Baltic to the Ukraine, still partly in feudalism, with an elective monarchy, the trophy of foreign intrigue, and a constitution which might have been designed for a cauldron of domestic broil. "Ceaselessly gnawed by aristocratic lawlessness,"[1] its throne a prey to all the princes and adventurers of Europe, its frontiers ravaged, its magnates bribed, Poland was the sport of Europe. There was to be an interlude of glorious independence under John Sobieski; but for the rest Louis XIV, the Emperor, and the Great Elector tirelessly spun their rival webs about the threatened state, and with each candidature for its throne put their competing influences to the test. No wonder the Great Elector, until a final phase which we shall presently reach, had to follow an equivocal policy.

On the eastern flank of Poland lay the huge, sprawling Muscovy Empire, until recent times called Russia, still almost barbarous and perpetually torn by the revolt of the Cossacks against the Tsar. Moscow was ravaged by the Cossack

1 R. Nisbet Bain, *Slavonic Europe.*

Hetman Stenk, who also brought "unspeakable horrors" upon an "oppressed peasantry."[1] The possibilities of contact with Western civilization were blocked by Sweden and Poland, which together also impeded Russia from any outlet on to the Baltic. In the south the Turks shut it out from the Black Sea. The Tsar Alexis (1645–76), a peace-loving and conscientious man, entrusted a reforming patriarch, the monk Nikon, with most of the affairs of State during the early part of his reign. Later, in 1671, Stenka was captured and quartered alive, and when Alexis died, although no one yet foresaw the emergence of these eastern barbarians as a Western Power, the way lay open for the work of Peter the Great.

In the north of Europe Sweden, the ancient rival of Denmark, was the strongest Power, and aimed at making the Baltic a Swedish lake. At this time the Swedish realm included Finland, Ingria, Esthonia, Livonia, and West Pomerania; and the house of Vasa had traditional designs on Denmark and parts of Poland. The hardy, valiant race of Swedes had impressed upon all Europe the startling effects of a well-trained, warlike professional army. For a spell in the Thirty Years War Gustavus Adolphus had overthrown the troops of every Central European state. But Gustavus and his victories now lay in the past. The chief desire of Prussia was to win Pomerania from the Swedish Crown. Soon, in the battle of Fehrbellin (1675), the Great Elector with his Prussian troops was to overthrow the famous army of Sweden. The antagonism between the two countries was keen and open. Only the unfailing strength of France saved Pomerania for a time from Prussian absorption. Although the bias of Sweden was towards Protestantism, no Dutch or German statesman in the last quarter of the seventeenth century could ever exclude the possibility that her doughty soldiery would be bought by France, or rallied to her cause. All these baffling potential reactions were well comprehended at Whitehall in the closet of King Charles II.

[1] R. Nisbet Bain, *op. cit.*, for this paragraph.

Continuing our progress, we reach the domain of the Holy Roman Empire. This organism of Central Europe, "the survival of a great tradition and a grandiose title,"[1] signified not territory but only a sense of membership. The member states covered roughly modern Germany, Austria, Switzerland, Czecho-Slovakia, and Belgium. The ruler was chosen for life by the hereditary Electors of seven states. The Hapsburgs, as sovereigns of Austria, laying claim to Silesia, Bohemia, and Hungary, were the most powerful candidates, and in practice became the hereditary bearers of the ceremonial office of Emperor.[2]

Austria proper and the Hapsburg dynasty were deeply Catholic; not violent, aggressive, or, except in Hungary, proselytizing, but dwelling solidly and sedately in spiritual loyalty to the Pope. Then, as in our own age, the Hapsburgs were represented by a sovereign who reigned for fifty troublous years over an empire already racked by the stresses which two centuries later were, amid world disaster, to rend it in pieces. Confronted and alarmed by the growing power and encroachments of France, at variance often with Prussia, Vienna had fearful preoccupations of its own. The Turk under fanatical Sultans still launched in the south-east of Europe that thrust of conquest which in earlier periods had been successively hurled back from France and Spain. At any time the Ottoman armies, drawing recruits and supplies from all those subjugated Christian peoples we now call the Balkan States, might present themselves in barbaric invasion at the gates of Vienna. And there were always the Magyars of Hungary, always in revolt. In general, the divided princes of Germany faced the united strength of France, and Austria struggled for life against the Turk; but the whole vague confederacy recognized common dangers and foes, and the majestic antagonisms of Bourbons and Hapsburgs were the main dividing line of Europe.

Italy in the seventeenth century was merely a geographical

---

1 *The Cambridge Modern History*, v, 338.
2 In this account we shall use ' the Empire,' ' Austria,' and ' the Court at Vienna ' as more or less interchangeable terms.

LITTLE ROCK PUBLIC LIBRARY

expression. In the north Savoy (Piedmont) was brought out of its obscurity at the beginning of the century by the genius of Charles Emmanuel I (1580–1630). Afterwards it poised precariously between France and the Empire, deserting them both in turn according to the apparent fortunes of war. It has been said that the geographical position of Savoy, "the doorkeeper of the Alps," made its rulers treacherous. At best they could only preserve themselves and their country from ruin by miracles of diplomatic alternation.

Such were the unpromising and divided components of a Europe in contrast with which the power and ambitions of France arose in menacing splendour. Such were the factors and forces amid which Charles II had to steer the fortunes of his kingdom.

The nineteenth-century historians, writing mainly in the triumphant serenity of the Victorian era, did not make proper allowance for the weak and precarious plight of our country in the period with which we are now concerned. They thought it sufficient to set forth the kind of policy which the opinion of their day would approve, and they judged severely every divergence from it. Particularly they inculcated the virtues of strong, plain, straightforward conduct, and pointed their censure upon deceit, intrigue, vacillation, double-dealing, and bad faith. Upon this there must, of course, be general agreement. It would have been possible for England in 1660 to take a more dignified course through all her perils and to solve the problems of Europe, if only she had at that time possessed the relative power and resources she commanded two centuries later.

The politics of a weak and threatened state cannot achieve the standards open to those who enjoy security and wealth. The ever-changing forms of the dangers by which they are oppressed impose continuous shifts and contradictions, and many manœuvres from which pride and virtue alike recoil. England in the seventeenth century was little better placed than were Balkan states like Roumania or Bulgaria, when in the advent or convulsion of Armageddon they found themselves bid for or struck at by several mighty empires. We

75

had to keep ourselves alive and free, and we did so. It is by no means sure that plain, honest, downright policies, however laudable, would have succeeded. The oak may butt the storm, but the reeds bow and quiver in the gale and also survive.

It is a mistake to judge English foreign policy from 1667 to 1670, from the Triple Alliance with Holland against France to the Secret Treaty of Dover with France against Holland, as if it meant simply alternating periods of good and evil, of light and darkness, and of the influence of Sir William Temple as against that of the Duchess of Orleans. In fact, both the problems and the controls were continuous and the same, and our policy rested throughout in the same hands, in those of Charles II and his Minister Arlington. Although devoid of both faith and illusions, they were certainly not unintelligent, nor entirely without patriotic feeling. The invasion of Belgium by Louis XIV in the late summer of 1667 confronted them both with a situation of the utmost perplexity. At this stage in his life, at any rate, Charles desired to play an independent part in Europe, while Arlington, with his Spanish sympathies and training and his Dutch wife, was positively anti-French. Their first impulse was to resist the invasion of Belgium.

Strange indeed why this patch of land should exercise such compelling influence upon our unsophisticated ancestors! Apparently in 1667 they forgot or expunged the burning of their battleships in the Medway and Thames and all the passions of hard-fought naval battles because France was about to invade Belgium. Why did Belgium count so much with them? Two hundred and fifty years later we saw the manhood of the British Empire hastening across all the seas and oceans of the world to conquer or die in defence of this same strip of fertile, undulating country about the mouth of the Scheldt. Every one felt he had to go, and no one asked for logical or historical explanations. But then, with our education, we understood many things for which convincing verbal arguments were lacking. So did our ancestors at this time. The Court, the Parliament, the

City, the country gentlemen, were all as sure in 1668 that Belgium must not be conquered by the greatest military power on the Continent as were all parties and classes in the British Empire in August 1914. A mystery veiling an instinct!

If resistance to France were possible, still more if it were profitable, the King and Arlington were prepared to make an effort. They sounded the Courts of Europe: but the replies which they received from every quarter were universally discouraging. Spain was utterly incapable of defending her assaulted province. Without English or Dutch shipping she could not even reach it. Yet voluntarily Spain would not yield an inch. The Dutch would not attack France. If strongly supported, they would seek to limit the French territorial gains, but would agree to many of them, and all at the expense of Spain. The Emperor, whatever his Ambassador in London might say, seemed curiously backward. He would make no offensive alliance, least of all with heretics. In fact, as we now know, he was during these very months framing a secret treaty with France for the future partition of the whole Spanish Empire. The Great Elector would not move without subsidies which the Dutch would not and the Spanish could not give him. He was nervous of Sweden, and if the French gave him a free hand in Poland he would not oppose their progress in the west. Truly a depressing prospect for a coalition against the dominating, centralized might of France, wielded by a single man.

In a spirit which it is easy to call 'cold-blooded' and 'cynical' Charles and Arlington next examined the possibility of persuading France to let England share in her winnings, in return for English support in a war against Holland. Here they encountered a sharp rebuff. Louis, who hoped to obtain Belgium without coming to actual war with Holland, was not prepared to barter Spanish colonies against an English alliance, or still less against English neutrality. Both alternatives having thus been unsentimentally explored, Charles, with natural and obvious misgivings, took his decision to oppose France. He sent Sir William Temple to The Hague to make the famous Triple Alliance between England, Holland, and Sweden. The two Governments—for Sweden was a mere mercenary—entered upon it with limited and different objectives, but both sought to extort the favour of France by the threat of war. The English ruling circle hoped to win the French alliance by teaching Louis XIV not to despise England; the Dutch thought they could still retain the friendship of France by compelling Spain to a compromise. Perverse as were the motives, flimsy as was the basis, the result emerged with startling force. Louis saw himself confronted by a Northern league, and simultaneously Arlington brought about a peace between Spain and Portugal which freed the Spanish forces for a more real resistance. The consequences were swift and impressive. The shadow of the Spanish succession fell across the world. Louis, by his aggression upon that Belgian soil so strangely sacred, had called into being in phantom outline the beginnings of the Grand Alliance which was eventually to lay him low. He recoiled from the apparition. By his Partition Treaty of 1668 with the Emperor he had assured himself by merely waiting future gains throughout the whole Spanish Empire incomparably greater than those which might now be won by serious war. He could afford to be patient. Recalling his armies, silencing the protests of his generals, he retreated within his bounds, content for the time being with the acquisition of Lille, Tournai, Armentières, and other fortresses that put Belgium at his mercy. In April 1668, under the pressure and guarantee of the Triple Alliance, France and Spain consequently signed the peace of Aix-la-Chapelle.

We now approach days fatal to the house of Stuart. The national foreign policy attempted in 1668 rested upon diverse motives and paper guarantees. The Triple Alliance must succumb to any strain or temptation. Its partners were bound to protect the *status quo* in Belgium by expeditionary forces in the event of aggression; for this they looked, and in vain, to Spanish subsidies. They were still divided by their old hatreds and recent injuries, by their ceaseless hostilities in the East Indies and in Guiana, and in their rivalry of

78

the Channel. Charles, whatever his subjects might feel, had never forgiven the burning of his ships in the Medway. He hated the Dutch, and though he had been forced by events to side with them for a while and they with him, he yearned for a day when he could unite himself to France. In 1669 he began with Croissy, the French Ambassador, negotiations which reached their fruition in 1670.

Louis's sister-in-law, Duchess of Orleans—the "Madame" of the French Court—was also Charles's sister and his "beloved Minette." She was in the final phase the agent of France. Romance, as well as history, has played around this delightful, tragic figure, so suddenly decisive, so swiftly extinguished. No one stood so high in the love and respect of both monarchs. They cherished her personality: they admired her mind. She was to Charles the purest and deepest affection of his life. Louis realized only too late what he had lost in not making her his Queen. Minette loved both her native and adopted countries, and longed to see them united; but her heart was all for England's interests, as she misunderstood them, and for the Old Faith, to which she was devoutly attached. She presented and pleaded with all her wit and charm the case for an accommodation—nay, an alliance with the Sun King. Why condemn England to an endless, desperate struggle against overwhelming force? Why not accept the friendly hand sincerely, generously extended, and share the triumph and the prize? With France and England united, success was sure, and all the kingdoms of the world would lie in fee. It often happens that when great projects have been brought to maturity, personal touch is needed to set them in action. Minette came to England in the summer of 1670, bringing in her train another charmer, who also was destined to play her part—Louise de Kéroualle. "Madame's" husband, jealous of her political power and of his own eclipse, grudged every day of the Princess's absence from the home he had made odious with his minions. But Charles welcomed her with unrestrained joy. He met her with his Navy, and for a few sunlit days the English Court made picnic revel at Dover. Louis awaited results in eager suspense. They were all he could desire. Minette bore with her back to France—signed, sealed, and delivered— the Secret Treaty. She returned to perish almost immediately of a mysterious illness. She left as her legacy and life's achievement an instrument ruinous to all she prized.

By the Secret Treaty of Dover Charles agreed to join with Louis in an attack on Holland which aimed at nothing less than the destruction of the United Provinces as a factor in Europe, and to take all measures needful to that end. Louis agreed to respect the integrity of Belgium; to place in British keeping much of the coastline of conquered Holland, including the isle of Walcheren, with its valuable ports of Sluys and Cadsand, and the mouths of the Scheldt. Every safeguard was furnished to English naval requirements and colonial ambition.[1] The mastery of the seas, the command of the Dutch outlets, and the exploitation of Asia and the Americas were inestimable temptations. For the young Stadtholder, William of Orange, a prince of Stuart blood, now just twenty, a dignified, if restricted, sphere would be reserved. He might reign as hereditary sovereign over the truncated domains of the former Dutch Republic, for which his great-grandfather William the Silent had battled with all that his life could give. Next there was to be money. Large subsidies, sufficient to make King Charles with his hereditary revenues almost independent in times of peace of his contumacious Parliament, would be provided. Money, very handy for mistresses and Court expenses, but also absolutely necessary to restore and maintain the strength of the Royal Navy, now decaying in its starved dockyards! Such were the secular clauses. But the pact contained what in those days was even graver matter. Charles was to try persistently and faithfully, by every means at his disposal, to bring his subjects back to the Catholic faith. Full allowance would be made for the obvious difficulties of such a task; but the effort was to be continuous and loyal. In any case, not only French money, but French troops were to be available to secure the English

1 Lingard, *History of England,* vol. vi, Appendix.

monarchy against the anger of Parliament or the revolt of the nation.

Such was the hideous bargain, struck by so fair a hand, upon which the execration of succeeding generations has fastened. Far be it from us to seek to reverse that verdict of history which every British heart must acclaim. It would not, however, have been difficult to state a case at Charles II's council board against any whole-hearted espousal of Dutch interests, nor to have pleaded and even justified a temporizing opportunist policy towards France, deceitful though it must be. "We cannot commit ourselves to Holland; at any moment she may outbid us with France. Spain is futile and penniless. Alone we cannot face the enmity of the Great King. Let us take his money to build our fleet, and wait and see what happens." As for religion, Charles had learned in a hard school the willpower of Protestant England. Whatever his own leanings to the Catholic faith, all his statecraft showed that he would never run any serious risk for the sake of reconverting the nation. Manœuvre, fence, and palter as he might, he always submitted, and always meant to submit, with expedition to the deep growl of his subjects and to the authority of their inexpugnable institutions.

The Secret Treaty of Dover was handled personally by Louis, Charles, and their intermediary, Minette. But, of course, Colbert and Croissy had long studied its terms, and in England Arlington's support was soon found indispensable. As the protocol began to take shape first Arlington and then Clifford and the rest of the Cabal were invited to approve its secular provisions. It was perhaps less of a turn-about for Arlington than it appeared on the surface, and we cannot measure the slow, persistent pressures to which he yielded. Ministers in those days considered themselves the servants of the King, in the sense of being bound to interpret his will up to the point of impeachment, and sometimes beyond it. The whole Cabal endorsed such parts of the treaty as were communicated to them. The religious plot—it deserves no other name—was locked in the royal breast. James had not been much consulted in the negotiations, but he learned all that had been done ·with an inexpressible joy. Most especially he admired the religious clauses. Here more clearly than ever before he saw the blessed hands of the Mother of God laid upon the tormented world.

If anyone in 1672 computed the relative forces of France and England, he could only feel that no contest was possible; and the apparent weakness and humiliation of the pensioner island was aggravated by the feeble, divided condition of Europe. No dreamer, however romantic, however remote his dreams from reason, could have foreseen a surely approaching day when, by the formation of mighty coalitions and across the struggles of a generation, the noble colossus of France would lie prostrate in the dust, while the small island, beginning to gather to itself the empires of India and America, stripping France and Holland of their colonial possessions, would emerge victorious, mistress of the Mediterranean, the Narrow Seas, and the oceans. Aye, and carry forward with her, intact and enshrined, all that peculiar structure of law and liberty, all her own inheritance of learning and letters, which are to-day the treasure of the most powerful family in the human race.

This prodigy was achieved by conflicting yet contributory forces, and by a succession of great islanders and their noble foreign comrades or guides. We owe our salvation to the sturdy independence of the House of Commons and to its creators, the aristocracy and country gentlemen. We owe it to our hardy tars and bold sea-captains, and to the quality of a British Army as yet unborn. We owe it to the inherent sanity and vigour of the political conceptions sprung from the genius of the English race. But those forces would have failed without the men to use them. For the quarter of a century from 1688 to 1712 England was to be led by two of the greatest warriors and statesmen in all history: William of Orange, and John, Duke of Marlborough. They broke the military power of France, and fatally weakened her economic and financial foundations. They championed the Protestant faith, crowned Parliamentary institutions with triumph, and opened the door to an age of reason and freedom. They reversed the proportions and balances of Europe. They turned into new courses the destinies of Asia and America. They united Great Britain, and raised her to the rank she holds to-day.

CHAPTER V

ARMS

(1672-73)

THERE are two main phases in the military career of John, Duke of Marlborough. In the first, which lasted four years, he rose swiftly from ensign to colonel by his conduct and personal qualities and by the impression he made on all who met him in the field. In the second, during ten campaigns he commanded the main army of the Grand Alliance with infallibility. An interval of more than a quarter of a century separates these two heroic periods. From 1671 to 1675 he exhibited all those qualities which were regarded as the forerunners in a regimental officer of the highest military distinction. He won his way up from grade to grade by undoubted merit and daring. But thereafter was a desert through which he toiled and wandered. A whole generation of small years intervened. He was like young men in the Great War who rose from nothing to the head of battalions and brigades, and then found life suddenly contract itself to its old limits after the Armistice. His sword never rusted in its sheath. It was found bright and sharp whenever it was needed, at Sedgemoor, at Walcourt, or in Ireland. There it lay, the sword of certain victory, ready for service whenever opportunity should come.

"Everybody agreed," wrote Anthony Hamilton, "that the man who was the favourite of the King's mistress and brother to the Duke's was starting well and could not fail to make his fortune." But the influence of royal concubines was not the explanation of the rise of Marlborough. That rise was gradual, intermittent, and long. He was a professional soldier. "And," wrote the old Duchess at the end of her life,

I think it is more Honour to rise from the lowest Step to the greatest, than, as is the fashion now, to be Admirals without

84

ever having seen Water but in a Bason, or to make Generals that never saw any action of war.[1]

By the time he arrived at the highest command he was passing the prime of life, and older than many of the leading generals of the day. The early success and repeated advancement which this chapter records were followed by lengthy intervals of stagnation. Arabella and Barbara had long ceased to count with him or anyone else,. while he was still regarded as a subordinate figure, when he had yet to make and remake his whole career. Continual checks, grave perplexities, extreme hazards, disgrace and imprisonment, constant skilful services, immense tenacity, perseverance and self-restraint, almost unerring political judgment, all the arts of the courtier, politician, and diplomatist, marked his middle life. For many long years his genius and recognized qualities seemed unlikely to carry him through the throng of securely established notabilities who then owned the fulness of the earth. At twenty-four he was a colonel. He was fifty-two before he commanded a large army.

In 1672 the slumbering Treaty of Dover awoke in the realm of action. Louis, having perfected his plans to the last detail, suddenly, without cause of quarrel, made his cavalry swim the Rhine and poured his armies into Holland. At the same time England also declared war upon the Dutch. The States-General, de Witt and his Amsterdammers, taken by surprise, were unable to stem the advance of 120,000 French troops, armed for the first time with the new weapon of the bayonet. Cities and strongholds fell like ninepins. The Dutch people, faced with extermination, set their despairing hopes upon William of Orange. The great-grandson of William the Silent did not fail them. He roused and animated their tough, all-enduring courage. John de Witt and his brother were torn to pieces by a frenzied mob in the streets of The Hague. William uttered the deathless battle-cry,

[1] " Some Instructions to the Historians for beginning the Duke of Marlborough's History," by Sarah, Duchess of Marlborough (Spencer MSS., 1744). See Appendix, II, for full text.

"We can die in the last ditch." The sluices in the dykes were opened; the bitter waters rolled in ever-widening deluge over the fertile land. Upon the wide inundation the fortified towns seemed to float like arks of refuge. All military operations became impossible. The French armies withdrew in bewilderment. Holland, her manhood, her navy, and her hero-Prince preserved their soul impregnable.

Meanwhile the French and English fleets united had set themselves to secure the mastery of the Narrow Seas. A contingent of six thousand English troops under Monmouth's command served with the French armies. Lediard and other early writers suppose that Churchill was among them. In fact he took part in a deadlier struggle afloat. The sea fighting began on March 13, before the declaration of war, with the surprise attack of Sir Robert Holmes's English squadron upon the Dutch Smyrna fleet while at anchor off the Isle of Wight. This treacherous venture miscarried, and the bulk of the Dutch vessels escaped. The companies of the Guards in which Churchill and his friend George Legge[1] were serving were embarked for the raid and took part in the action.[2]
The handling of the Dutch navy under De Ruyter in this campaign commands lasting admiration. He pressed into the jaws of the Channel to forestall the concentration of the French and English fleets. But the Duke of York, setting sail from the Thames in good time, made his junction with the French fleet from Brest, and De Ruyter was glad to extricate himself from the Channel and return safely to the North Sea. Here he lay off Walcheren and Texel, watching his chance to strike at superior forces and shielding his country meanwhile from an additional invasion. The Duke of York understood that if he could place the Anglo-French fleet about the Dogger Bank (we now know these waters as well as he) the Dutch fleet would be cut off from home as the Germans might have been after Jutland. But the English fleet,

---

1 Afterwards Lord Dartmouth.
2 Atkinson, *Marlborough and the Rise of the British Army,* (p. 39) is the only writer who has noted this incident in Churchill's career. His account is exact; but his reference should be *C.S.P.* (*Dom.*), 1671–72, p. 609.

starved by Parliament, was ill-found and short of men, and in any case it was necessary to replenish before sailing across the communications of the enemy. The combined fleets therefore proceeded through the Straits of Dover to Sole Bay (or Southwold), on the Suffolk coast, to fit themselves for their enterprise. Here from London several thousand seamen and soldiers, together with a crowd of gentlemen volunteers hurrying from the Court, joined them. For three days all the ships lay in the open roadstead busily embarking men, food, and munitions. But this was the opportunity which De Ruyter sought. Lord S a n d w i c h, whose name revives from one generation to another in battleships christened *Montagu*, was a wary, hard-bitten salt. At the council of war

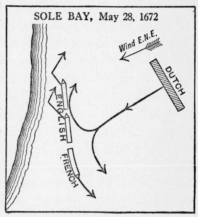

SOLE BAY, May 28, 1672

he complained of the posture and wished to put to sea. His warnings were ill-received and attributed to excess of caution. Anyhow, everything was being done as fast as possible. But on the morning of May 28/June 7 a French frigate, hotly pursued, brought the news that the whole Dutch fleet was at her heels. Every one scrambled on board, and a hundred and one ships endeavoured to form their line of battle. The French division, under D'Estrées, whether from policy or necessity or because James's orders were lacking in precision, sailed upon a divergent course from the English fleet. De Ruyter, playing with the French and sending Van Ghent to attack the ships of Lord Sandwich, fell himself upon the Duke of York's division, of which at first not more than twenty were in their stations. In all he had ninety-one vessels and a superiority of at least two to one in the first part of the battle.

> I cannot stay to name the names
> Of all the ships that fought with James,
> Their number and their tonnage;

87

But this I say: the noble host
Right gallantly did take its post,
And covered all the hollow coast,
From Walderswyck to Dunwich.[1]

Grievous and cruel was the long struggle which ensued. The Suffolk shores were crowded with frantic spectators, the cannonade was heard two hundred miles away. From noon till dusk the battle raged at close quarters. The Dutch desperately staked their superiority with cannon and fire-ships against the English, tethered upon a lee shore. The Duke of York's flagship, the *Prince*, was the central target of the attack. Upon her decks stood the 1st Company of the Guards—Captain Daniels, Lieutenant Picks, and Ensign Churchill. Smitten by the batteries of several Dutchmen, assailed by two successive fire-ship attacks, and swept by musketry, she was so wrecked in hull and rigging that by eleven o'clock she could no longer serve as a flagship. The Duke of York, who in the actual battle of Sole Bay displayed the courage expected of an English prince and admiral, was forced to shift his flag to the *St Michael*, and when this ship became unmanageable in turn he was rowed with his staff to the *London*. The Guards company had remained upon the *Prince*. The captain of the ship and more than two hundred men, a third of the complement, were killed or wounded. Both sides fought with the doggedness on which their races pride themselves. Lord Sandwich, brought to a standstill by a small Dutch vessel, wedged with extreme audacity under the bowsprit of the *Royal James*, became the prey of fire-ships. With his personal officers he paced his quarter-deck till the flames drove him overboard, where he perished. Both sides awaited the explosion of the magazines. The magazines of the *Royal James* did not explode. All her powder had been fired when she sank. Sunset and the possible return of the French ended a battle described by De Ruyter as the hardest of his thirty-two actions, and the Dutch withdrew, having destroyed for

---

1 "A Song on the Duke's late Glorious Success over the Dutch," from *Naval Songs and Ballads* (ed. Firth, 1906), p. 82.

JAMES II
John Riley
National Portrait Gallery

88

many weeks the offensive power of the superior combined fleets.[1]

Not one single word has come down to us of John's part in this deadly business, through which he passed unscathed. No reference to it exists in his correspondence or conversation. This was before the age when everybody kept diaries or wrote memoirs. It was just in the day's work. All we know is that his conduct gained him remarkable advancement. No fewer than four captains of the Admiralty Regiment had been killed, and he received double promotion from a Guards ensign to a Marine captaincy.[2]

Lieutenant Edward Picks complained to Sir Joseph Williamson, Arlington's Under-Secretary, that:

> Mr Churchill, who was my ensign in the engagement, is made a Captain and I, without my Lord Arlington's kindness and yours, I fear may still continue a lieutenant, though I am confident my greatest enemies cannot say I misbehaved myself in the engagement. . . .

He further declared:

> . . . if you will oblige me with your kindness to get me a company, I will present you with four hundred guineas when I receive my commission. Sir, I am confident it may be done by my Lord Arlington, for the King will not deny him anything.[3]

We do not know the details of the action. Favouritism there may have been in the double step, but it was favouritism founded upon exceptional conduct. In such rough times, when chiefs and subalterns faced the fire together, many wholesome correctives were at work. The Duke of York, coming himself out of heavy battle, would have acted in accordance with what he had seen and with what men said of Churchill's conduct.

Sole Bay for the time being knocked out the fleet, and only

1 A full account of this battle with admirable contemporary picture-plans is given by Corbett (Navy Records Society, 1908). Mahan's comments are also instructive (*The Influence of Sea Power on History*, 1896, chapter iii).

2 The commission, dated June 13, 1672, is at Blenheim. Cf. *C.S.P.* (*Dom.*), 1671–72, pp. 218, 222, and C. Dalton, *Army Lists*, i, 127–128.

3 October 20, 1672, printed in full in F. W. Hamilton, *History of the Grenadier Guards*, i, 166.

meagre funds were found to refit and repair it. The infantry and gentlemen volunteers came ashore, and the Guards were ordered to France. The courtiers forgathered at Whitehall to celebrate their experiences in revel and carouse, and John, fresh from danger and in the flush of promotion, was welcomed, we doubt not, in the arms of Barbara. It is believed that at this time she paid the purchase money which enabled him to take up the captaincy his sword had gained. We apologize for mentioning such shocking facts to the reader; but it is our duty, for such was the depravity of these fierce and hectic times.

In 1673 Louis XIV again made war in person. Condé with weak forces occupied the Dutch in the north. Turenne similarly engaged the Imperialists in Alsace. The Great King advanced in the centre with the mass and magnificence of the French Army. His Majesty quitted Saint-Germains on May 1, accompanied by the Queen, Madame de Montespan, and the Court. It is understood that the presence of the Queen was indispensable to cover that of the mistress, and thus prevent scandal arising. The proprieties being observed, the assemblage arrived in due course at Tournai, where Madame de Montespan, who was with child, gave birth to a daughter. This happy event having been accomplished with full decorum, the hero-monarch took leave of his Court and his ladies, and, attended only by a personal retinue of several hundred persons, including a sufficiency of painters, poets, and historians, set himself to the stern business of war, entered his coach, and marched upon Courtrai. All the world wondered where he would strike. It soon appeared that he had honoured Maestricht, a strong Dutch fortress garrisoned by about five thousand men, as the scene of his intended triumph. He felt his military qualities more suited to sieges than to battles; and "Big sieges," he remarked, "please me more than the others."[1] Maestricht was accordingly invested on June 17.

It will be well for the reader to accustom himself at this

---

[1] Lavisse, *Histoire de France*, vii, 2, 317–318.

point to the routine and ritual of siege operations in this period; for unhappily these pages must speak of many. A network of fortresses, great and small, covered the frontiers of France and Holland. All were constructed upon the principles of Vauban or his Dutch competitor, Cohorn. We often gaze at these star-shaped plans without comprehending the marvellous intricacy of the defences they portray. Each salient angle (or ravelin), each pentagon (or bastion), was a self-contained compartment with its proper guns and garrison. Every line was so drawn as to be protected by flanking fire of cannon, or at least musketry, at right-angles. Around these ramparts, and conforming geometrically to their trace, ran the 'open ditch,' a stone-faced alley perhaps 20 feet deep and 40 feet wide, upon the farther side of which stretched the smooth glacis with its 'covered way,' often guarded by minor advanced defences, all commanded in reverse from the main line. The wall of the ditch nearest the rampart was called the scarp, and the opposite wall nearest the besiegers the counterscarp. The counterscarp was, where necessary, lined with galleries subterraneously connected with the fortress. From the stone-faced loopholes of these galleries annihilating fire, additional to all flanking fire, could be poured into the backs of any hostile troops who entered the ditch. Such, in short, was the defence.

The procedure of the attack was as follows. First the fortress was invested—*i.e.*, surrounded by a superior army and, so far as possible, cut off entirely from the world. Next on the side chosen for attack the trenches were opened. In general there were three parallels, the first being dug just beyond the range of the fortress cannon. From this first parallel zigzag approaches were dug to the second, and from this again, the zigzags getting ever more acute, to the third. The third parallel should have carried the assailants to the edge or within striking distances of the fortifications. Then by mining and close hand-to-hand fighting the counterscarp galleries of the sector under attack were seized and large portions of the counterscarp blown into the ditch. Meanwhile the besieging batteries planted in or behind the second parallel, and protected against sorties by strong entrenchments and infantry garrisons, had been firing day after day, and sometimes week after week, upon the ramparts, silencing the defenders' cannon and breaching their parapets. Thus when the moment was ripe a rough but continuous road lay open from the first parallel into the fortress or into such ravelins or bastions of the fortress as had been battered.

The crisis of the assault was now imminent. Superior masses of troops, headed by their 'forlorn hopes' of volun-

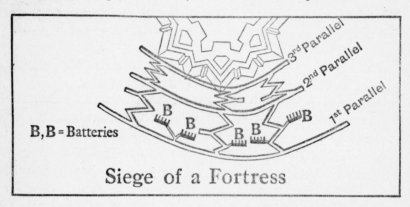

B, B = Batteries

Siege of a Fortress

teers, were assembled in the third parallel and other slits dug close by and in the captured counterscarp galleries; and on the signal these charged across the *débris* which filled the covered way, climbed through the breach in the pulverized ramparts, and, storming whatever improvised breastworks or barricades the defenders had been able to construct broke into the city.

However, the conflict rarely reached this culmination. A minute and rigorous etiquette governed both sides in a siege during the half-century of war with which we are concerned. The governor of a fortress was expected by his own Government as well as by his assailants to use it for what it was worth, and no more. If he stood an assault and repelled it, even though he afterwards was forced to surrender, his fame was great. If he resisted until the breaches were practicable, he might make a bargain to save needless loss of life which entitled the garrisons to march out with all the honours of war—"bag and baggage, drums beating, matches lighted, bullet in the

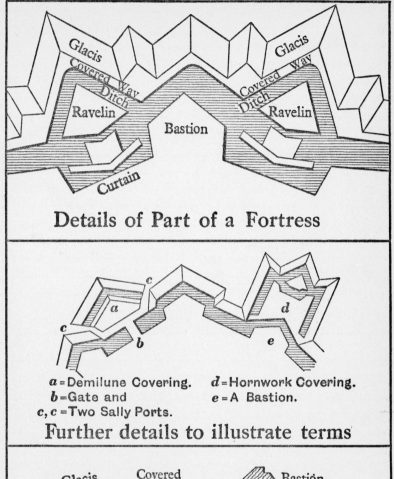

Details of Part of a Fortress

a = Demilune Covering.   *d* = Hornwork Covering.
b = Gate and   *e* = A Bastion.
c, c = Two Sally Ports.

Further details to illustrate terms

a = Scarp   *b* = Counterscarp
c = Counterscarp Gallery

Section through a Bastion

THE DEFENCES OF A FORTRESS

mouth, etc." The city then passed peacefully into the hands of the besiegers, who usually treated the inhabitants with all proper consideration. But if the governor, presuming too much on fortune, forced the besiegers to a needless assault which in fact he well knew he could not resist, and if the place was taken by storm, then the whole city was given up to sack, rape, and flame. Very nice questions therefore arose for all governors and for the civil inhabitants once the assault was imminent, and their conduct in these circumstances was judged by highly standardized expert opinion on both sides and in all the armies of Europe.

We have, of course, explained only the conventional features of a seventeenth- or eighteenth-century siege. Each case among the many hundreds that occurred presented peculiarities of its own. Sometimes in the greatest operations a relieving army strong enough to break the investment, if not to beat the besiegers, approached the scene. This had to be warded off in one of two ways. Either a covering army manœuvred continually between the fortress and its would-be rescuers, or else the besiegers constructed what are called 'lines of circumvallation'—*i.e.*, they built an improvised fortress around themselves, enclosing the doomed city in its midst, and were besieged from without, while pressing their attack within. We shall presently see the Duke of Marlborough besieging cities whose garrisons were almost as strong as his own army, while his covering forces confronted a relieving army capable at any moment of fighting an equal battle in the field.

Nothing of this kind, however, presented itself at the siege of Maestricht. It was less like a serious war struggle than a sanguinary tournament in which the common soldiers were slaughtered as well as the knights and nobles. The strength of the French army was unchallengeable, and no relieving forces durst appear. Vauban prescribed the stages and method of the attack, and the Great King took the credit. "Vauban," he explained modestly, "proposed me the steps which I thought the best." Above all, the master enjoined prudence. Nothing was to be hurried, no stage was to be slurred. The operation was to be a model. "Let us go surely, taking even unnecessary precautions." We are assured that he set a personal example in the endurance of hardships—no doubt for an hour or two by day or night; and that he exposed his sacred person from time to time to the fire of the enemy. And all was duly immortalized in the French poetry, tapestries, pictures, and engravings of the age.

We do not know precisely what happened to Captain Churchill between the battle of Sole Bay and the siege of Maestricht. The Admiralty regiment in which he now held a company went to France in December. Various English contingents were serving in Alsace or in garrison with the French. It seems probable that once it became clear that the centre of the war was to be in Flanders and that the Great King would be there, himself, Monmouth allowed or encouraged a handful of swells and their personal attendants to leave the different units of the army and come to the bull's-eye of the fighting under his personal direction. At any rate, England was represented at Maestricht only by the Duke of Monmouth with a score of gentlemen volunteers, prominent among whom was Churchill, and an escort of thirty gentlemen troopers of the Life Guards. Louis XIV treated the distinguished delegation with the ceremony due to the bastard son of his royal brother. Monmouth was assigned his turn as 'General of the Trenches,' and ample opportunity was offered to him and his friends of winning distinction before the most critical and fashionable military assemblage of the period. Every one of them was on his mettle, eager to hazard his life in the arena and wrest renown from beneath so many jealous and competent eyes. Little did this gay company trouble themselves about the rights and wrongs of the war, or the majestic balance of power in Europe; and we cannot doubt that our young officer shared their reckless mood to the full. Comradeship and adventure and the hopes of glory and promotion seemed all-sufficing to the eyes and sword of youth.

The trenches were opened ten days after the investment,

and a week later the siege works justified an attempt to break in upon the fortress. The attack, timed for ten o'clock at night, was arranged to fall in Monmouth's tour of duty. Picked detachments from the best regiments, including the King's Musketeers, formed the storming forces. The King came and stood at the end of the trenches to watch. The signal was given, and Monmouth, with Churchill and his English-men at his side, led the French assault. With heavy losses from close and deadly fire, amid the explosion of two mines and of six thousand grenades, the counterscarp galleries were occupied, and a half-moon work in front of the Brussels gate was attacked. Three times the assailants were driven partly out of their lodgments and three times they renewed the assault, until finally Churchill is said to have planted the French standard on the parapet of the half-moon. The rest of the night was spent in consolidating the defence and dig-ging new communications, and at daylight Monmouth handed over the captured works to supporting troops. The English-men were resting in their tents, and Monmouth was about to dine, when near noon of the next day the dull roar of a mine and heavy firing proclaimed the Dutch counter-stroke. The governor, M. de Fariaux, a Frenchman in the service of the States-General, gallantly leading his men, had sallied out upon the captured works.

The episode which followed belongs to romance rather than to history or war, but the most detailed and authentic records exist about it. We have two first-hand accounts in letters written to Arlington; one is from Duras, a French Huguenot noble of high rank who as early as 1665—flying from the wrath to come—had naturalized himself an English subject. Duras, like Churchill, was personally attached to the Duke of York, and seems to have enjoyed his unbounded confidence and favour. He subsequently became the Earl of Feversham, whom we shall meet again presently at Sedgemoor. A further account (from which we shall quote) is from Lord Alington, who was himself in the thick of the fighting.

Monmouth sent appeals to a company of musketeers at hand. Their officer, a certain M. d'Artagnan, then famous in the Army and since deathless in Dumas's fiction, responded instantly. There was no time to go through the zigzags of the communication trenches. De Fariaux was already in the half-moon. Monmouth, fleet of foot, led straight for the struggle across the top of the ground. With him came Churchill, twelve Life Guardsmen, and a handful of Englishmen of quality, with some valiant pages and servants. They reached the half-moon from an unexpected direction at the moment when the fighting was at its height. D'Artagnan and his musketeers joined them. The Life Guards threw away their carbines (twelve were subsequently reissued from the English ordnance stores) and drew their swords. Monmouth, Churchill, and d'Artagnan forced their way in. Here Lord Alington's letter to Lord Arlington[1] will best carry on the account.

After the Duke had put on his arms, we went not out at the ordinary place, but leapt over the banke of the Trenches, in the face of our Enemy. Those that hapned to be with the Duke were Mr Charles Obrien, Mr Villars,[2] Lord Rockingham's two sons, and Capt. Watson their kinsman, Sir Tho. Armstrong, Capt. Churchille, Capt. Godfrey, Mr. Roe and myselfe, with the Duke's two Pages and three or four more of his servants, thus we marcht with our swords in our hands to a baricade of the Enemys, where only one man could passe att a time. There was Monsieur Artaignan with his musketeers who did very bravely. This Gentleman was one of the greatest reputation in the Army, he would have perswaded the Duke not to have past that place, but that beeing not to be done, this Gentleman would goe along with him, but in pasing that narrow place was kill'd with a shot through his head, upon wch the Duke and we past where Mr O'Brien had a shot through his leages. The souldiers att this tooke heart the Duke twice leading them on with Great Courage; when his Grace found the enemy being to retire, he was prevail'd with to retire to the Trenche, the better to give his Comands as there should be occasion. Then he sent Mr Villars to the King for 500 fresh

[1] S.P., 78/137, f. 142. Confusion between Alington and Arlington has led to error in many books.

[2] Or Villiers, son of Lord Grandison. Several writers confuse him at this point with Louis Hector de Villars, afterwards the famous French Marshal, who fought in a different part of the same attack.

men and to give him an account of what had past. When those men came, our Enemys left us wthout any farther disturbance, masters of what we had gained the night before. so that to the Dukes' great Honor we not only tooke more than was expected, but maintain'd it after we had been in possession of it, but wth the losse of a great many men and many brave officers. One of their Great Fournoes blewe into the aire near 50 men, just before they made their sally. And I truly believe we had killed and wounded from the time we went into the Trenches to our comeing out, about 1500. Some old Commanders say, this was the bravest and briskest action they had seen in their lives, and our Duke did the part of a much older and more experienced General, and the King was very kinde to him last night.

Churchill, who was wounded at Monmouth's side, was also held to have distinguished himself. He was, in fact, publicly thanked upon a great parade by Louis XIV, who assured him that his good conduct would be reported to his own sovereign. Another subaltern fought in this attack whose name will recur in these pages: Louis Hector de Villars against orders joined the assault. His gallantry won forgiveness for his disobedience. We do not know whether he and Churchill became acquainted at Maestricht. They certainly met at Malplaquet.

The governor of Maestricht, satisfied with the resistance he had made and strongly pressed by the townsfolk to capitulate while time remained, beat a parley, and was allowed to march out with the honours of war. The severity of the losses, especially among persons of note in the storming troops, made a strong impression throughout the camps and the Courts concerned. Monmouth was praised and petted by Louis not only from policy, but on the undoubted merit of his performance. He and his English team received the unstinted tributes of "the finest army in the world." The brief and spectacular campaign was soon brought to a close. Louis XIV rejoined his anxious Court, who burned before him the incense of flattery with all the delicate address of which the French are peculiarly capable. The armies retired into winter quarters, and Monmouth and his hunting party were welcomed again into the bosom of Whitehall.

LITTLE ROCK PUB

Churchill's favour stood high at this time. Monmouth commended him to Charles with the words, "Here is the brave man who saved my life." To this there was to be a grim sequel. The King, who was by this time in full flight with the charming Louise de Kéroualle, and was perhaps not so sorry as he ought to have been to have Barbara taken off his hands and made thoroughly happy, was gracious to a degree. England seemed to have shared the honours of the siege of Maestricht without any of the trouble, expense, and loss of sending an army.

Meanwhile Captain Churchill and the Duchess of Cleveland continued to make the running at the Court. That a virile young officer should be the lover of a beautiful, voluptuous, and immoral woman is not inexplicable to human nature. The fact that she was a few years his senior is by no means a bar. On the contrary, the charms of thirty are rarely more effective than when exerted on the impressionable personality of twenty-three. No one is invited to applaud such relationships, but few, especially in time of war, will hold them unpardonable, and only malignancy would seek to score them for ever upon a young man's record. How disgusting to pretend, with Lord Macaulay, a filthy, sordid motive for actions prompted by those overpowering compulsions which leap flaming from the crucible of life itself! Inconstant Barbara loved her youthful soldier tenderly and followed with eager, anxious eyes his many adventures and perils from steel and fire. He returned her love with the passion of youth. She was rich and could have money for the asking. He had no property but his sword and sash. But they were equals, they were kin, they lived in the same world. She was now the mother of his child.

Contemporaries vie with one another in describing her charms. She was by all accounts a picture of transcendent loveliness. Already the hopes of the future gleamed upon John's shapely frame and noble countenance. Why need we seek farther for the impulses that drew and held these two together? Why make of their romance a shameful scarecrow of mercenary vice? Naturally she wished to help him in the way

99

that would help him most; naturally she gave him money, and was proud to have it to give. The wars lay on the coasts, and from time to time the sound of hostile guns thudded in the English air. Death stood very near a captain of the Guards, and love drew majesty and sanction from that sombre presence. He, serving ashore and afloat under the shot of the enemy, must have felt no shame and earned no scorn in taking from her hands the modest necessary sums without which he could not have pursued his career or taken his promotions as he gained them. But it would, of course, have been much better if John had been wealthy and chaste, and if Barbara had remained the faithful spouse of Roger Palmer. The association brought him the frowns—if increasingly perfunctory—rather than the favour of the Royal Power. The only reward which the King bestowed upon the presumptuous rival in his waning affections was to set him in the forefront of the battle. But this was a reward of which the recipient was prepared to take the fullest advantage.

He was back at the front in the early autumn. The Admiralty Regiment was now with Turenne in Westphalia. There is little doubt that Churchill served as a captain with them during the rest of 1673. Although no great operations were in progress, he made his way in the Army. There is always the story of Turenne wagering, when some defile had been ill defended, that the "handsome Englishman" would retake it with half the number of troops used when it was lost; and how this was accordingly and punctually done. No one has been able to assign the date or the place, but at any rate the newly made captain in the Admiralty Regiment was a figure well known in Turenne's army and high in the favour of the Marshal himself before the year closed.

CHAPTER VI

THE DANBY ADMINISTRATION

(1673–74)

FOR some time King Charles proceeded on the lines of the Secret Treaty of Dover. He had issued his Declaration of Indulgence, which in the name of toleration gave to Catholics the freedom they were denying to Protestants in every country where they were in the ascendant. But the French subsidies, though quite convenient for paying a peace-time navy, were utterly inadequate to maintain a costly war. The expenses of the two great sea battles, Sole Bay and the Texel, and the repair of the fleet were enormous. Even the contingent of six thousand men in France was a heavy charge. The King was forced to repudiate the interest upon his loans from the goldsmiths and the bankers in the celebrated "Stop of the Exchequer." Parliament had been prorogued for fifteen months: it must now be called together.

Accordingly in February 1673 the once enthusiastic Cavalier Parliament reassembled in a mood of pent-up passion. We have invaluable reports of their debates in the records kept by Mr. Grey, the Member for Derby. The Commons demanded the immediate withdrawal of the Declaration of Indulgence as a precedent condition of all supply. They did not at this stage attack the Dutch war. Indeed, Shaftesbury's Ministerial fulmination against Holland, *Delenda est Carthago*, received silent approval. They do not seem to have been moved by the heroic spectacle of Protestant resistance to Louis. The war at sea against so dangerous a naval rival as Holland aroused their partisanship. It was the pro-Catholic inclination of the Crown which excited their wrath. Louis XIV, on the other hand, was more interested in victory over the Dutch than in the fortunes of the English Catholics. His Ambassador was instructed to advise Charles to give way upon the Declaration of Indulgence, and even to accept a Test Act which excluded Papists from all offices of State. Charles agreed, and the Commons voted a liberal supply of £1,200,000.

Stern, curious eyes were now turned upon the Duke of York. Rumours of his conversion to Rome had long been rife. How would he stand the Test? The answer was soon forthcoming. The heir to the throne renounced all his offices, and Prince Rupert succeeded him in the command of the fleet. So it was true, then, that James was a resolute Papist, ready to sacrifice all material advantages to the faith his countrymen abhorred. And now there came a trickle of allegations and disclosures about the Secret Treaty of Dover. Rumours of decisions taken by the King, by his brother, and his Ministers to convert England to Rome were rife during all the summer and autumn of 1673.

Moreover, the war went ill. Like so many wars, it looked easy and sure at the outset. There is always the other side, who have their own point of view and think, often with surprising reason, that they also have a chance of victory. The cutting of the dykes had marred the opening French campaign. The Dutch defensive at sea in 1672 and 1673 was magnificent. Rupert's battles against De Ruyter were bloody and drawn. The situation of Holland had vastly improved. The Prince of Orange, Stadtholder and Captain-General, stood at the head of truly 'United Provinces,' and in August both the Empire and Spain entered into alliance with the Dutch to maintain the European balance. Diplomatically and militarily the Anglo-French compact had failed. On top of all this came the news that Charles had allowed a most obnoxious marriage between the Duke of York and the Catholic princess Mary of Modena.

A standing army of ten thousand men, commanded by a Frenchman, assembled first at Blackheath and then at Yarmouth, was believed by many to be designed for a forcible conversion of England to Popery. Our affairs had already reached a sufficient refinement for the passage of subsidies across the Channel to be reflected in Anglo-French exchange.

When Parliament met in October all sections were united in the demand for peace with Holland and the end of the alliance with France. Vehement opponents demanded the overthrow of the Ministry. But by this date the Cabal was already splintering into its original elements. It had held together upon the principle of toleration for Catholics and Dissenters. Now Parliament deliberately rejected, and, indeed, reversed, this policy. Clifford, himself almost certainly a Catholic, finally wrecked the Cabal by his refusal to take the Test, and he retired to his estates to die so swiftly that men spoke of suicide or a broken heart. Arlington became Lord Chamberlain and passed out of power into Court life and the pursuit of wealth and security. Ashley, soon to succeed to the earldom of Shaftesbury, and Buckingham made terms with the Whig Opposition, from whom, as Puritans, they had originally come. Henceforward they led the assault upon the King, for whose misguided policy they had been partly responsible. Lauderdale, the first to be assailed, alone survived to continue his skilful maltreatment of Scotland.

A new scene, and, indeed, a new era, now opened. The man upon whom the King began increasingly to rely was Sir Thomas Osborne, who had been made a baron and had succeeded Clifford as Lord Treasurer in June 1673. A year later he was created Earl of Danby, the one of his five titles best known to history. Sprung from a Yorkshire family faithfully Cavalier, Danby had a large, though highly critical, following in the House of Commons. More than most statesmen of this period he had a sense of England as a personality. He was in many ways a typical 'John Bull.' Equally averse from Catholics and Dissenters, he sought to rally the nation to the throne upon the old Royalist cry of "Church and King." He set himself to manage the House of Commons, not only by a policy generally agreeable to them, but by pretty bold corruption of individual members such as was afterwards perfected by Sir Robert Walpole. Although the King differed from Danby both on the French alliance and the Catholic succession, he leaned upon him, and already felt the need of an organized following, besides the

Court party, behind Ministers in the House of Commons. Danby did his work with robust vigour. The King swung steadily and smoothly with the change of the tide like a ship at anchor, and his prow and guns were soon pointing in exactly the opposite direction.

Through Spanish mediation peace was signed with Holland on February 19, 1674. The Dutch, stubborn though they were, gave in their sore straits the fullest satisfaction to English naval pride. Within six years of the Medway, within two years of Sole Bay, and within a year of De Ruyter's proud encounters with Rupert, Holland accepted with every circumstance of humility the naval supremacy of England. The States-General confirmed the agreement of the Treaty of Breda (1667) that all Dutch ships should dip their flag and topsails whenever, north of Cape Finisterre, they sighted an English man-of-war. Not only were Dutch fleets and squadrons to make their salute to similar forces of the Royal Navy, but even the whole of the Dutch fleet was to make its submission to a single English vessel, however small, which flew the royal flag. The history books which dwell upon our shame in the Medway and the Thames do not do justice to this turning of the tables. Callous, unmoral, unscrupulous as had been Charles's policy, he might now on this account at least exclaim, "He laughs best who laughs last."

Peace had relieved the finances from an insupportable strain. The continuance of the war on the Continent gave the English many profits as traders and as carriers for both sides. The Dutch indemnity came to hand. In two years Danby rescued the country from bankruptcy. Profiting by a period of expanding trade and an increased yield from customs and excise, and freed from the gigantic war-charges, he was able to make the King comfortable. He wielded the axe of economy in all directions, laying up the fleet and disbanding the greater part of the Army. The Danby Administration—for such, indeed, it was in modern Parliamentary parlance—although the first of its kind, gave effect to the will of the people more fully than is usually done now as the result of popular elections.

104

The King was conscious of a great relief. He had become, in fact, for the moment a constitutional sovereign with a popular Minister to bear the brunt. But as soon as the national tension diminished, politics became more complex. Neither King nor Minister had really trusted each other, or pursued a single policy. Charles had not unnaturally some feelings of compunction, as between one gentleman and another, about Louis, whom he had unquestionably cheated. He did not wish to risk open personal rupture with so dangerous a potentate. The late hostilities against the Dutch had been described as "war without anger." Could not the desertion of France be accomplished at least without impoliteness? Charles was therefore anxious to keep in touch with the French King, and especially to receive his money; and from time to time there were minor secret agreements, largely arising out of the failure to implement the original Treaty of Dover. Something had, for instance, to be patched up about the British troops serving in the pay of France and other matters of that kind, so as not to make the reversal of policy an utterly impudent breach of contract.

This policy quickly developed into an interlude of political blackmail used simultaneously against Parliament on the one hand and Louis on the other. Danby, in full accord with the Prince of Orange, moved towards a breach with France. But Louis, in spite of previous disappointments, thought it worth while to purchase English neutrality. This was just the kind of game which King Charles could play extremely well, and apart from its squalid aspect no great harm was done to English interests. The King got money from the House of Commons by saying, "If you are hostile to France, we must get our fleet and army into order: give me money." To Louis he said, "Unless you keep me in a position of complete independence of the House of Commons, they will make me join the Dutch: give me money." Very considerable sums were paid from both quarters, while all the time nothing was done to satisfy either. Like Danton, a century later, Charles was "paid for, but not bought."

The King got on well with his Minister—too well, in fact, for the fortunes of the latter. We had unconsciously arrived at a kind of dyarchy in which the distinctive forces of Crown and Parliament held each other in play with many a compromise and reservation, and, in spite of much friction, arrived often at some agreed step. The Ministers generally considered they must obey the King and take responsibility for his actions up to the point, at any rate, where their own heads came into danger. Danby had no direct correspondence with the French, and though he feathered his own nest in accordance with custom and saw that his numerous relations did not lack jobs, he took no money himself from Louis. Nevertheless, he shouldered the burden of the French intrigue as a necessary part of what was in its initiation his successful policy. He acquiesced in the King's habit of taking French money. He even signed "by the King's command" the receipts for important sums. Montagu, the English Ambassador in Paris, urged the plan. "Now is the time to ask the French; they can refuse you nothing," he counselled. When there was much suspicion and talk Danby adopted a brazen attitude. He said in effect to important intimates, "Let us spoil the Amalekites; let us make the French pay through the nose. They are getting nothing in return." Charles for his part was well content that this double auction should go on indefinitely. He kept on urging Louis to moderate his ambitions, and to make peace with the Dutch. He expatiated on the difficulties of his position, and warned his royal brother that, unless large payments arrived punctually, he would be forced into war against him. He took all the money he could get from Parliament to increase his armaments, ostensibly for hostilities against France. So ran affairs during 1676 and 1677.

There were in 1674 five or six thousand English troops in French pay; but these had to be reduced after the Anglo-Dutch treaty, and as many of the men returned home and no drafts were sent out, the strength of the various regiments soon fell, and it became necessary to amalgamate units. Thus Skelton's regiment became merged with Peterborough's.

LITTLE ROCK PUBLIC LIBRARY

Peterborough resigned. Who was to take his place? Who should command the combined regiment but the brilliant officer who had planted the lilies of France on the parapet of the Maestricht half-moon, whose quality was known throughout the French Army, who had been thanked by Louis in the field, and whose advancement was so entirely agreeable to Charles II, to the Duke of York, and to both their lady-loves? A news-letter from Paris on March 19, 1674, says:

> Lord Peterborough's regiment, now in France, is to be broken up and some companies of it joined to the companies that went out of the Guards last summer, and be incorporated into one regiment, and to remain there for the present under the command of Captain Churchill, son of Sir Winston.[1]

But before Churchill could receive the colonelcy he had to be presented at Versailles and receive the personal approval of the Great King. He therefore proceeded to Paris furnished with a letter from Monmouth to Louvois, the French Minister of War, which explained the proposed amalgamation of regiments. On March 21 Louvois wrote to thank Monmouth for his letter, to announce that Churchill had been accepted as a colonel in the French service by Louis XIV, and to suggest that companies not merely from Skelton's, but also from Sackville's and Hewetson's regiments, should be included in his command.[2] On April 3 the commission was granted, and John Churchill found himself Colonel in the service of France and at the head of a regiment of English infantry.[3] He was just twenty-four. He had skipped the rank of lieutenant after Sole Bay; he now, in the French service, skips the ranks of Major and Lieutenant-Colonel at a bound. He retained his substantive rank of Captain in the English Army until January 1675,

[1] Le Fleming Papers, *H.M.C.*, p. 108.
[2] Louvois to Monmouth, March 31 (N.S.), 1674; *Dépôt de la guerre*, 391, pièce 204. *Cf.* Lockhart to Arlington of the same date (S.P., 78/139, f. 73).
[3] The original commission, dated April 3/13, is at Blenheim. Lord Wolseley has made two errors in connexion with this commission. In the first place he has dated it March 3/13, and in the second place he has linked it with a correspondence of Louvois throwing doubts on Churchill's suitability for the post, which belongs to nearly three years later.

when he was promoted Lieutenant-Colonel in the Duke of York's regiment. He had evidently at this time impressed his personality on the French Court. He had been there a year before with half a dozen English officers on the way to the Maestricht campaign. Once again the Great King acknowledged the bows of the young Adonis in scarlet and gold, of whose exploits under the planets of Mars and Venus he had already been well informed through the regular channels. He would certainly not have allowed the royal radiance to play upon this elegant, graceful figure if there were not veils which shroud the future.

No historian has examined the scanty records of Churchill's movements from 1674 to 1677 with the care and accuracy of Atkinson. It is surprising that he should cast doubts upon Churchill's presence at the battle of Sinzheim. The foundations of this are solid. Mr Hare, some day the Duke of Marlborough's chaplain, afterwards Bishop of Chichester, accompanied him on several of his campaigns. His well-known journal was read by Marlborough himself, and is one of our comparatively few indisputable documents. Hare, writing about the campaign of 1704, states that on June 15 the Duke advanced to Sinzheim, "which he could not but remember since the year 1674, when he there commanded an English regiment under that great general Marshal Turenne, in the memorable battle fought between him and the Imperial generals, the Duke of Loraine and Count Caprara."[1]

This passage is familiar. It is confirmed by a manuscript account of the battle of Sinzheim which a search of the French military archives has revealed.[2] By this document Churchill is shown serving apart from his own regiment as a volunteer, as at Maestricht, with Douglas's regiment of foot in the French reconnaissance before the battle.

As it was known that there was no news of the enemy army about Heidelberg, and thinking that it was stationed far off to the right in the direction of the Margravate of Baden, Douglas was immediately ordered to advance with 1500 musketeers and 6 guns. On the third day after his departure from Hagenau he

1 Coxe, i, 8 n.   2 *Dépôt de la guerre*, 413, pièce 138.

arrived near Wisloch, three hours from Heidelberg in the direction of Heilbron; he had taken with him M. de Montgaillard and Mr Hamilton, Mr Churchill and M. Duvivier, Quartermaster of the Languedoc regiment, these latter as volunteers.

This detachment rejoined Turenne on June 15, and on the 16th the whole army marched on Sinzheim, on the left bank of the Elsatz. The battle began with Turenne's seizure of the town and the forcing of the stream. The fighting lasted for seven hours and ended in the retreat of the enemy with heavy loss. Although unaccompanied by strategic results, it is claimed as a perfect example in miniature of Turenne's handling of all three arms. Turenne after various manœuvres received reinforcements, and proceeded to ravage the Palatinate, partly to fill his own magazines and partly to impede its reoccupation by a still unbeaten enemy.[1] This military execution of the province dictated by the needs of war must be distinguished from the systematic devastation of the same region ordered by Louis XIV seven years later as a measure of policy.

We have a letter from an old lady—the widow Saint-Just —one of the few residents who did not suffer from Turenne's severities in 1674, written to the Duke of Marlborough from Metz on July 16, 1711, in which she says:

> It would be indeed difficult for me to forget you, Monseigneur, and I have an indispensable duty to remember all my life the kindness which you showed me in Metz *thirty-four years ago*.[2] You were very young then, Monseigneur, but you gave already by your excellent qualities the hope of that valour, politeness and conduct which have raised you with justice to the rank where you command all men. And what is more glorious, Monseigneur, is that the whole world, friends and enemies, bear witness to the truth of what I have the honour to write; and I have no doubt that it was your generosity on my account which [then] made itself felt, because the troops who came and burnt everything around my land at Mezeray in the plain spared my estate, saying that they were so ordered by high authority.[3]

[1] *Cf.* J. Revol, *Turenne*, pp. 316 *seq.*
[2] Author's italics.
[3] Coxe, i, 8 *n.*

Whether this letter stirred some scented memory, long cherished in Churchill's retentive mind, which after the lapse of thirty-four years would make the shielding of this little plot and homestead from the ravages of war an incident he would not forget, we cannot tell. We think, however, that the widow is wrong in her dates. It is, of course, possible

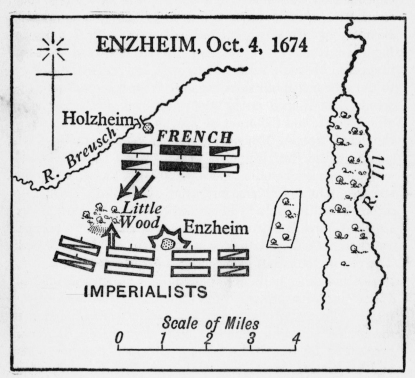

ENZHEIM, Oct. 4, 1674

Holzheim
R. Breusch
FRENCH
Little Wood
Enzheim
R. Ill
IMPERIALISTS

Scale of Miles
0   1   2   3   4

—though the evidence is against it—that Churchill was in Metz on some military duty in 1677. But it is far more likely that the letter refers to the year 1674, when indeed the troops "came and burnt everything around . . . Mezeray."

There is no dispute, however, about Churchill's presence at the head of his regiment in the battle of Enzheim in October. Here all is certain and grim. We have one of his matter-of-fact letters written to Monmouth about the action. We have also a much fuller account by the future Lord Feversham. Turenne had ten thousand horse and twelve thousand foot against enemy forces almost double. Nevertheless, he crossed the Breusch river and attacked the Imperialists by surprise. All turned upon what was called the 'Little Wood,' which lay on the French right between the armies. The development of the main action depended on who held the wood, and the fight for it constituted the crux of the battle. A competent French colonel, Boufflers by name, whom we shall meet several times in higher situations later, was sent to clear the wood with his dragoons. He could make no headway, and resigned his effort to the infantry. Both sides began to cram battalions into the wood. The French rarely stint their own, and never their allies' blood; and the brunt of Turenne's battle was borne by the hired troops. Dongan's battalion of Hamilton's Irish regiment, the third battalion of Warwick's Loyal English, and Churchill's battalion were successively thrown into the struggle. Duras (Feversham) wrote, "One and all assuredly accomplished marvels." They certainly suffered most severe losses. Churchill's battalion, which was the last to engage, had half its officers killed or wounded in the Little Wood. The rest of the island mercenaries suffered almost as heavily in this and other parts of the field. The three squadrons of Monmouth's horse charged the Imperialists who were attacking the French left and centre at a critical moment, and won much honour with almost total destruction. Turenne bivouacked on the field, claiming a victory at heavy odds, and his strategic theme was vindicated. But the battle must take its place in that large category 'bloody and indecisive.'

Feversham, reporting to the Government, wrote, "No one in the world could possibly have done better than Mr Churchill has done and M. de Turenne is very well pleased with all our nation." Turenne also mentioned Churchill and his battalion in his despatches. It was a very rough, savage fight in a cause not reconcilable with any English interest. We print in full Churchill's report to Monmouth because it shows an aspect of his character. Nothing is spent in trappings and explanations. It gives a bald, dour recital of such service facts as it was necessary that Monmouth should know.

Its restraint does not conceal the resentment of a Colonel whose soldiers have been ill-used and slaughtered in a foreign quarrel.[1]

Sept. 25/Oct. 5 1674

COL. JOHN CHURCHILL TO THE DUKE OF MONMOUTH

The 4th of this month M. de Turenne proffered battle to the enemies' army, but they would not advance out of their post to fight us, though they were much stronger, so we were forced to attack them as well as we could. The enemy had a village in their rear and a wood in their front, so M. de Turenne made 8 battalions of us and the dragoons to march out into the wood and push till we came to the head of it, where they had a battery of 5 cannon, which we beat them from and took the cannon and afterwards pushed their foot about 100 yards from the wood's side, so that there was room for squadrons of horse to draw up with us, which being done, we advanced towards them, and beat them out of that post, which was a very good ditch; which being done M. de Vaubrun, one of our lieutenant-generals, commanded us to guard that, and advance no forwarder so that we advanced all that day afterward no forwarder. Half of our foot was so posted that they did not fight at all. Your Grace's last battalion was on this attack, and both those of Hamilton and mine, so we have lost a great many officers, Hamilton, his brother and several others of his regiment. In your battalion Captains Cassels and Lee were killed and 2 wounded. I had Captain Dillon killed, Captains Piggott and Tute wounded, Lieutenants Butler and Mordant and Ensign Donmere wounded, and Lieutenants Watts, Howard, Tucker and Field killed. I had with me but 22 officers, of which I have given your Grace account of 11. Yet your regiment of horse was used much worse than we, for Lieut-colonel Littleton, Captain Gremes and Sheldon and 4 cornets with several lieutenants were killed. The Major, Captain Kirke and most of the officers not killed are wounded, and above half the regiment lost with also several of their colours.

I durst not brag much of our victory, but it is certain they left the field as soon as we. We have three of their cannon and several of their colours and some prisoners. The village where the battle was fought is called Waldheim.

[1] *C.S.P.* (*Dom.*), 1674-75, p. 367. *Cf.* Atkinson, pp. 55 *seq.*

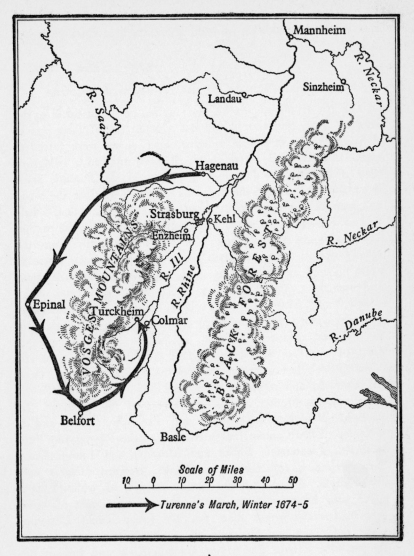

Scale of Miles

10 0 10 20 30 40 50

Turenne's March, Winter 1674-5

TURENNE'S MARCH

Even before the battle it seems likely that Churchill was well esteemed in the army. We find him selected by Turenne with five hundred picked men for an attack upon the Imperialist rearguard at a moment when it was recrossing the Rhine. But only here and there does his figure catch a fleeting gleam. Lots of others, for whom no one has rummaged, did as well. All that can be said is that he did his duty and bore a solid reputation in this hard-pressed, over-weighted, and yet victorious army. There is no doubt that he fought too in the mid-winter attack on Turckheim. In those days the armies reposed from October till April, the condition of such roads as there were alone imposing immobility upon them; but Turenne, starting from Haguenau on November 19, broke into the Imperialist cantonments, and after cutting up various detachments gained a considerable success on Christmas Day. Churchill's regiment marched with him. Duras and other English officers had already been given leave to Paris, it being essential to Turenne's design to pretend that the year's campaign was over. Although a letter on December 15 states that Churchill was daily expected in Paris, he was certainly with the troops.[1]

It is customary to say that he learned the art of war from Turenne, and attempts have been made to draw comparisons between the attacks across the Breusch at Enzheim and across the Nebel at Blenheim. This is going too far. No competent officer of that age could watch the composed genius of Turenne in action without being enriched thereby. But no battle ever repeats itself. The success of a commander does not arise from following rules or models. It consists in an absolutely new comprehension of the dominant facts of the situation at the time, and all the forces at work. Cooks use recipes for dishes and doctors have prescriptions for diseases, but every great operation of war is unique. The kind of intelligence capable of grasping in its complete integrity what is actually happening in the field is not taught by the tactics of commanders on one side or the other—though these may train the mind—but by a profound

1 S.P., 78/139, cf. ff. 145, 172.

appreciation of the actual event. There is no surer road to ill-success in war than to imitate the plans of bygone heroes and to fit them to novel situations. The Enzheim letter is by no means a tribute of admiration to Turenne. On the contrary, the laconic remark, "Half of our foot was so posted that they did not fight at all," is a damaging criticism of an action fought necessarily against superior forces. It comes with peculiar weight from Churchill, who knew so well how to keep unhelpful opinions to himself and hardly ever committed them to paper. We do not know what part, other than has been described, Churchill played in these campaigns. But he must have been thinking intensely about war ever since he came of age, and he certainly had many opportunities of watching it at close quarters under one of its most famous masters, and of learning in a responsible but subordinate position every detail of active service.

CHAPTER VII

SARAH

(1675–76)

IN the early seventies a new star began to shine in the constellations of the English Court. Frances Jennings—"la belle Jenyns" of Grammont—beautiful as "Aurora or the promise of Spring," haughty, correct, mistress of herself, became a waiting-woman of the Duchess of York. She soon had no lack of suitors. The Duke himself cast favourable glances towards her, which were suavely but firmly deflected. Fair and impregnable, she shone upon that merry, easy-going, pleasure-loving society.

Her father, Richard Jennings, of Sandridge, came of a Somersetshire family who, though long entitled to bear arms, had no crest before the reign of King Henry VIII. For some time they had been settled in Hertfordshire, near St Albans, at Holywell House, on the banks of the Ver. Her grandfather was High Sheriff of Herts in 1625, and, like his son Richard, was repeatedly returned to the House of Commons as Member for St Albans. Their property also included land in Somersetshire and Kent, and may have amounted at this period to about £4000 a year. Curiously enough—in after-light—the Manor of Churchill, in Somersetshire, was, as we have seen, in the possession of the Jennings family for a hundred years.

About Frances Jennings' widowed mother various reports exist. We find references in Somersetshire letters to "your noble mother." In *The New Atalantis* she is described as a sorceress: "the famous Mother Shipton, who by the power and influence of her magic art had placed her daughter in the Court." She certainly bore a questionable reputation, suffered from a violent temper, and found in St James's Palace, where she had apartments, a refuge from hungry creditors who, armed with the law, bayed outside.

In 1673 Frances brought her younger sister Sarah, a child of twelve, into the Court circle. She too was attached to the household of the Duke of York. There she grew up, and at the mature age of fifteen was already a precocious, charming figure. She was not so dazzling as her sister, but she had a brilliancy all her own; fair, flaxen hair, blue eyes sparkling with vivacity, a clear, rosy complexion, firm, engaging lips, and a nose well chiselled, but with a slightly audacious upward tilt. She also, from her tenderest years, was entirely self-possessed and self-confident, and by inheritance she owned, when roused, the temper of the devil.

Towards the end of 1675 she began to dance with John Churchill at balls and parties. He, of course, must have been acquainted with her ever since she arrived at St James's, but after one night of dancing at the end of that year they fell in love with each other. It was a case of love, not at first sight indeed, but at first recognition. It lasted for ever; neither of them thenceforward loved anyone else in their whole lives, though Sarah hated many. The courtship was obstructed and prolonged. Meanwhile Sarah grew to her beauty and power, and her personality, full of force, woman's wiles, and masculine sagacity, became manifest.

She soon quarrelled with her mother. "Mrs Jennings and her daughter, Maid of Honour to the Dutchesse," says a contemporary letter,

> have had so great a falling out that they fought; the young one complained to the Dutchesse that if her mother was not put out of St James's where she had lodgings to sanctuary her from debt, she would run way; so Sir Alleyn Apsley was sent to bid the mother remove, who answered "with all her heart; she should never dispute the Duke and Dutchesse's commands, but with the Grace of God she would take her daughter away with her." . . . So rather than part with her, the mother must stay, and all breaches are made up again.[1]

But this was only the first round; and a month later we read:

> Mrs [Mistress] Sarah Jennings has got the better of her mother, who is commanded to leave the Court and her daughter in itt,

[1] Rutland Papers, *H.M.C.*, XII, ii, *32, 34.*

notwithstanding the mother's petition, that she might have her girle with her, the girle saying she is a mad woman.

However, once the eviction had taken place relations were restored between mother and daughter, and they seem to have been attached to one another so long as they dwelt apart.[1]

Such is the first we hear of the young lady who now entered John Churchill's life and was eventually to play as large a part in English history as any woman not a sovereign. It is odd that, in spite of all the glare which has beaten upon the story of Sarah Jennings, we do not know with certitude either the house in which she was born, nor that in which she was married to John, nor even the house in which—octogenarian, millionairess, and world figure—she died. Lengthy arguments are exchanged by her train of biographers on all these simple points of fact. Still, it seems probable that she died in London, and still more probable that she was born at St Albans, which she always calls "her native town."

At Blenheim Palace there is a bundle of thirty-seven love-letters of John and Sarah covering a period of about three years, from 1675 to 1677. All are unsigned and all are provokingly undated. All but eight are his. Her contributions are short, severe, and almost repellent. She must have written many more letters, and it is surmised that these were in a more tender vein. She seems, however, only to have kept copies of her warlike missives. She asked him to destroy all

[1] Among the Blenheim MSS. there are a few letters, written from Sarah to her mother after her marriage, which show the terms on which they lived.

Sarah Churchill to Mrs Jennings

"I have thought very often since I left, dear Mother, what was the reason of all the disorder and ill humour the night and morning before I came away; and if I thought I had done anything that you had reason to take ill I should be very angry with myself, but I am very sure I did not intend anything but give you the duty I ought, and if against my will and knowledge I have committed any fault I hope you will forgive it and I beg you will consider how often I stopped the coach as we came home and begged you to come in which I could do for no other reason but for leave [fear] you should get your death, and what reason had you when you came here to say so many cruel things to me and Betty Moody [Mowdie] which I can't but take to myself. The post is going and I can say no more but that I hope I shall see you or hear from you very soon, and that I will ever be your most dutiful daughter whatever you are to me.

"CHURCHILL"

SARAH JENNINGS BEFORE SHE MARRIED
Simon Verelst
This portrait always hung in her dressing-room at Holywell.
By permission of Earl Spencer 118

LITTLE ROCK PUBLIC LIBRARY

SARAH

her letters, and he must have done so, for none survives except this bundle of thirty-seven, of which hers are copies and his only are originals. In her old age the Duchess several times fondled and reread this correspondence. Her own letters are endorsed in her handwriting, "Some coppys of my letters to Mr Churchill before I was married & not more than 15 years old." She left a request that her chief woman-in-waiting, or secretary, Grace Ridley, should after her death be given the letters in order that she might "burn without reading them." There is an endorsement in the quivering hand of age stating that she had read over all these letters in 1736. Finally, the year before her death, "Read over in 1743 desiring to burn them, but I could not doe it."

The reader shall be the judge of the correspondence.[1] The first batch consists entirely of John's letters.

John to Sarah

* My Soul, I love you so truly well that I hope you will be so kind as to let me see you somewhere to-day, since you will not be at Whitehall. I will not name any time, for all hours are alike to me when you will bless me with your sight. You are, and ever shall be, the dear object of my life, for by heavens I will never love anybody but yourself.

* I am just come and have no thought of any joy but that of seeing you. Wherefore I hope you will send me word that you will see me this night.

* My head did ache yesterday to that degree and I was so out of order that nothing should have persuaded me to have gone abroad but the meeting of you who is much dearer than all the world besides to me. If you are not otherwise engaged, I beg you will give me leave to come at eight o'clock.

* I fancy by this time that you are awake, which makes me now send to know how you do, and if your foot will permit you to give me the joy of seeing you in the drawing-room this night.

---

[1] The letters are here printed from the originals in the Blenheim MSS. with the spelling and punctuation modernized. Those hitherto unpublished are marked with an asterisk.

119

Pray let me hear from you, for when I am not with you, the only joy I have is hearing from you.

* My Soul, it is a cruel thing to be forced in a place when I have no hopes of seeing you, for on my word last night seemed very tedious to me; wherefore I beg you will be so kind to me as to come as often as you can this week, since I am forced to wait [to be in waiting]. I hope you will send me word that you are well and that I shall see you here to-night.

* The reason that I write thus early to you is for fear you should be gone abroad, and this would be a very long day, if you should be so unkind as not to write. I hope, although you do go to Mrs Fortrey, that you will be dressed at night, so that I may see you in the drawing-room. Pray write two words before you go. You ought to do it, for I love you with all my heart and soul.

* I did no sooner know that you were not well, but upon my faith without affectation I was also sick. I hope your keeping your bed yesterday and this night has made you perfectly well, which if it has, I beg that I may then have leave to see you to-night at eight, for believe me that it is an age since I was with you. I do love you so well that I have no patience when I have not hopes of seeing my dear angel, wherefore pray send me word that I shall be blessed and come at eight, till when, my Soul, I will do nothing else but think kindly of you.

* I was so sick all day yesterday that I would have got somebody to have written for me, but the desire I had to see you made me endure all and wait. If you will be at Mrs Berkley's or anywhere else this afternoon where I may see you I will come, if you send me word what hour.

* I hope you were so wise as to value your own health before your duty to the Duchess, so that you did not walk with her at five this morning.

I hope your sitting up has done you no harm, so that you will see me this afternoon, for upon my soul I do love you with all my heart and take joy in nothing but yourself. I do love you with all the truth imaginable, but have patience but for one

LITTLE ROCK PUBLIC LIBRARY

week, you shall then see that I will never more do aught that shall look like a fault.

If your happiness can depend upon the esteem and love I have for you, you ought to be the happiest thing breathing, for I have never anybody loved to that height I do you. I love you so well that your happiness I prefer much above my own; and if you think meeting me is what you ought not to do, or that it will disquiet you, I do promise you I will never press you more to do it. As I prefer your happiness above my own, so I hope you will sometimes think how well I love you; and what you can do without doing yourself an injury, I hope you will be so kind as to do it—I mean in letting me see that you wish me better than the rest of mankind; and in return I swear to you that I never will love anything but your dear self, which has made so sure a conquest of me that, had I the will, I have not the power ever to break my chains. Pray let me hear from you, and know if I shall be so happy as to see you to-night.

I was last night at the ball, in hopes to have seen what I love above my own soul, but I was not so happy, for I could see you nowhere, so that I did not stay above an hour. I would have written sooner, but that I was afraid you went to bed so late that it would disturb you.

Pray see which of these two puppies you like best, and that keep; for the bitch cannot let them suck any longer. They are above three weeks old, so that if you give it warm milk it will not die. Pray let me hear from you, and at what time you will be so kind as to let me come to you to-night. Pray, if you have nothing to do, let it be the latest [earliest], for I never am truly happy but when I am with you.

We now see the falling of shadows upon the sunlit path. We cannot tell their cause, whether they come from passing clouds or from some solid obstruction. We do not know the reason, nor even the year. We must realize that these written fragments, luckily preserved, represent only a tiny part of all that happened in nearly a thousand days of two young lives.

* I stayed last night in the drawing-room expecting your coming back, for I could have wished that we had not parted until you had given me hopes of seeing you, for, my soul, there is no pain

121

so great to me, as that when I fear you do not love me; but I hope I shall never live to see you less kind to me than you are. I am sure I will never deserve it, for I will by all that is good love you as long as I live. I beg you will let me see you as often as you can, which I am sure you ought to do if you care for my love, since every time I see you I still find new charms in you; therefore do not be so ill-natured as to believe any lies that may be told you of me, for on my faith I do not only now love you but do desire to do it as long as I live. If you can have time before you go to church, pray let me hear from you.

* I was last night above an hour in the Bedchamber still expecting every one that came in it should be you, but at last I went to Mrs Brownley's, where I found Mrs Mowdie,[1] who told me that you were with your sister, so that you would not be seen that night; so I went to Whitehall to find out the Duke, for when I know that you will not appear I do not care to be at St James's. For 'tis you and you only I care to see, for by all that is good I do with all the truth imaginable love you. Pray let me hear from you, and I beg that I may be blessed this night in being with you. I hope you will like the waistcoat; I do assure you there is not such another to be had in England.

* My Lord Mulgrave's page is come to let me know that they stay for me, but I cannot stir before I write to know how you do, and if you will be at Mrs Berkley's and whether you would have me come or no, for I will never do aught that you will not have me do.

My Soul, I go with the heaviest heart that ever man did, for by all that is good I love you with all my heart and soul, and I am sure that as long as I live you shall have no just reason to believe the contrary. If you are unkind, I love [you] so well that I cannot live, for you are my life, my soul, my all that I hold dear in this world; therefore do not make so ungrateful a return as not to write. If you have charity you will not only write, but you will write kindly, for it is on you that depends the quiet of my soul. Had I fitting words to express my love, it would not then be in your power to refuse what I beg with tears in my eyes, that you would love me as I will by heavens do you.

1 Mrs Mowdie was Sarah's waiting-woman and to some extent chaperone.

134

I am Just come, and have
noe thoughts of anny Joye,
but that of seeing you,
wherfore I hope you will
send me word that you
will see me this night,

FRAGMENT FROM ONE OF MARLBOROUGH'S LOVE-LETTERS
Blenheim MSS.

To show you how unreasonable you are in accusing me, I dare swear you yourself will own that your going from me in the Duchess's drawing-room did show as much contempt as was possible. I may grieve at it, but I will no more complain when you do it, for I suppose it is what pleases your humour. I cannot imagine what you meant by your saying I laughed at you at the Duke's side, for I was so far from that, that had it not been for shame I could have cried. And [as] for being in haste to go to the Park, after you went, I stood near a quarter of an hour, I believe, without knowing what I did. Although at Whitehall you told me I should not come, yet I walked twice to the Duke's back-stairs, but there was no Mrs Mowdie; and when I went to my Lord Duras's, I would not go the same way they did but came again down the back-stairs; and when I went away, I did not go in my chair, but made it follow me, because I would see if there was any light in your chamber, but I saw none. Could you see my heart you would not be so cruel as to say I do not love you, for by all that is good I love you and only you. If I may have the happiness of seeing you to-night, pray let me know, and believe that I am never truly pleased but when I am with you.

Thus time slipped by, and ardent courtship must have lasted far into its second year. Sarah's sister Frances, after rejecting so many suitors, royal or honourable, was already married to Lord Hamilton, a man of charm and distinction, but of no great wealth. Sarah, approaching seventeen, was alone. She had chased away her mother, and the man she loved and who loved her so well had not yet spoken the decisive word.

Meanwhile the war continued; but such few records of John Churchill as exist for the years 1675, 1676, and 1677 are conclusive against his having fought any more on the Continent. His name is never mentioned in any of the operations.[1] The regiment which he had formerly commanded, withering for lack of drafts, was incorporated in

[1] On April 13, 1675, the Jesuit Father St Germaine wrote from Flanders to his correspondent in England, " I have wrote many times these three months about being assured that neither Churchill nor Clarke would come over any more, . . . but hearing nothing from you it makes me conclude . . . there is nothing to be done in it." (St Germaine to E. Coleman, April 13, 1675; *H.M.C.*, xiii, App. vi, p. 108.)

Monmouth's Royal English regiment in May 1675. It is
therefore almost certain that he took no part in this year's
campaign either with Turenne or elsewhere.[1]

In August we read of him hastening to Paris. We can
but guess at his mission. Since 1673 he had been Gentleman
of the Bedchamber to the Duke of York. On August 9,
1675, the French Ambassador in England wrote to Louis XIV
describing an interview with James at which the Duke
had asked for an immediate subsidy from the French King
to free his brother from the need of summoning Parliament.[2]
In view of the fact that four years later James was to send
Churchill over to Paris to make a similar request for a subsidy, and that he was already well known at Versailles, it is
not unlikely that he was sent to Paris to reinforce his master's
petition. A warrant showing that in October he had permission to import from France free of duty his silver plate
seems to mark the end of his stay abroad.[3] In September
1676 he was a member of a court-martial convened in
London to try an officer for an assault on the governor of
Plymouth. There is therefore no doubt that he spent these
years mainly at Court, and that he was increasingly employed
in diplomatic work and at his ordinary duties in the Duke
of York's household.

Towards the end of this year the Duke of Monmouth
expressed his dissatisfaction with the Lieutenant-Colonel
of his Royal English regiment, which was serving with
the French Army against the Dutch, and proposed to
Louis XIV that the command should be transferred to
Churchill. Justin MacCartie, a nephew of the Duke of
Ormonde, who when an ensign had accompanied Feversham to the siege of Maestricht, also sought this appoint-

1 Cf. Atkinson, pp. 65–66.
2 Correspondance politique, Angleterre, t. 116, ff. 173 seq.
3 C.S.P. (Treasury Books), 1672–75, p. 830, describes the contents of Churchill's
two trunks of silver recently brought out of France in October—to wit, " one basin,
2 great dishes, 12 small dishes, 2 massarines, 3 doz. of plates, 2 flagons, 4 candle-
sticks, 2 ewers, 2 stands, 2 chafing dishes, 1 vinegar pot, 1 sugar pot, 1 mustard pot, 1
pair of snuffers and its case, 4 salts, 6 cups, 12 spoons, 12 forks, 12 hafts, one great
spoon, one chamber pot, one tea pot, one chocolate pot, one great cup, one skillet, 2
Turkey cups." Several pieces of this plate of French make are still preserved at
Althorp.

ment. Courtin, the French Ambassador, laid the situation before Louvois, together with elaborate and scandalous accounts of John's love-affairs. Louvois replied that Churchill appeared to be too much taken up with the ladies to devote his whole-hearted affection to a regiment. He would give, Louvois said, "more satisfaction to a rich and faded mistress, than to a monarch who did not want to have dishonourable and dishonoured carpet knights in his armies." Courtin, however, considered Churchill a far abler officer than his competitor, and the post was undoubtedly offered him. It was Churchill who refused. "Mr Churchill," reported the Ambassador, whose news was now certainly up to date, "prefers to serve the very pretty sister [Sarah Jennings] of Lady Hamilton than to be lieutenant-colonel in Monmouth's regiment."[1]

This phase in Churchill's life is significant. It marks more clearly than anything else the intensity of his passion for Sarah, before which adventure, ambition, and "lucre" alike lost their power. There may, of course, have been more general reasons as well for his not wishing to take further service under the French. He had probably begun to share the prejudices of most Englishmen of this time against Louis XIV's assaults on the Protestant Dutch. He had experienced at Enzheim the French profusion with their hired troops. Better to "sport with Amaryllis in the shade" than lease himself as a French popinjay! Anyhow, he refused. Mars was quite decidedly set aside for Venus. However, the estrangement was not final.

During this same year, 1676, Sir Winston Churchill and his wife became concerned at the attachment of their son to Sarah Jennings. They did not see how he could make a career for himself unless he married money. To this, with his looks and prowess, he might well aspire. They fixed their eyes upon Catharine Sedley, daughter and heiress of Sir Charles Sedley, a man renowned for his wit and his wealth. Catharine

1 November 19/29, 1676. *Correspondance politique, Angleterre*, t. 120 C, f. 231; *cf*. ff. 206, 248, etc. This account is based on the original letters in the French Foreign Office, and corrects erroneous accounts in Wolseley and in Forneron's *Louise de Kéroualle*. Wolseley, indeed, places part of this story in 1674 and part in 1676.

Sedley was also of the household of the Duke of York. By some accounts she was tall, plain, thin, angular, but had a pair of fine eyes. Her portrait, however, is by no means unprepossessing; and she already inherited her father's caustic wit. She exerted her attractions in her own way, and, though not admired, was both liked and feared. Ultimately, after the parental hopes had failed to unite her to John Churchill, she became, in what seemed almost rotation for the maids of honour, the Duke of York's mistress. Although she was a staunch Protestant with an unconcealed scorn of priests and Papists, he was for some years devoted to her, and a time was to come when she seemed about to play a decisive part in politics. Several of her sayings have been preserved. When, after the Revolution, Queen Mary slighted her at Court, she boldly reproached her, saying, "Remember, ma'am, if I broke one of the commandments *with* your father, you have broken another *against* him." Speaking generally of James II's mistresses, including Arabella, Lady Bellasis, and herself, she remarked with much detachment, "What he saw in any of us, I cannot tell. We were all plain, and if any of us had had wit, he would not have understood it." Altogether she was by no means a negligible personality, and had treasures of her own to bestow besides her father's fortune.

The news of these parental machinations must have been swiftly carried to Sarah. How far, if at all, John lent himself to them, at what point they begin to darken the love-letters, we cannot tell. Certainly the arguments which Sir Winston and his wife could deploy were as serious and matter-of-fact as any which could ever be brought to bear upon a son. We may imagine some of them.

"You have your foot on the ladder of fortune. You have already mounted several important rungs. Every one says you have a great future before you. Every one knows you have not got—apart from the annuity or your pay— a penny behind you. How can you on a mere whim compromise your whole future life? Catharine Sedley is known to be a most agreeable woman. She holds her own in any company. The Duke listens to all she says, and the whole

Court laughs at her jests. She is asked everywhere. Women have beauties of mind quite as attractive, except to enamoured youth, as those of body. Sir Charles is a really wealthy man, solid, long-established, with fine houses, broad acres, and failing health. She is his only child. With his fortune and her humour and sagacity behind you, all these anxieties which have gnawed your life, all that poverty which has pursued us since your infancy, would be swept away. You could look any man in the face and your career would be assured.

"Moreover, do you really think this little Jennings could be a companion to you? Although she is only a child, little more than half your age, she has proved herself a spitfire and a termagant. Look at the way she treats you—as if you were a lackey. You have told us enough of your relations with her—and, indeed, it is the talk of the Court—to show that she is just humiliating you, twirling you round her finger for her own glorification. Did she not say only last week to So-and-so how she could make you do this, that, or anything? Even if she had all Catharine's money we would beg you for your peace of mind, with all the experience of the older generation, not to take this foolish step. It would be a decision utterly out of keeping with your character, with your frugal life—never throwing any expense on us, always living within your income—with all your prudence and care for the future. You would be committing a folly, and the one kind of folly we were always sure you would never commit.

"Lastly, think of her. Are you really doing her justice in marrying her? She has come to Court under good protection. She could never hold a candle to her sister, but she may well hope to marry into the peerage. There is the Earl of Lindsay, who could give her a fine position. He is paying her a great deal of attention. Would she ever be happy with love in a cottage? Would she not drag you down and sink with you?" "Believe me, my son, I, your father," Sir Winston might have said, "pillaged by the Roundheads, uprooted from my lands for my loyalty, have had a hard time. I can give nothing to you or your bride but the shelter of my roof at Mintern. You know how we live there. How would she put up with that? We have never been able to do more than hold up our heads. These are rough times. They are not getting better. By yielding to this absurd fancy you will ruin her life as well as your own, and throw a burden upon us which, as you know, we cannot bear. I am to meet Sir Charles next week. He is a great believer in you. He has heard things about you from the French. It is said that among the younger men none is your master in the land service. I never commanded more than a cavalry troop, but you at half my age are almost a general.* But are you not throwing away your military career as well?"

How far did John yield to all this? He was no paragon. All around was the corrupt, intriguing Court with its busy marriage market. In those days English parents disposed their children's fortunes much as the French do now. Winston himself had perhaps been betrothed at fourteen or fifteen, and had made a happy, successful family life. We do not believe that John ever weakened in his purpose. Certainly he never wavered in his love. No doubt he weighed with deep anxiety the course which he should take. All the habit of his mind was farsighted. "In the bloom of his youth," says Macaulay, "he loved lucre more than wine or women." However, he loved Sarah more than all. But how were they to live? This was the cold, brutal, commonplace, inexorable question that baffled his judgment and tied his tongue.

Her situation, as she learned about the family negotiations and saw her lover oppressed and abstracted, was cruel. Already, with discerning feminine eye, she had marked him for her own. Now wealth and worldly wisdom were to intervene and snatch him from her. Already barriers seemed to be growing between them, and it was here that the vital truth of her purpose saved all. Weakness on her part in dealing with him might perhaps have been fatal. She maintained towards him a steady, bayonet-bristling front. Between perfect love, absolute unity, and scorn and fury such as few souls are capable of, there was no middle choice. Sometimes, indeed, her ordeal in public was more than she could bear. Scores of peering, knowing eyes were upon her. Her tears were seen at some revel, and the French Ambassador wrote a sneering letter about them for the gossips of Versailles.

> * There was a small ball last Friday at the Duchess of York's where Lady Hamilton's sister who is uncommonly good-looking had far more wish to cry than to dance. Churchill who is her suitor says that he is attacked by consumption and must take the air in France. I only wish I were as well as he. The truth is that he wishes to free himself from intrigues. His father urges him to marry one of his relations who is very rich and very ugly, and will not consent to his marriage with Miss Jennings. He is also said to be not a little avaricious and I hear from the various Court ladies that he has pillaged the Duchess of Cleveland, and that she has given him more than the value of 100,000 livres. They make out that it is he who has quitted her and that she has taken herself off in chagrin to France to rearrange her affairs. If Churchill crosses the sea, she will be able to patch things up with him. Meanwhile she writes agreeably to the Duchess of Sussex conjuring her to go with her husband to the country and to follow her advice but not her example.[1]

Thus Courtin. We must make allowance for his own love of scandal, and for the palates he sought to spice: but here, at any rate, we have a definite situation. Courtin's letter is dated November 27, 1676. We see that John's relations with Barbara have ended; that his father is pressing him to marry Catharine Sedley; that he is deeply in love with Sarah, but does not feel justified in his poverty in proposing marriage; that she is indignant at his delay and miserable about the other women and all the uncertainty and the gossip. We see her magnificent in her prolonged ordeal. We see John for the only time in these pages meditating flight from a field the difficulties of which seemed for the moment beyond his sagacious strength. Well is it said that the course of true love never did run smooth. The next chapter will, however, carry the lovers to their hearts' desire.

---

[1] Courtin to Louvois, November 27/December 7, 1676; *Correspondance politique, Angleterre*, t. 120 C, f. 248.

CHAPTER VIII

MARRIAGE

(1676–78)

WE now approach the delicate question of how John freed himself from the Duchess of Cleveland. Unquestionably towards the end of 1676 he quitted Barbara for Sarah. Was he "off with the old love before he was on with the new"? Or was it one of those familiar dissolving views, where one picture fades gradually away and the other grows into gleaming, vivid life? Gossip and scandal there is a-plenty; evidence there is none. Of course, a married woman separated from her husband, unfaithful to him, notoriously licentious, who has a young man in the twenties as her lover, must expect that a time will come when her gay companion will turn serious, when all the charms and pleasures she can bestow will pall and cloy, and when he will obey the mysterious command of a man's spirit to unite himself for ever, by every tie which nature and faith can proffer, to a being all his own. But Barbara took it very ill, and after a brief attempt to console herself with Wycherley, the playwright, she withdrew from England altogether and took up her abode in Paris. Here she became intimate with Montagu, the English Ambassador already mentioned, with results which after a while emerged upon the stage of history.

We cannot dismiss this topic without recourse to Mrs Manley. She is Lord Macaulay's witness; and, countersigned by his great name, cannot be swept incontinently back into the cesspool from which she should never have crawled. The witness is voluble where trustworthy records are silent upon this transference of Churchill's affections. She throws light of a certain character where the lamps of truth are dim. In her masterpieces, *The New Atalantis* and *Queen Zarah*, she gives two mutually destructive accounts of the breach between John and Barbara. *The New Atalantis* describes how Church-

130

ill, tired of the Duchess of Cleveland and having fallen in love with Sarah Jennings, used the following stratagem to give himself the best of the argument.

He persuaded a young lord—Mrs Manley says Lord Dover, but this is plainly impossible—who was Barbara's ardent admirer to lodge in his apartments. One day after his bath, when he was in scanty attire upon the couch, with his face concealed, apparently sleeping, Barbara, coming to see John, entered the room. Macaulay's witness, Mrs Manley, asserts that, struck by the beauty of the young lord's form, she embraced him, and that not until much had passed did his voice recall her to the fact that he was a comparative stranger. Hot-foot upon this surprise came a knocking at the door. Churchill broke in and, suitably scandalized at the scene, delivered himself up to transports of simulated fury. He averred that she was the most inconstant of women, that he would never see her again, and would that very day marry Sarah Jennings, of whom she was already jealous. On which he departed, free. Such is Mrs Manley's first account.

The second account, published some years after in *Queen Zarah*, is different.[1] The technique is the same, but the facts are opposite. The parts played by the characters and their sexes are reversed. Here the tale begins with Sarah deeply in love with John. She has met him at balls and parties where he was so attractive and danced so well that "every step he took carried death with it." Sarah's mother, represented by Mrs Manley as an experienced, disreputable woman, resolved to aid her daughter's sentiments. She therefore contrived to bring Barbara and Sarah together. Barbara, who took a great liking to Sarah and did not know that she was her rival, invited Sarah to her apartments—those beautiful, elegant rooms where she was wont in her ordinary duty to receive the King. Thither Sarah repaired, and as her hostess was late—lured away upon a pretext—for better security disrobed and got into bed. Again suddenly the door opened, and John

---

1 It is not quite certain that Mrs Manley was the author of *Queen Zarah,* but if she was not, the pamphlet was certainly a product of the same factory and by a scribe of the same kidney.

on one of his customary visits to Barbara entered. Struck and inspired by Sarah's dazzling beauty, he immediately declared his overwhelming love for her. Thereupon once more the door opened, and this time it was her mother who appeared. She in her turn was scandalized. Alleging that her daughter was now hopelessly compromised, and urging that John had declared his love for her in her hearing, she demanded immediate marriage as the only method of preventing the humiliation of her daughter, and as the surest way by which John could sever once and for all the ties which bound him to Barbara. While the future Captain-General was temporarily disconcerted by this turn of events, Mrs Jennings produced a priest, and before anyone could say Jack Robinson the marriage ceremony was accomplished. The modern reader, accustomed to the Hollywood films, will have already foreseen the last act of the drama: the incursion of the Duchess of Cleveland, and her fury as she gradually discovered that her rival had been married to her lover in her own apartments, to which she had herself invited her.

We have set out these two tales as told by Macaulay's witness in abridged and expurgated form. The reader may choose the one or the other, but evidently not both. Or, again, he may believe that these are only the lying inventions of a prurient and filthy-minded underworld, served up to those who relish them and paid for by party interest and political malice. We shall not attempt to sway his judgment. It will depend entirely upon his character.

Let us return to the love-letters, which plead John's cause to posterity, as well as to Sarah. The deadlock in their affairs continued, and she rightly challenged him to end it or to leave her.

Sarah to John

If it were true that you have that passion for me which you say you have, you would find out some way to make yourself happy—it is in your power. Therefore press me no more to see you, since it is what I cannot in honour approve of, and if I have done too much, be so just as to consider who was the cause of it.

MARRIAGE

John to Sarah

As for the power you say you have over yourself, I do no ways
at all doubt of it, for I swear to you I do not think you love me,
so that I am very easily persuaded that my letters have no charms
for you, since I am so much a slave to your charms as to own
to you that I love you above my own life, which by all that is
holy I do. You must give me leave to beg that you will not
condemn me for a vain fool that I did believe you did love me,
since both you and your actions did oblige me to that belief in
which heaven knows I took so much joy that from henceforward
my life must be a torment to me for it. You say I pretend a
passion to you when I have other things in my head. I cannot
imagine what you mean by it, for I vow to God you do so entirely possess my thoughts that I think of nothing else in this
world but your dear self. I do not, by all that is good, say this
that I think it will move you to pity me, for I do despair of your
love; but it is to let you see how unjust you are, and that I must
ever love you as long as I have breath, do what you will. I do
not expect in return that you should either write or speak to me,
since you think it is what may do you a prejudice; but I have a
thing to beg which I hope you will not be so barbarous as to
deny me. It is that you will give me leave to do what I cannot
help, which is to adore you as long as I live, and in return I will
study how I may deserve, although not have, your love. I am
persuaded that I have said impertinent things enough to anger
you, for which I do with all my heart beg your pardon, and do
assure you that from henceforward I will approach and think of
you with the same devotion as to my God.

John to Sarah

You complain of my unkindness, but would not be kind yourself in answering my letter, although I begged you to do it. The
Duchess goes to a new play to-day, and afterwards to the Duchess
of Monmouth's, there to dance. I desire that you will not go
thither, but make an excuse, and give me leave to come to you.
Pray let me know what you do intend, and if you go to the play;
for if you do, then I will do what I can to go, if [although] the
Duke does not. Your not writing to me made me very uneasy,
for I was afraid it was want of kindness in you, which I am sure
I will never deserve by any action of mine.

Sarah to John

As for seeing you I am resolved I never will in private nor in public if I could help it. As for the last I fear it will be some time before I can order so as to be out of your way of seeing me. But surely you must confess that you have been the falsest creature[1] upon earth to me. I must own that I believe that I shall suffer a great deal of trouble, but I will bear it, and give God thanks, though too late I see my error.

Here the door is firmly closed, and then opened with a chink again.

John to Sarah

It is not reasonable that you should have a doubt but that I love you above all expression, which by heaven I do. It is not possible to do anything to let you see your power more than my obedience to your commands of leaving you, when my tyrant-heart aches me to make me disobey; but it were much better it should break than to displease you. I will not, dearest, ask or hope to hear from you unless your charity pities me and will so far plead for me as to tell you that a man dying for you may hope that you will be so kind to him as to make a distinction betwixt him and the rest of his sex. I do love and adore you with all my heart and soul—so much that by all that is good I do and ever will be better pleased with your happiness than my own; but oh, my soul, if we might be both happy, what inexpressible joy would that be! But I will not think of any content but what you shall think fit to give, for 'tis you alone I love, so that if you are kind but one minute, that will make me happier than all the world can besides. I will not dare to expect more favour than you shall think fit to give, but could you ever love me, I think the happiness would be so great that it would make me immortal.

Sarah to John

I am as little satisfied with this letter as I have been with many others, for I find all you will say is only to amuse me and make me think you have a passion for me, when in reality there is no such thing. You have reason to think it strange that I write to you after my last, where I protested that I would never write nor speak to you more; but as you know how much kindness

1 Perhaps a reference to the Catharine Sedley episode.

I had for you, you can't wonder or blame me if I try once more, to hear what you can say for your justification. But this I must warn you of—that you don't hold disputes, as you have done always, and to keep me from answering of you, and yourself from saying what I expect from you, for if you go on in that manner I will leave you that moment, and never hear you speak more whilst I have life. Therefore pray consider if, with honour to me and satisfaction to yourself, I can see you; for if it be only to repeat those things which you said so oft, I shall think you the worst of men, and the most ungrateful; and 'tis to no purpose to imagine that I will be made ridiculous in the world when it is in your power to make me otherwise.

John to Sarah

Yours last night found me so sick that I thought I should have died, and I have now so excessive a headache that I should not stir out all day but that the Duchess has sent me word that the Duke will see me this afternoon, so that at night I shall have the happiness to see you in the drawing-room. I cannot remember what it was I said to you that you took so ill, but one thing I do assure you, that I will never say or do aught willingly that I think you may take ill. Ah, my soul, did you love so well as I, you could never have refused my letter so barbarously as you did, for if reason had bade you do it, love would never have permitted it. But I will complain no more of it, but hope time and the truth of my love will make you love better.

John to Sarah

I have been so extreme ill with the headache all this morning that I have not had courage to write to know how you do; but your being well is what I prefer much above my own health. Therefore pray send me word, for if you are not in pain I cannot then be much troubled, for were it not for the joy I take in the thought that you love me, I should not care how soon I died; for by all that is good I love you so well that I wish from my soul that that minute that you leave loving me, that I may die, for life after that would be to me but one perpetual torment. If the Duchess sees company, I hope you will be there; but if she does not, I beg you will then let me see you in your chamber, if it be but for one hour. If you are not in the drawing-room, you must then send me word at what hour I shall come.

Sarah to John

At four o'clock I would see you, but that would hinder you from seeing the play, which I fear would be a great affliction to you, and increase the pain in your head, which would be out of anybody's power to ease until the next new play. Therefore, pray consider, and without any compliment to me, send me word if you can come to me without any prejudice to your health.

This unkind sarcasm drew probably the only resentful reply which John ever penned in all his correspondence with Sarah. The letter does not exist; but we can judge its character by his covering note to her waiting-woman, whose support he had doubtless enlisted.

Colonel John Churchill to Mrs Elizabeth Mowdie

Your mistress's usage to me is so barbarous that sure she must be the worst woman in the world, or else she would not be thus ill-natured. I have sent a letter which I desire you will give her. It is very reasonable for her to take it, because it will be then in her power never to be troubled with me more, if she pleases. I do love her with all my soul, but will not trouble her, for if I cannot have her love, I shall despise her pity. For the sake of what she has already done, let her read my letter and answer it, and not use me thus like a footman.

This was the climax of the correspondence. Sarah's response shows that she realized how deeply he was distressed and how critical their relations had become. She held out an offended hand, and he made haste to clasp it. Some days evidently passed before he wrote again, and this time his rebellious mood had vanished.

Sarah to John

I have done nothing to deserve such a kind of letter as you have writ to me, and therefore I don't know what answer to give; but I find you have a very ill opinion of me, and therefore I can't help being angry with myself for having had too good a one of you; for if I had as little love as yourself, I have been told enough of you to make me hate you, and then I believe I should have been more happy than I am like to be now. However, if you can be so well contented never to see me as

I think you can by what you say, I will believe you; though I have not other people; and after you are satisfied that I have not broke my word, you shall have it in your power to see me or not—and if you are contented without it I shall be extremely pleased.

John to Sarah

It would have been much kinder in you, if you had been pleased to have been so good-natured to have found time to have written to me yesterday, especially since you are resolved not to appear when I might see you. But I am resolved to take nothing ill but to be your slave as long as I live, and so to think all things well that you do.

This was the only surrender to which the Duke of Marlborough was ever forced. It was to the fan of a chit of seventeen. Moreover, so far as we have been able to ascertain, his courtship of Sarah affords the only occasions in his life of hazards and heart-shaking ordeals when he was ever frightened. Neither the heat of battle nor the long-drawn anxieties of conspiracy, neither the unsanctioned responsibilities of the march to the Danube nor the tortuous secret negotiations with the Jacobite Court, ever disturbed the poise of that calm, reasonable, resolute mind. But in this love-story we see him plainly panic-stricken. The terror that he and Sarah might miss one another, might drift apart, might pass and sail away like ships in the night, overpowered him. A man who cared less could have played this game of love with the sprightly Sarah much better than he. A little calculation, a little adroitness, some studied withdrawals, some counter-flirtation, all these were the arts which in every other field he used with innate skill. He has none of them now. He begs and prays with bald, homely, pitiful reiteration. We see the power of the light which sometimes shines upon the soul. These two belonged to one another, and, with all their faults, placarded as we know them, their union was true as few things of which we have experience here are true. And at this moment in the depth of his spirit, with the urge of uncounted generations pressing forward, he feared lest it might be cast away.

137

We now reach at least the year 1677, and with it the final phase of the correspondence. It seems plain that they are engaged. The difficulties that remain are only those of time and means. He writes of an interview with his father, of the importance of Sarah not angering the Duchess of York, and of business arrangements for their future.

John to Sarah

It was unkind of you to go away last night since you knew that I came for no other purpose but to have the joy of seeing you, but I will not believe it was for want of love, for you are all goodness, the thought of which makes me love you above my own soul. If you shall be in the drawing-room to-night, send me word at what hour, so that I may order it so to be there at the same hour. I am now in my chamber, and will stay there as long as I can in hopes I may hear from you.

Sarah to John

I am willing to satisfy the world and you that I am not now in the wrong, and therefore I give you leave to come to-night —not that I can be persuaded you can ever justify yourself, but I do it that I may be freed from the troubles of ever hearing from you more.

John to Sarah

When I left my father last night, on purpose to come and speak with you, I did not believe that you would have been so unkind as to have gone away the minute I came in, fearing that I might else have spoke to you, which indeed I should have been very glad to have done. I beg you will give me leave to see you this night, at what hour you please. Pray let me hear from you, and if you do not think me impertinent for asking, I should be glad to know what made you go away.

John to Sarah

* I am just going to Richmond, but would not go until I had first paid my duty to you, who is and ever shall be the first thing in my thought. I shall come back time enough to be according as you appointed, but I believe it will be better if you let it be at ten, for I would be glad you would wait [be in waiting],

138

you having not waited last night. I am sure if you love me, you will not at this anger the Duchess; therefore pray do wait, and be so kind to me as to believe that I have no thought but what is all kindness to you, for I despair to live but to convince you how truly well I love you. Pray let me at my return find two words of answer.

John to Sarah

* You are very unjust in saying that I love you less than I did, for by all that is good I think I love better than ever I did. I am very sorry that you are not well and that I shall not see you to-day. I was three acts at the play for no other reason but that of seeing you. I was in the drawing-room almost an hour expecting you, which Mr Berkley can witness for me, for he was with me. I desire you will not choose any [trustees?] or do anything in that business until I speak with you. Pray be so kind to me as to write and assure me that you can be happy if I love you ever, as by heavens I will.

Frances, Lady Hamilton, had now arrived upon the scene, and Sarah seems to have threatened him with plans for going abroad with her.

John to Sarah

When I writ to you last night I thought I writ to the one that loved me; but your unkind, indifferent letter this morning confirms me of what I have before been afraid of, which is that your sister can govern your passion as she pleases. My heart is ready to break. I wish 'twere over, for since you are grown so indifferent, death is the only thing that can ease me. If that the Duchess could not have effected this, I was resolved to have made another proposal to her, which I am confident she might have effected, but it would not have brought so much money as this. But now I must think no more on it, since you say we cannot be happy. If they should do the first I wish with all my soul that my fortune had been so considerable as that it might have made you happier than your going out with your sister to France will do; for I know 'tis the joy you propose in that, that makes you think me faulty. I do, and must as long as I live, love you to distraction, but would not, to make myself the happiest man breathing, press you to ought that you think will make you unhappy. Madame, methinks it is no unreasonable

139

request to beg to see you in your chamber to-night. Pray let me hear presently two words, and say I shall; and, in return, I swear to you if you command my death I will die.

This last is endorsed in Sarah's handwriting, "This leter was when he was to settle the time of marrying me with the Dutches." One by one, as in a methodical siege, he had removed the obstacles which had barred the way. He had put aside his military prospects. Barbara was gone. Catharine was gone. The parents, still perhaps protesting, had given way. Evidently he had now in sight some means of livelihood sufficient for him and Sarah. Even now she did not soften her hectoring tone. But everything was settled.

Sarah to John

If your intentions are honourable,[1] and what I have reason to expect, you need not fear my sister's coming can make any change in me, or that it is in the power of anybody to alter me but yourself, and I am at this time satisfied that you will never do anything out of reason, which you must do if you ever are untrue to me.

Sarah to John

I have made many reflections upon what you said to me last night, and I am of the opinion that could the Duchess obtain what you ask her, you might be more unhappy than if it cannot be had. Therefore, as I have always shown more kindness for you than perhaps I ought, I am resolved to give you one mark more—and that is, to desire you to say nothing of it to the Duchess upon my account; and your own interest when I am not concerned in it, will probably compass what will make you much happier than this can ever do.

We now come to the marriage. No one knows exactly or for certain when or where it took place. For several months it was kept secret. That poverty rather than parental opposition was the cause is proved by a remarkable fact. John's grandfather had strictly entailed his estates, and Sir Winston was only tenant for life. He was heavily in debt, and was now forced to appeal to his son for help. Just at the

---

1 This phrase has been fastened on by some to suggest that Churchill was not seeking marriage. The natural sequence of the letters shows that he was at this very time arranging the basis of their future married life.

moment when some assured prospects were most necessary to his heart's desire, John was asked to surrender his inheritance. He did so for his father's sake. Part of the property was realized, and Sir Winston's debts were paid. At his death the remnant went to the other children. John, therefore, by his own act disinherited himself.[1] This was a singular example of filial duty in a young man desperately in love and longing to marry.

He could not keep his wife in any suitable conditions at the Court. Once the marriage was announced all sorts of things would be expected. Mary of Modena, "the Dutchesse" of the letters, was the good fairy. She was the partisan of this love-match; she used all her power to help the lovers. Evidently something had to be done to provide them with some means of living. Although Sarah had expectations, and John had his pay and, of course, his £500 a year, "the infamous wages," these were very small resources for the world in which they lived. The future Queen threw herself into the marriage, and her generous, feminine, and romantic instincts were stirred. "None but the brave," she might well have exclaimed, "deserves the fair." We have seen in the letters traces of various plans which the Duchess favoured or tried in order to make some provision for the lovers. We do not know what arrangements were made. Something, at any rate, was assured. Some time in the winter of 1677–78, probably in Mary of Modena's apartments, the sacred words were pronounced, and John and Sarah were man and wife. There is a strong local tradition at Newsells Park, Royston, Hertfordshire, then in the possession of a branch of the Jennings family, that the dining-room had been specially built for the festivities of Sarah Jennings' marriage. Probably they passed their honeymoon here.[2]

1 See Appendix, II.

2 A writer in *Notes and Queries* (No. 151, 1926, p. 199) says, " Newsells Park, Royston, . . . had its dining-room specially built in order to give room for the festivities of the marriage of Sarah Jennings and John Churchill." The present owner of Newsells Park, Captain Sir Humphrey de Trafford, very kindly had the local parish registers examined to see if the marriage took place there, but there is no trace of it.

Macaulay tells the love-story of John and Sarah in the following passage:[1]

> He must have been enamoured indeed. For he had little property except the annuity which he had bought with the infamous wages bestowed on him by the Duchess of Cleveland: he was insatiable of riches: Sarah was poor; and a plain girl with a large fortune was proposed to him. His love, after a struggle, prevailed over his avarice: marriage only strengthened his passion; and, to the last hour of his life, Sarah enjoyed the pleasure and distinction of being the one human being who was able to mislead that farsighted and sure-footed judgment, who was fervently loved by that cold heart, and who was servilely feared by that intrepid spirit.

How often men reveal their own secrets unconsciously when affronting others! This sentence, "He must have been enamoured indeed," shows the sphere to which Macaulay relegates love and the limits within which, from his personal experiences, he supposed it to be confined. It is to him a localized aberration which distorts judgment, and not a sublime passion which expresses and dominates all being. On this Paget has written finely:

> Lord Macaulay's intimate acquaintance, if not with human nature, at any rate with the writings of those who, in all ages and all languages, have most deeply stirred the heart of man, might have told him that [that] tale of young passionate love mellowing into deep and tender affection, living on linked to eternity, stronger than death and deeper than the grave, was fitly the object of feelings far different from those which it appears to waken in his breast. . . . It is a singular fact that two of the most vigorous writers of the English language appear to be in total ignorance of all the feelings which take their rise from the passion of love. We know of no single line that has fallen from the pen of Swift or from that of Lord Macaulay, which indicates any sympathy with that passion which affords in the greater number of minds the most powerful of all motives. The love of Churchill and Sarah Jennings seems to inspire Lord Macaulay with much the same feelings as those with which a certain

[1] *History*, ii, 317.

personage, whom Dr Johnson used to call "the first Whig," regarded the happiness of our first parents in the Garden of Eden.[1]

The explanation of Macaulay's sourness is not, however, obscure. He had decided in the plan of his history that Marlborough was to be presented as the most odious figure in his cast. He was the villain who "in the bloom of youth loved lucre more than wine or women . . . and who at the height of greatness loved lucre more than power or fame." This indictment, the most detestable that can be conceived, had to be sustained. The whole story of the courtship, marriage, and lifelong union of John and Sarah was in brutal conflict with the great historian's theme. The facts could not be disputed. They proclaim the glory of that wedlock in which the vast majority of civilized mankind find happiness and salvation in a precarious world. After nearly a quarter of a century of married life Churchill, sailing for the wars from Margate quay, wrote to his wife:

It is impossible to express with what a heavy heart I parted with you when I was at the waterside. I could have given my life to have come back, though I knew my own weakness so much I durst not, for I should have exposed myself to the company. I did for a great while have a perspective glass looking upon the cliffs in hopes I might have had one sight of you.[2]

Sarah, in a letter certainly later than 1689, and probably when he was in the Tower, wrote:

Wherever you are, whilst I have life, my soul shall follow you, my ever dear Lord Marl and wherever I am I should only kill the time wishing for night that I may sleep and hope the next day to hear from you.

Finally when, after his death, her hand was sought by the Duke of Somerset:

If I were young and handsome as I was, instead of old and faded as I am, and you could lay the empire of the world at my feet, you should never share the heart and hand that once belonged to John, Duke of Marlborough.

[1] *Op cit.*, p. 9.   [2] Coxe, i, 158.

These are tremendous facts, lifting the relations of men and women above the human scene with all its faults and cares. They rekindle in every generous bosom the hope that things may happen here in the life of the humblest mortals which roll round the universe and win everlasting sanction

> Above Time's troubled fountains
> On the great Atlantic mountains,
> In my golden house on high.[1]

All this vexed the mind of Lord Macaulay. It marred the design of his history. It ruptured whole sets of epigrams and antitheses which had already become his literary pets. There was nothing for it but to sneer; and sneer he did, with all the resources of his nimble, sharp, unscrupulous pen.

His literary descendant, Professor Trevelyan, whose faithful, fair, and deeply informed writings are establishing a new view of these times and the men who made them, has offered the best defence in his power for the historical malversations of his great-uncle. He says (in effect) that Macaulay, with his sense of the dramatic, vilified Marlborough's early life in order by contrast to make the glories of his great period stand out more vividly. He had completed the black background, but died before he could paint upon it "the scarlet coat and flashing eye of the victor of Blenheim." We need not reject this apologia nor the confession which it implies. But what a way to write history! On this showing—the best that can be provided—Lord Macaulay stands convicted of deliberately falsifying facts and making the most revolting accusations upon evidence which he knew, and in other connexions even admitted, was worthless, for the purpose of bringing more startling contrasts and colour into his imaginative picture and of making the crowds gape at it. Macaulay's life-work lay in the region of words, and few have been finer word-spinners. Marlborough's life is only known by his deeds. The comparison is unequal, because words are easy and many, while great deeds are difficult and rare. But there is no treachery or misconduct of which Macaulay's

1 Blake.

where ever you are whilst I have life my
soul shall follow you my ever dear D^r mad: if
whereever I am I shall only kill the time, with
the wish that I may sleep, & hope the next
day to hear from you ——

FRAGMENT OF A LETTER FROM SARAH TO MARLBOROUGH
Blenheim MSS.

malice has accused Marlborough in the field of action which is not equalled, were it true, by his own behaviour in this domain of history and letters over which he has sought to reign.

Mrs Manley, the French Ambassador Courtin, and other scurrilous writers have dwelt upon the enormous wealth which John had extracted from the Duchess of Cleveland. However, it was five years after he had married the girl he loved before he could buy her a house of his own. They shifted from one place to another according as his duties or employment led him. They followed the Duke or the drum. For five years Churchill kept on his bachelor lodgings in Germaine Street (Jermyn Street), five doors off St James's Street, and here they stayed during their rare visits to town. Meanwhile at first she lived at Mintern with Sir Winston and his wife, both now getting on in years and increasingly impoverished. Well may Sir Winston have said, "There is this poor roof—all that is left to us, in spite of our loyalty; you are ever welcome here. You have been the best of sons. But how you have thrown away your chances! Did I not, and your mother too, tell you how hard is the world, and how imprudent young people are? Still, there is always hope. Your mother and I in our young days went through eleven years of utter poverty. Had it not been for your grandmother, Eleanor Drake, we should have starved. We cared about one another, and we came through. It may well be, although I have nothing to leave, that you two will be able to keep going. It is little enough that I and your mother can do. We will do what we can, and it may be that some day you will have enough money to have a home of your own."

It must have been a very sharp descent for the glittering blade, lover of the King's mistress, daring Colonel of England and France, and friend or rival of the highest in the land, and for the much-sought-after Sarah, to come down to the prosaic, exacting necessities of family life. However, they loved each other well enough not to worry too much about external things. This was a strange beginning for the life of a man who "in the bloom of youth loved lucre more than wine or women."

It is beyond our hopes to overtake Lord Macaulay. The grandeur and sweep of his story-telling style carries him swiftly along, and with every generation he enters new fields. We can only hope that Truth will follow swiftly enough to fasten the label "Liar" to his genteel coat-tails.

CHAPTER IX

MASTER AND SERVANT

(1678–79)

DANBY, humouring the King and compromising himself deeply in his service, nevertheless had pursued his own policy, and by 1678 he reached the culmination of his power. He had effected in 1677, to the immense disgust of Louis, the marriage between William of Orange and the Duke of York's elder daughter, Mary. This event, so potent in our history and in that of Europe, was to Danby only a feature in his anti-French policy. Since 1674 Holland, Prussia, the Empire, and Spain had all been ranged against Louis. Vast as were his resources, the weight of so many opponents began to tell. The appearance of England in the anti-French coalition seemed likely to turn the scale decisively against France. Charles continued to press peace and moderation on Louis, and marketed his remaining hesitations at the highest price. There is no doubt that, had the King now followed Danby's advice wholeheartedly, he could have brought an almost united nation, restored and revived by a breathing-spell, into war against France. He would have had much popular support and large supplies from Parliament. We came, in fact, to the very verge at the beginning of 1678.

During his three years in England Churchill had gained repute in the diplomatic work upon which, without losing his military status, he was increasingly employed. When the foreign crisis arose on the morrow of his marriage he was deemed equally apt for diplomacy or war. The alliance with Holland and the raising of the English Army to thirty thousand men opened important prospects in both spheres. On February 18, 1678, he was gazetted Colonel of one of the new regiments of foot. In March he was summoned from

Mintern by the Duke of York, as the following letter to Sarah explains:

I got to Town by a little after three, very weary. However I dressed and went to the Duke for to know what he had to command me. He told me that the reason that he sent for me was that he did believe that there would be occasion to send me to Holland and Flanders, and that he would have me here to be ready to go. By the French letters on Saturday, they expect to know whether we shall have peace or war; but whatever happens I believe you may be satisfied that I shall not be in danger this year.[1]

The State Papers show the character of the mission now entrusted to him. He was to act with the King's authority, and not only to settle directly with the Dutch and the Spaniards the strength of the land and sea forces to be maintained against France by the new alliance, but to arrange the military details for the co-operation of the armies and the precedence of the English and Dutch officers of the various ranks. Lastly there was the safety of four English battalions at Bruges, who were in danger through the change of policy. These were grave functions to be entrusted—upon instructions largely verbal—to a Colonel of twenty-eight. At the same time Churchill's friend, Sidney Godolphin, was sent over to manage the political side of the negotiation and to elicit from the Dutch the lowest terms on which they would conclude peace.

Churchill left England on April 5 and went first to Brussels, where he reached an agreement with the Duke of Villa Hermosa.[2] Thence he travelled *via* Breda to The Hague, and after meeting with some difficulties successfully negotiated a military convention with William of Orange, to whom he had been instructed to offer twenty thousand men "and guns proportionable." The hitch in the arrangements was mentioned both in a letter from Churchill to his wife and one from William to Danby.[3] William wrote from The Hague on April 23/May 3, 1678:

1 Wolseley, i, 202–203.
2 This agreement dated April 13 (O.S.) is in Add. MSS., 28397, f. 289.
3 Churchill to his wife, April 12, 1678, Brussels: "I met with some difficulties in my business with the Prince of Orange." (Wolseley, i, 204.) The convention dated April 23 (O.S.) is at Blenheim and in Add. MSS., 28397, f. 291.

I will not tell you anything of the way in which we have arranged matters with Mr Churchill, since he will tell you about it himself. Mr Godolphin arrived yesterday evening. I am much distressed at not being able to carry out very promptly what the King desired and was so necessary.

Lord Wolseley fell into error and confusion about this convention and letter, and tells the identical story twice in two different chapters, dating it first in May and then in August, and quoting William's same letter first in French and then in English.[1] There is no doubt that Churchill concluded all his agreements in April, and then returned to England. When he next sailed for the Continent, in September, it was as a soldier.

He got on extremely well with William of Orange. No doubt he set himself to do so. They must have met frequently in 1677–78, not only on business, but in society.[2] They were exactly the same age. If the conversation turned on religion, they were agreed. If the aggrandizement of France became the topic, was this not the campaign in prospect? If talk ran upon the art of war, here was the profession of their lives. All the actions of the still continuing war in which they had fought, though in different theatres and on opposite sides, furnished an inexhaustible theme. Their talks may have ranged very far. We can in imagination see them poring over the map of Europe with eyes that understood so much about it. William, who was not hostile to young men, must greatly have liked to talk with his agreeable contemporary, who seemed to have the ear of every one at the English Court and had such grounding in the secrets of politics and power as was usually the privilege of princes.

The Duke of York's attitude at this time reveals the blunt, downright side of his nature, devoid of subtlety or artifice, and throws a light forward to the events of 1688. His whole outlook in religion and politics favoured an arrangement with

---

1 *Cf.* Wolseley, i, 205, 211.
2 *Cf.* S.P., 84/206, f. 151. The English envoy at The Hague reported that on April 19/29, 1678, Colonel Churchill arrived there with the Prince of Orange, and that the latter immediately spent three hours at the "Assembly of the States of Holland" deciding the question of whether it was to be peace or war.

France against Holland. But he had no patience with French
domination. England must stand on her dignity and brook
no patronage. An alliance having been made—rightly or
not—with Holland, let the war proceed with vigour, as wars
should always do. There must be no half-measures: one
thing or the other![1] We thus see him press his trusted agent
Churchill into the centre of the business. Irritated by French
obstructiveness at Nimwegen, James wrote to William of
Orange in July that if the Dutch would do their part the King
of England would sustain them. He and Monmouth—
Catholic heir-presumptive and bastard Protestant claimant to
the Crown—worked together with energy. On May 1
Churchill was appointed Brigadier of Foot with power to enlist recruits. He wrote from London to Sir Charles Lyttelton
(June 12, 1678), "We are again very furious upon the war;
so that I hope it will not be long before I have orders to come
over."[2] At last, on September 3, he received orders to proceed to Flanders in company with another Brigadier, Sir
John Fenwick, who was to play a significant part in his later
life. Churchill's brigade consisted of "two battalions of
guards and one battalion each of the Holland, the Duchess'
and Lord Arlington's regiments."[3] Monmouth, with about
eight thousand men drawn from the English troops in
Flanders, had actually come into action in William's attack
on Saint-Denis (August 4, 1678). Charles surveyed these
loyal activities with cynical amusement, and pursued his
negotiations with Louis. He wanted peace; he meant peace;
and in the end he secured it.

Thus we see John Churchill well established in his famous
dual capacity of soldier and diplomatist, entrusted in the space
of a few months with delicate and weighty negotiations, and
placed at the head of the first fighting troops in the Army.

---

[1] C.S.P. (Dom.), 1678, p. 91. Danby to William of Orange: "I suppose you
are before now convinced how earnest the Duke of York is for the war and how he
is resolved to go over with the army himself." The conventions that Churchill concluded relating to the precedency of officers both stipulated that James should be
commander-in-chief. See also James's own letters in Campane de Cavelli, Les
Derniers Stuarts, i, 208, etc.

[2] H.M.C., ii, 36.

[3] The various commissions are at Blenheim.

Already in 1678 he had the foretaste of what his great period was to bring him. Already he was by natural selection, as it seems, the chosen man, though not yet on the grand scale, for the vital situations of parley or arms. Now (September 3) he was to go to the front. However, he knew too many secrets to believe at this date in the continuance of the war, and his letters to Sarah show his accurate prosaic judgment of the tangled scene.

> You may rest satisfied that there will be certain peace in a very few days. This news I do assure you is true; therefore be not concerned when I tell you that I am ordered over and that to-morrow I go. You shall be sure by all opportunities to hear from me, for I do, if possible, love you better than I ever did. I believe it will be about the beginning of October before I shall get back, which time will appear an age to me, since in all that time I shall not be made happy with the sight of you. Pray write constantly to me. Send your letters as you did before to my house, and there I will take order how they shall be sent off to me. So, dearest soul of my life, farewell.
>
> My duty to my Father and Mother and remember me to everybody else.
>
> *Tuesday night.* My will I have here sent you for fear of accident.

This letter is endorsed in the Duchess's handwriting, "Lord Marlborough to ease me when I might be frighted at his going into danger."

The various treaties constituting the Peace of Nimwegen were signed during the autumn of 1678. Confronted by the coalition of more than half Europe, Louis had come off with solid advantages. He had failed in his prime and fell design of destroying the Dutch Republic, but he had absorbed and annexed Franche-Comté; Lorraine was virtually in his hands, and by his perfidious failure to observe the terms of the treaties he remained in possession of a large part of Belgium, including many of the most important fortresses. Nevertheless, Nimwegen registered in his mind an unmistakable sense of being checked. He had secured valuable booty; he had widely extended the boundaries of France; but he had felt the thrust of definite and formidable resistances to his onward career. He was dissatisfied in the midst of his triumphs, and turned a baleful eye towards the quarter from which he knew he had been thwarted. In 1668 he had recoiled from Belgium to prepare the punishment of Holland. In 1678 he recoiled from Holland to prepare the punishment of Danby. This was an easier matter.

That Minister's hour of reckoning had now come. Hostile, jealous forces had been gathering against him during his four years of power. A strange loose combination of Whigs under Shaftesbury, of Dissenters, of Catholics, and of malcontents under Arlington, was fostered by Barillon into an Opposition, and fed, like Charles, with French gold. It was found that "'Church and King,' in the sense of exclusive Anglicanism and unfettered monarchy, had ceased to be possible, when a Protestant Church was governed by a King with a Catholic policy."[1]

Already before Nimwegen the sinister figure of Titus Oates had begun to present himself to the Council at Whitehall, weaving out of much fact and more falsehood the monstrous terror of the "Popish Plot." Danby tried for his own ends to exploit the plot against the Duke of York and thus turn the lightning from himself. It was too late. The Anglican champion became the victim of the "No Popery!" cry. All England was already agog with passion when Louis launched his thunderbolt against the Minister. Montagu was the tool. This Ambassador had fallen in with Barbara, Duchess of Cleveland, in her Paris sojourn, had at first consoled her by becoming her lover, but had later transferred his affections to her eldest daughter. The Duchess, doubly indignant, had written revengefully to Charles. Montagu, who hurried back to London to defend himself, was dismissed summarily from his office. He forthwith offered himself willingly to the bribes of Louis.[2] For 100,000 crowns he would expose the financial skeletons of

---

1 Keith Feiling, *History of the Tory Party, 1640–1714*, p. 174.
2 For various versions of the Montagu-Cleveland incident see Ormond Papers, *H.M.C.*, iv, 441–445; Bath Papers, *H.M.C.*, ii, 166.

the Danby Administration to Parliament. Conducted to the bar of the House of Commons by the vindictive Shaftesbury, he produced from a carefully guarded box the proofs that Danby—the patriot, Protestant, anti-French Danby, as he had been acclaimed—had all the time been responsible for taking French subsidies. There was his name upon the receipts, and the Ambassador (who had counselled the policy) was the most competent witness to denounce it.

The natural, righteous wrath of the Commons knew no bounds. All Ministerial attempts to explain or justify were drowned in furious clamour. The King proved powerless to save his Minister. Danby was impeached, dismissed from office, and hustled to the Tower. Titus Oates about this time became the hero of the hour, and there then began that awful reign of terror and hatred which for the next five years was to scorch and sear the political life of England, was to involve both Scotland and Ireland in its frenzy, was amid the shedding of much innocent blood almost to disintegrate the society and institutions of the three kingdoms, and was, above all, to render England utterly impotent abroad. Thus was Louis XIV avenged upon Danby for his policy and upon Charles for his swindles.

When Churchill returned to England after the Treaty of Nimwegen in the winter of 1678 he found grievous changes in the atmosphere of English society. Not even the Civil Wars had given rise to such vitriolic hatreds and suspicions as had now broken loose. "No kind of thing is thought of here," wrote Robert, Earl of Sunderland, "but Mr Oates and who he has accused, and who he will accuse. . . . The whole people is enraged for fear of the King['s safety]. Everybody is in pain [alarmed for his sake] but himself."[1] As long as the prospect of war against France filled men's minds there was at least one point upon which the nation could unite. But with the disappearance of this motive the passions of parties seemed to blast and wither the whole national life. Even the faithful Cavalier Parliament was

1 Sunderland to Henry Savile, October 31, 1678. The original letter is among the Spencer MSS.

utterly estranged. Its composition had naturally changed with time. It had already, in 1673, passed the Test Act excluding Papists from all public office. It was now proceeding with the impeachment of Danby. It had lost all confidence in the King. For eighteen years this Pensionary Parliament had served him loyally; now he and they could go no farther together. Accordingly in January 1679 this second Long Parliament was dissolved. The King was never to find so friendly a one again.

The election was fought in all the fury of the Popish Plot. Shaftesbury and the Whig leaders, who had dreaded the dissolution, found themselves fortified by its results. The new House of Commons made their one object the exclusion of James or any other Popish prince from succession to the throne. Till this should be the law they refused all supply. Many were firmly persuaded that a deep design was on foot to subvert the Protestant religion, to kill the King and crown James in his stead. A pervasive propaganda was organized that the King had really married Lucy Walter in his exile, and that her son Monmouth, "our beloved Protestant Duke," was the rightful heir to the throne. The theory was inculcated with the same vigour and had almost the same vogue as the warming-pan myth of 1688. The King stood to his main principles. He solemnly proclaimed the bastardy of Monmouth: he resisted the Exclusion Bill with uncompromising grit; but he found it expedient to send James out of the kingdom even before Parliament reassembled.

In March, therefore, the Duke of York and his household went into exile first at The Hague and then in Brussels, taking up their abode in the same house in which Charles had lived before the Restoration. Churchill, therefore, had scarcely returned to England when he had to set out again, this time upon a melancholy pilgrimage. Sarah too was fetched from Mintern with her small belongings, and joined the forlorn party. By April James was reluctantly making plans to settle in Brussels: "I fear," he told Legge,

for the longer people are used to be without me, the harder it will [be] in my mind [as I see it] to come back, and though I do

154

not doubt of the continuance of his Majesty's kindness to me, yet you know there are those about him who would be glad to keep me from coming back to him. . . . In the mean time it is very uneasy for me to be without coach and horses here.

A few months later he proposed to have his fox-hounds and huntsman sent over, as "I now begin to have plenty of stag-hunting and the country looks as if the fox-hunting would be very good."[1] In August Princess Anne came over to join her father. Gradually a shadow Court grew up in Brussels, of which Lady Peterborough, Lady Bellasis, and the Churchills were the mainstays. To these we must add the beautiful Frances Jennings. The reader of Grammont will remember her haughty constancy in all the temptations of Charles's Court: how she had rebuffed the Duke of York: how even the seductive monarch himself had not attained the goal: how she had been courted in vain by "Mad Dick Talbot" and had eventually married Lord Hamilton. But Lord Hamilton had fallen in battle at Ziebernstern, and Frances had now been for nearly three years a widow, fair to see. The two sisters were very happy to come together again for a space. Meanwhile the exiles were tormented by the news from home. The growth of Monmouth's popu-larity with the people, the violence of the Whig faction, the progress of the Exclusion Bill, filled them with dismay. Churchill was sent hot-foot on unpromising errands, now to Charles in England, now to Louis in Paris, in the interests of his unhappy master. He knew everybody and how to approach them. He was well received everywhere—as a Protestant by the Whigs, as James's agent by the Catholics—and could plead or whisper into the ear of power. He used every resource.

In August the King fell ill. Deep alarm was felt by those who saw his symptoms and knew how his excesses had worn him out. Churchill was in England at the time. Sunderland, Halifax, Godolphin, Feversham, and La Kéroualle, buzzing together, all felt that James should be sent for. A demise of the Crown in James's absence meant certainly a Whig attempt

1 For these letters see Dartmouth Papers, *H.M.C.*, xi, 34 *seq.*

to set Monmouth on the throne, and Churchill was sent to fetch James over. He came at once most obviously disguised. We have a spirited account by Lord Longford of his journey.

LONDON
Sept. 6, 1679

* To LORD ARRAN

In my last I gave your Lordship an account of the surprizal we all had at the Duke's arrival on Monday night. He left Brussels in a disguise of a black perruque only and a plain stuff suit without his Star and Garter, rode post to Calais with my Lord Peterborough, Colonel Churchill, Mr Doyley and two footmen but not in their livery. He then took ship and it was so bad a sail that though he had no ill wind he was nineteen hours at sea before he landed at Dover. He went immediately to the post house where Churchill like a French officer in his scarf represented the best man in the company and being known to the post master, he [the postmaster] welcomed him, took him by the hand, said he was glad to see him, but swore by God he should be much gladder to see a better man than he and at an instant looked full in the Duke's face, when he knew it would not seem [be seemly] to take notice of him, because he saw him in disguise. Churchill was mounting upon the best horse and just as the Duke was mounting, another man who belonged to the post office went to the other side of the Duke, looked full in his face, and whispered so softly to himself that nobody could have heard him but the Duke took no notice, but rode on. These were the only persons that knew him upon the road. And yet they kept his secret. My Lord Peterborough and Doyley were outridden so that only His Highness and Churchill with one footman arrived on Monday in the evening at seven of the clock at the Barbican in Smithfield where they took a hackney coach and drove to the law office in Lombard Street, where Churchill alighted and went to see if Phil Froude was at home, but he being abroad, Churchill left a letter for him to follow him to Sir Allen Apsley's when he came home, not acquainting him that the Duke was come. At Sir Allen's the Duke supped and went to bed there, and at three in the morning took coach for Windsor, his arrival being kept secret till he was gone thither, where he arrived about seven, and came into the King's withdrawing room at the moment my Lord Sussex, who

156

was then in waiting in the bedchamber, opened the door; at which the Duke entered and when he came to the King's bedside he with great submission threw himself upon his knees, asking the King's pardon for his coming into England and into his presence without his leave, saying he was so confounded at the news of His Majesty's illness that he could have no satisfaction or content in his mind till he had seen His Majesty. And since that now he had that happiness to find him past all danger (for which he blessed God) he was ready to return again that morning if it was his Majesty's pleasure; for he came with resolutions to be absolutely governed and disposed of by His Majesty in all things. Upon this His Majesty cast his arms about him, kissed him and received him with all kindness imaginable and 'tis said by the standers-by that they both shed tears of joy at the interview.[1]

The temper of the nation was such that Charles durst not keep his brother at his side. He destroyed the first Exclusion Bill by dissolving the Parliament which brought it forward; but the election produced a House of Commons of the old hue and even sharper resolve. A new Exclusion Bill rolled through its stages, and all money was refused the Crown. The fury of the times had even destroyed the loyalty of the King's own circle; Ministers, courtiers, and favourites—mistresses, indeed—sided with the Opposition. Louise de Kéroualle, now Duchess of Portsmouth, used the most persuasive arguments of all. She had become attached to Charles, and, careless of French interests, advised him for his own good. Why should he ruin himself for this hated, unreasonable brother? Her antagonism to James became henceforward a definite factor in the broil. Godolphin, pliable and moderate, held his office, but voted for exclusion. The King's situation was poignant. He loved his brother dearly, and in no part of his life did he show such wisdom and courage. He kept rigidly within the letter of the Constitution, but he used all the resources of law and of time with patient adroitness. He now bowed to the storm and sent James back to Brussels.

Churchill had no sooner announced his arrival with the Duke in England to his wife at Brussels than he was dispatched upon a mission to Paris. The object was to further

[1] Carte MSS., 232, f. 51.

James's design of knitting up again the arrangement with
France and the renewal of subsidies which would render
Charles less dependent upon Parliament and James less in
jeopardy of exclusion. In the letter which Churchill bore
from James he is described as "Master of my Wardrobe to
whom you may give entire credit." The King approved, and
Churchill's expenses (£300) were paid from the royal exchequer. Churchill was instructed to promise on behalf of
James that he would in future identify himself completely
with the interests of the French King, and to apologize for
his master's conduct in the last two years when he had been
so active in aid of William of Orange and had even permitted
this arch-enemy of France to marry his own daughter Mary.
The negotiation was abortive. Louis XIV refused to offer
an adequate sum.[1] He saw better uses for his money in
England. It was October before Churchill returned to
Brussels.

But James's patience was already at an end. He refused
to stay any longer in Belgium. He forthwith dispatched
Churchill in advance of him to England "to get leave [for
him] to go to London and thence by land to Scotland."[2]
This was granted. At the same time, to reassure James,
the King sent Monmouth out of the kingdom too. The
health of the monarch was henceforth to be watched from
abroad by three pairs of interested, vigilant eyes: by James
from Edinburgh, and by Monmouth and William of Orange
from The Hague. The far-seeing William elaborated his
courtesies to both his rivals, and was eminently correct in
his demeanour to Charles.

Accordingly, in October James, having kissed his daughter
Mary at The Hague—as it fell out, for the last time—travelled through London by land for Edinburgh. The journey
was made as if it were a progress; and the large towns and great

1 Louis XIV to Barillon, September 21 (N.S.), 1679, from Fontainebleau by special messenger, *Correspondance politique, Angleterre*, t. 137, ff. 87–89. This letter
gives the most detailed account of Churchill's mission. Other notes from the
French archives are printed in Dalrymple, *Memoirs of Great Britain and Ireland*,
i, 321 *seq.* For Churchill's expenses see *C.S.P.* (*Treasury Books*), 1679–80, pp.
216, 233, 240.
2 James to Legge, October 14, 1679; Foljambe Papers, *H.M.C.*, p. 139.

houses all along the road offered dutiful hospitality. It was thirty-eight days before he reached Edinburgh, and set up his Court there with suitable celebrations. Churchill was ever at his side; but Sarah, who was expecting a baby, had to stay behind in his lodgings in Jermyn Street. Here the beautiful Frances joined her, and the two sisters kept house together. The baby, "Harriot," was born at the end of October, and died in infancy. The young couple had had a much disturbed year and a half of married life, with no home or resting-place of any kind. They were now widely separated. Scotland was as far off in those days as Canada is now, and the journey by land or sea was incomparably toilsome and dangerous. Such are the vicissitudes which poverty imposes.

CHAPTER X

THE UNSEEN RIFT

(1679–82)

THIS chapter is gloomy for our tale. While the French power grew and overhung Europe, the political and religious storms which raged in England from 1679 to 1683 concentrated their fury upon the Duke of York. His change of religion seemed to be the origin of the evils that had fallen upon the realm. There was impatience with individual conscientious processes which disturbed the lives of millions of people. That one man should have it in his power, even from the most respectable of motives, to involve so many others in distress and throw the whole nation into disorder, weighed heavily on the minds of responsible people. Even the most faithful servants of the King, the most convinced exponents of Divine Right, looked upon James with resentment. They saw in him the prime cause of the dangers and difficulties which his loving royal brother had to bear. There he was, a public nuisance, the Papist heir whose bigotry and obstinacy were shaking the throne. His isolation became marked; the circle about him narrowed severely. Forced into exile in Belgium and now to be marooned in Scotland, his lot was cast in dismal years. With all the strength and obstinacy of his nature he retorted scorn and anger upon his innumerable foes—the subjects he hoped to rule. The ordeal left a definite and ineffaceable imprint upon his character. He felt some of the glories of martyrdom. Henceforward he would dare all and inflict all for the faith that was in him.

It was in the household of this threatened, harassed, and indignant Prince that the first four or five years of the married life of John and Sarah were to lie. The wars had stopped, and with them for John not only pay and promotion, but all

160

chance to use that military gift of which he had become conscious. He must follow a master, united to him by many ties, but a man unlovable, from whom his whole outlook and nature diverged—nay, if the truth be told, recoiled; a master who was at times an outcast, and whose public odium his personal servants to some extent shared. Between him and that master opened the almost unbridgeable gulf which separated Protestant and Catholic. Faithful and skilful were the services which Churchill rendered to James. Many a secret or delicate negotiation with the French King or with Charles II and the Court or with English political parties was entrusted to the discreet and persuasive henchman. The invaluable character of these services and the sense of having been his patron from boyhood onwards were the bonds which held James to him. But no services, however zealous and successful, could fill the hiatus between contrary religions. The English Catholics, and above all James, their fanatical champion, and his immediate friends, were united not only by their creed, but by the comradeship which springs from being persecuted for conscience' sake. They thought thoughts and spoke a language of their own. Relations they must have with Protestants. Indeed, the Churchills formed for them indispensable contacts with the outer world. The fact that these two well-known Protestants were high in James's confidence could be paraded as a proof of the toleration of the heir to the throne. But at this time, when religion held the first place in men's minds, and when Catholics were a sect hunted and proscribed, there could be no perfect union of hearts. "They are with us," James might have exclaimed to his close, fervent necklace of priests and co-religionists, "with us, and serviceable; but, alas, not of us." And so it continued to the end.

However, the joys and responsibilities of the early years of married life redeemed for John and Sarah their harsh, anxious, and disturbed surroundings. They had in their family life an inner circle of their own, against which the difficulties of the Duke's household and the nation-wide hostility with which that household was regarded, might beat in vain. We must record their trapesings to and fro as the fortunes of their master ebbed and flowed.

There are a few letters from John on the northern road or in Scotland to Sarah in Jermyn Street.[1]

* You may guess by yourself how uneasy I have been since I left you, for nothing breathing ever loved another so well as I do you, and I do swear to you as long as I live I will never love another; and if you do ever love me, I will always love you. I have spoke to Mr Frowde so that you have but to send your letters to him, and he will always send them safe to me. After I saw you my Lady Sunderland spoke to me herself, and told me that she took it very unkindly that I had not left you in her care, but however she said she would take care of you in spite of me. Therefore pray when you see her be very civil to her, for as things now stand it is very fit you should be well with her. Mr Legge leaves us this night so that then I will write to you again; till when, my soul's soul, farewell.

STILTON
Monday night [November 2, 1679?]

* You will see by this that I am got safe to this place, and to-morrow night I intend to lie at Doncaster. I am a great deal wearier in riding this day than I ever was when I have ridden twice as far; if I continue so to-morrow, I shall hardly get to Scotland on Saturday, but sooner I promise you I will not, for all that I pretend to, is to be at Berwick on Friday night. You will be sure to hear from me as soon as I get to my journey's end, and pray believe that I love nobody in the world but yourself, and I do assure you I do at this present with all my heart wish we were together. Therefore pray be ready to come away as soon as you may, for if I should not come back, I would beg hard you would come away the day after you know it, and I do assure you, you shall be extreme welcome to me.

Pray kiss the child once for me.

EDINBURGH
Jan. 15, 1680

I have received yours of the 10th with a copy of the letter you writ to my Mother, which if she takes anything ill that is in that

---

1 Those letters marked with an asterisk have not been previously published. The others are in Wolseley, chapter xxix.

LITTLE ROCK PUBLIC LIBRARY

letter, you must attribute it to the peevishness of old age, for really there is nothing in it that she ought to take ill. I take it very kindly that you have writ to her again, for she is my Mother, and I hope at last that she will be sensible that she is to blame in being peevish. I long extremely to have this month over so that I may be leaving this country, which is very uneasy since you were not in it, for I do assure you that my thoughts are so fond of you that I cannot be happy when I am from you, for I love you so well that you cannot yourself wish to be loved better.

He adds this message for Frances:

Pray present my services to the widow and tell her that I am very glad she is not married, and if she stays for my consent she never will be.

Frances did not take his advice, and "mad Dick Talbot," afterwards Duke of Tyrconnel and James's viceroy in Ireland, renewed the suit he had pressed so ardently six years before. This time he was successful. Thus the delectable Frances was caught up in the Catholic-Jacobite world, and after 1688 consumed her life in exile.

January 17th, 1680

I do with all my soul wish myself with you; and now that I am from you I do assure you that I have no satisfaction but that of receiving yours and writing to you, and flattering myself that it will not now be long before I shall be truly happy in being with you again. You are so well beloved by me that if that will make you happy, you ought to be the happiest woman living, for none is so well beloved as you are by me. I hope by the first post of next month to send you word what day I shall leave this country, which is very much desired by me—not for any dislike to the country, but from the great desire I have to be with you, for you are dearer to me than ever you were in your life.

He adds quaintly, "My sarvice to Hariote," who was at that time about ten weeks old.

And a few days later:

Although I believe you love me, yet you do not love so well as I, so that you cannot be truly sensible how much I desire to

163

be with you. I swear to you the first night in which I was blessed in having you in my arms was not more earnestly wished for by me than now I do to be again with you, for if ever man loved woman truly well, I now do you, for I swear to you were we not married I would beg you on my knees to be my wife, which I could not do did I not esteem you as well as I love you.

If you please my service to your sister.

His earnest wish was to return from Scotland to England to see his wife and baby.

EDINBURGH
Jan. 29, 1680

* [I have received] yours of the 22nd. and also this to-day of the 24th. both doubting that I will leave this place the beginning of next month as I promised you, but before now I do not doubt but that you are satisfied I shall, for in my last I wrote to you to write no more. . . . London and Edinburgh are [not the?] same, for you [one] may find pleasure in being abroad at London, but it is not the same here, so that I will never send you that excuse for my not writing. About an hour after I had written to you last post night, I was taken ill of my old fits, and last night I had another of them so that for this two days I have had very violent headachings as ever I had in my life; I have this day taken physic so that I think I am better but . . . [torn] which makes me melancholy, for I love you so well that I cannot think with patience of dying, for then we must part for ever, which is a dreadful thing to me that loves you above all expression. The doctor is come in and will let me write no more, for he says it is the worst thing I can do. So, my All, farewell.

John's hopes of coming south were not ill-founded, for on the very day this last letter was written Charles sent a welcome command to his brother to return. James lost no time in taking leave of his Scottish Government, and at the end of February transported himself and his household in the royal yachts from Leith to Deptford.

Churchill on the eve of the voyage begged his wife to

pray for fair winds, so that we may not stay here, nor be long at sea, for should we be long at sea, and very sick, I am afraid it would do me great hurt, for really I am not well, for in my whole

LITTLE ROCK PUBLIC LIBRARY

lifetime I never had so long a fit of headaching as now: I hope all the red spots of the child will be gone against I see her, and her nose straight, so that I may fancy it be like the Mother, for as she has your coloured hair, so I would have her be like you in all things else.

The family were united in Jermyn Street in the beginning of March, and John saw his child for the first time. We do not know how long the infant lived. It may well be that the sorrow of her death came upon them almost as soon as they were together again.

James spent the summer of 1680 in England, and hoped, with the King, that the new Parliament summoned for October might be more tolerant to him. It is plain that in this interval Churchill was most anxious to secure some employment which would give him and his family a secure habitation. The command of one of the permanent regiments like the Admiralty Regiment, the governorship of Sheerness, or a foreign embassy were posts to which he might reasonably aspire. James was pleased with his services and made every effort to promote his interests, subject to one fatal condition. "So long as I am from him [Charles II]," he wrote to Hyde in December 1680,[1] "I would not willingly have Churchill from me." When James's hopes were high he tried to find an appointment for his servant, and when they fell he could not spare him.

Thus in the summer of 1680 James favoured Churchill's fitness to be Ambassador either to France or to Holland. In the latter case he was warmly seconded by William. Barillon's account of May 20, 1680, may serve.

Mr Sidney [the English Minister at The Hague] will come home soon. It is believed he will not return and I am told that Mr Churchill [*le sieur Chercheil*] may well succeed him. If this is done, it will be to satisfy the Duke of York and to reassure him on all possible negotiations with the Prince of Orange. He [James] distrusts Mr Sidney, and has hated him for a long time. Mr Churchill on the contrary has the entire confidence of his master, as your Majesty could see when he had the honour of

[1] Clarendon, *Correspondence and Diary*, i, 51.

165

presenting himself to you last year. He is not a man who has any experience of affairs. It is also said that the Prince of Orange has declared that there should be no other Ambassador of England in Holland but him, and that it is only necessary to send docile personages who let themselves be led.[1]

The talk about the Paris embassy gave offence to its occupant, Henry Savile, who wrote in protest to his brother, Lord Halifax:

> I am told that Mr Churchill likes my station so well that he has a mind to it, and got his master to work for him, and by very cunning artifice endeavours to make my friends willing to have me recalled upon pretext I live too high and shall ruin myself.

Halifax, who had already formed a firm and lasting friendship with John, wrote back at once saying, "Churchill, whatever inclination he may have to be minister, will never give such a price for it as the supplanting of a friend." Savile, reassured, explained to Halifax that he had now found out that the report had arisen from a remark of the Duke of York "which was improved into a story round the town."[2]

But all these hopes and projects, real or shadowy, came to naught. The new Parliament was fiercer than its predecessor. Shaftesbury was at the head of a flaming Opposition. A fresh Exclusion Bill advanced by leaps and bounds. The ferocity of the Whigs knew no limit, and their turpitude lay not far behind. Their cause was the cause of England, and is the dominant theme of this tale. Their conduct was sullied by corruption and double-dealing unusual even in that age. Their leaders without exception all took for either personal or party purposes French gold, while they shouted against Papist intrigues and denounced all arrangements with France. Upon this squalid scene Louis XIV gloated with cynical eyes. His agent Barillon, presiding over the dizzy whirlpools of Westminster and Whitehall, bribed both sides judiciously to maintain the faction fight. Many illustrious names, Whig and Tory, figure impartially on his pay-rolls. Lady Harvey joined her brother Montagu, the treacherous

1 Barillon to Louis XIV, May 20, 1680, R. O. Transcripts.
2 *Savile Correspondence* (Camden Society), pp 124, 128–129.

ex-Ambassador, upon them. Lord Holles, Hampden, the son of a famous father, and the Duke of Buckingham pocketed each a thousand guineas. Algernon Sidney, soon to give his life, took a solatium of five hundred guineas. The mood was that, if the King and his Ministers and courtiers could get gold out of France for their Popish leanings, why should not the honest Protestant Opposition have their share of the mischief-money too? Thus Louis stoked the fires which burned away the English strength.

One name is conspicuous in its absence from these lists of shame—Churchill's. Yet how glad Barillon would have been to have slipped a thousand guineas into the palm of this needy Colonel and struggling family man! The artful Ambassador, as we see by his correspondence, was no friend to John. Any tittle of spiteful gossip or depreciatory opinion which he could gather he sedulously reported. Churchill, this influential, ubiquitous go-between, the Protestant agent of the Duke of York, was well worth tainting, even if he could not be squared. Sarah long afterwards wrote, "The Duke of Marlborough never took a bribe." Think how these lists have been scanned by the eyes of Marlborough's detractors. See how every scrap of fouling evidence has been paraded and exploited. Yet nothing has been found to challenge Sarah's assertion.

The approaching assembly of this hostile Parliament was sufficient to force the King again to expatriate the brother of whom he was so fond. The Duke, desperate, asked Churchill to fetch Barillon to him, and begged the Ambassador to procure from Louis the funds which would obviate recourse to the dreaded House of Commons. James was obstinately determined not to be banished from London a third time. It took the combined efforts of the King and the two Secretaries of State, Sunderland and Jenkins, aided by Halifax and Essex, to persuade him.[1] The pressures were extreme. On October 20 James and his household most reluctantly again set out by sea for Edinburgh. This time both the Churchills could go together. They endured a rough voyage

[1] Dalrymple, i, Part I, 344 *seq.*

of five days. James was received in Scotland with due ceremony; but the famous cannon known as 'Mons Meg' burst in firing its salute, and many were the superstitious head-waggings which followed the occurrence. This time James seriously undertook the government of Scotland, and set his seal upon a melancholy epoch.

Scotland was at once the origin and the end of the Stuarts. No feature of Charles II's reign is more lamentable than the government of his northern kingdom. The Duke of Lauderdale, the ablest, the most wicked, and the sole survivor in office of the Cabal, was its mainspring for nearly twenty years. He had married Lady Dysart, a woman of appalling greed, whom Burnet describes as "ravenously covetous" and as one "who would have stuck at nothing by which she might compass her ends."[1] He was himself a former Covenanter, probably a freethinker, and exploited and applied all the local feuds and fanaticisms with callous craft. Nationalism at this time in ˙Scotland stood not upon a political basis, as in England, but upon the Kirk. The Reformation in Scotland had meant a period of violent mob-law and a revolutionary break with the past. Cold, sour, unchanging hatreds divided the Scottish race. Lauderdale used the quarrel between the Lowlands and the Highlands and the religious rifts to make a balance by which the Kings authority could stand. Cromwell had given Scotland Parliamentary union with England. A freer trade had flourished across the Border, and domestic peace reigned upon the overthrow of Presbyterian dominance. Under King Charles the Parliamentary union was dissolved, and hostile tariffs froze the streams of trade and wealth. Lauderdale held the country down. He extracted good revenues for the Crown, maintained a trustworthy standing army, and broke up by ruthless methods the fervent resistance of the Covenanters. Archbishop Sharp was brutally murdered in revenge on Magus Muir. A fierce rebellion in 1679 had been skilfully and temperately suppressed by Monmouth. Terror and counter-terror grew together.

[1] *History of My Own Time,* ii, 437.

It was over this scene that James now began actively to preside. On his first visit to Scotland his rule had seemed a mitigation of the severities of Lauderdale.[1] "I live there," he wrote, "as cautiously as I can, and am very careful to give offence to none." But now, between 1680 and 1682, embittered by ill-usage, emboldened by anger, his thoroughgoing temperament led him to support the strongest assertions of authority. When, in June 1681, Churchill brought him from London his patent as Royal Commissioner he decided to make use of the Scottish Parliament to obtain an emphatic and untrammelled assertion of his right of succession. He summoned the first Parliament held in Scotland since 1673. He set himself to demonstrate here on a minor scale the policy which he thought his brother should follow in England. He passed through the Parliament of 1681 an anti-Exclusion Bill. He developed with care the anti-national Scottish army. He used the wild Highlanders, the only Catholics available, to suppress the contumacy of the Lowlanders. The torture of the boot was inflicted freely upon Covenanters and persons of obstinate religious opinions. On these occasions most of the high personages upon the Privy Council would make some excuse to leave the room. But accusing pens allege that the Duke of York was always at his post. Dark and hateful days for Scotland!

Churchill's closest friend in James's circle at this time was George Legge. He was a faithful man with a fine record as a sea-captain in all the wars with the Dutch. He had long been in the Duke of York's service as Groom, and later Gentleman of his Bedchamber and his Master of the Horse. He had been Lieutenant-Governor of Portsmouth for some years, and in January 1681 was appointed Master-General of the Ordnance. The Duke, whose relations with him were almost those of father and son, tried his best to secure him the enjoyment of both offices. In the end Legge was obliged to "part with Portsmouth." He was related to Churchill on his mother's side by that same strain of Villiers blood of which mention has been made. He ranked far

1 Burnet, *History of My Own Time*, ii, 292–293.

higher in favour than Churchill, who must have greatly desired the comfortable office of the Ordnance. However, John wrote him a handsome and characteristic letter upon his appointment:

> I see by yours to the Duke that came this day that you are now Master of the Ordnance. I do not doubt but you are satisfied that I am glad of it, and I do assure you that I wish that you may live long to enjoy it, and as I wish you as well as any friend you have, so I will take the liberty to tell you that you will not be just to your family if you do not now order your affairs so as that you may by living within yourself be able in time to clear your estates. I will say no more on this subject at present but when we meet you must expect me to be troublesome if I find you prefer your own living before your children's good.[1]

He signs himself "your affectionate kinsman and faithful friend and servant." We shall follow Legge's tragic fortunes as Lord Dartmouth later.

Churchill, apart from his aversion from cruelties of all kinds, was now placed in a most difficult and delicate position. James relied on him to make every effort to secure his return to Court, and to support his claims against Monmouth and the Exclusionists; while, on the other hand, Churchill's powerful friends in London, Sunderland, Halifax, Godolphin, and Hyde, told him to keep James in Scotland at all costs. On December 22, 1680, Sunderland wrote to him, "I must join with [Hyde] in desiring you to help in persuading the Duke that whatever appears ungrateful to him in these letters is intended the kindlyest by the King."[2] Yet a month later (January 22, 1681) Churchill arrived in London on a confidential mission from James to press the King not to allow Parliament to sit, and to enter into an alliance with France and thus obtain his return.[3] Amid these conflicting currents no man was more capable of steering a shrewd and sensible course. He carried out his instructions from James with proper diligence and discretion; but, on the other hand,

1 January 5, 1681. Dartmouth Papers, *H.M.C.*, xi, Appendix v, 55–56.
2 Sunderland to Churchill, Blenheim MSS.
3 Clarke, *James II*, pp. 659–660.

LITTLE ROCK PUBLIC LIBRARY

his cautious temper prevented the wilder threats of his master (about raising the Scots or the Irish in his own defence) from being "attended with consequences"; for he "frankly owned" to the French Ambassador that James "was not in a condition to maintain himself in Scotland, if the King his brother did not support him there."[1]

In Scotland James's only possible opponent was the somewhat lackadaisical ninth Earl of Argyll.[2] "The Duke of York," wrote Burnet, "seeing how great a man the Earl of Argyll was, concluded it was necessary either to gain him or to ruin him." He first tried vainly to convert him by asking him to "exchange the worst of religions for the best." When Parliament met, Argyll opposed a clause in the Scottish Test Act exempting members of the royal household from the Protestant Oath of Allegiance. This angered James, and immediately on the adjournment of Parliament schemes hostile to the Earl were revived in a new form. It was proposed to apply to the King for the appointment of a commission to review his rights, deprive him of his heritable offices, and impose upon his property the debts which had been alleged against it. Argyll left Edinburgh to obtain the documents which confirmed him in his offices, and on his return interviewed James after supper in his bedroom at Holyrood to protest against his dismissal from one of his posts in his absence. If, Argyll said, this were "to express a frown, it is the first I have had from His Majesty these thirty years. I know I have enemies, but they shall never make me alter my duty and resolution to serve His Majesty. . . ."

The Churchills were in no sort of agreement with their patron in his Scottish courses, and it is clear that they regarded both the policy and its author with increasing repugnance. The old Duchess nearly three generations later in her comments on Lediard's history writes:

* All the account that is given in this History of the Duke's arbitrary Proceedings in Scotland was true; for I saw it myself, and was much grieved at the Trials of several People that were

1 Dalrymple, i, Part I, 344.
2 The following account is based mainly upon J. Willcock's *Life of Argyll* (1907).

171

hang'd for no Reason in the World, but because they would not disown what they had said, that King Charles the Second had broke his Covenant. I have cried at some of these Trials, to see the Cruelty that was done to these Men only for their choosing to die rather than tell a Lye. How happy would this Country be if we had more of those Sort of Men! I remember the Duke of Marlborough was mightily grieved one Day at a Conversation he had heard between the Earl of Argyle (who was beheaded afterwards for explaining the Test in saying he took it in such a Sense as was agreeable to his duty to God and the King) and the Duke of York. The Duke of Marlborough told me he never heard a man speak more Reason than he did to the Duke [of York] and after he had said what he at first resolved, the Duke would never make Answer to any Thing, But You shall excuse me, my Lord, You shall excuse me My Lord; And so continued for a long Time whatever he said without answering otherwise. Another thing I remember the Duke of Marlborough told me when we were in Scotland, there came a Letter from Lewis the Grand to the Duke of York, writ by himself; which put all the Family into a great Disorder; For no body could read it. But it was enough to shew there was a strict [secret] Correspondence between the Duke and the King of France. All these things the Duke of Marlborough told me with great Grief; But it was not at all in his Power to help any of them.[1]

We may make all allowances for the bias of this statement, but it certainly reveals the breach which had opened. The Duchess was eighty, but an old person's memory generally recalls faithfully the impressions of youth, while it often fails to record the events of later life.

In August 1681 the Duke of York's affairs in England were going from bad to worse, and the King was in desperate grapple with his brother's pursuers. An intense effort was concerted to persuade James to conform at least in outward semblance to the religion of his future subjects. His appeals to be recalled to England were made use of against him. The King offered to allow him to return if he would but come to church. After all, had he not consented to be present during the prayers of the Scottish Parliament? Surely what all his

1 Letter of October 6, 1744, in Spencer MSS.

well-wishers now asked was but an extension of that wise concession to political exigencies of the first order. Halifax, strong in the prestige of having destroyed the first Exclusion Bill, used hard words. Unless, he declared, the Duke complied, "his friends would be obliged to leave him like a garrison one could no longer defend." Every one could see what a simplification his assent would make; and what a boon to all! His first wife's brother, Laurence Hyde, afterwards Earl of Rochester, was entrusted with the difficult task of his conversion to conformity, upon which the strongest family, social, and State pressures were engaged. Hyde, Churchill, and Legge were James's three most intimate personal servants. They had been with him for many years. His partiality for them had long been proved. Legge was absent, but we cannot doubt that Churchill supported Hyde with any influence he could command. Nothing availed. James was advised by his confessor that there could be no paltering with heresy. Such advice was decisive.

This incident deserves prominence because it evoked from Churchill one of those very rare disclosures of his political-religious convictions in this period which survive. He wrote to Legge the following letter:

Sept. 12, 1681, *Berwick*

DEAR COUSIN,

I should make you both excuses and compliments for the trouble you have been at in sending my wife to me, but I hope it is not that time of day between you and I, for without compliment as long as I live I will be your friend and servant. My Lord Hyde, who is the best man living, will give you an account of all that has passed. You will find that nothing is done in what was so much desired, *so that sooner or later we must be all undone.*[1] As soon as Lewen has his papers the Duke would have [wish to] take the first opportunity by sea and come from Scotland. My heart is very full, so that should I write to you of the sad prospect I fear we have, I should tire your patience; therefore I refer myself wholly to my Lord Hyde and assure you that wherever I am, you and my Lord Hyde have a faithful servant of [in] me.[2]

[1] Author's italics.   [2] Dartmouth Papers, *H.M.C.*, xi, Appendix v, 67–68.

This letter, written so secretly to his intimate friend and kinsman seven years before the revolution of 1688, must not be forgotten in the unfolding of our story.

On December 12, 1681, Argyll was brought to trial for treason for explaining that he took the Oath of Allegiance "as far as it was consistent with the Protestant religion," and "not repugnant to it or his loyalty." By the exertions of James he was condemned to death. On the eve of his execution he escaped by a romantic artifice and for a time lay hidden in London. When the news of his refuge was brought to the King by officious spies, the tolerant Charles brushed them away with the remark, "Pooh, pooh, a hunted partridge!" His brother had a different outlook.

Churchill had deplored Argyll's sentence. He wrote to Sir John Werden, the Duke of York's secretary, and told him he hoped on account of their old friendship that Argyll would receive no punishment; and he wrote to George Legge that he trusted Argyll's escape from prison would be looked on as a thing of no great consequence.[1]

The author of *The Lives of the Two Illustrious Generals* relates that when in Scotland Churchill had "preserved from ruin and destruction several poor people whose scruples of conscience rendered them obnoxious to the laws then in force." We have therefore not only Sarah's octogenarian recollections, but Churchill's conversation with Barillon, the reliance that Sunderland put on him to moderate James, and Churchill's clear dislike of the treatment of Argyll. All these are trustworthy proofs of the growth of honest, grievous differences in political temper and outlook between James and his trusted servant.

The leaders of Scottish society were not men of half-measures. Affronted to the core by the ill-usage of their country as it continued year after year, they devoted their

---

1 Churchill's letter to Werden does not survive, but the reply (Blenheim MSS.) proves its tenor. He wrote on December 22, 1681, to Churchill, "Your's of the 13th is ye freshest yt I have had from you ; & by others service [?] I find ye Issue to the Ea. of Argille's Tryall such as was expected ; & now (in regard to Yr old ffriendship, which you put me in mind of) I hope he will have the Kings Pardon, & ye Effects of His Bounty, & hereafter in some Measure deserve both." See also Churchill to Legge, January 5, 1682, Dartmouth Papers, *H.M.C.*, pp. 55–56 (wrongly dated 1681).

lives to practical schemes of vengeance, and they turned resolutely to the Prince of Orange. The flower of the Scottish nobility emigrated to Holland with deep, bitter intent to return sword in hand. All became unrelenting enemies of the House of Stuart. In the revolution of 1688 Lowland Scotland swung to William as one man.

In 1682 Churchill was able to render a service to his patron of which James was profoundly sensible. The Duchess of Portsmouth was anxious about her future financial position. She sought £5000 a year secured upon the almost unimpeachable revenues of the Post Office. She pressed Charles hard upon the point. But all the revenues of the Post Office had been granted to the Duke of York for life, and the Duke was then still an impatient exile in Scotland. Churchill spent as much time and trouble upon the bargain that James should cede to "Madame Carwell" her £5000 from the Post Office, in exchange for his being allowed to return home, as in later years upon the combinations of the Grand Alliance or the strategy of the world war. In the first instance James was allowed to come to London to take part in the negotiations. Although these fell through because an Act of Parliament was required to alienate the Post Office revenues, fraternal contacts were re-established. At this time, as the next chapter will explain, the King felt his power returning to him. He was, moreover, anxious to gratify Louis XIV by restoring his Papist brother to his place at Court. The long-sought permission was granted. James, with a considerable retinue of nobles and servants, embarked in the frigate *Gloucester* on May 4, 1682, to wind up his affairs in Scotland and bring his household home.

The catastrophe which followed very nearly brought this and many important tales to an end. But another revealing beam of light is thrown by it upon Churchill's attitude towards his master. The royal vessel was accompanied by a small squadron and several yachts, on one of which was Samuel Pepys himself. Two days out the *Gloucester* grounded in the night upon a dangerous sandbank three miles off Cromer, on the Norfolk coast, known as the 'Lemon and

Ore."[1] After about an hour she slipped off the bank and foundered almost immediately in deep water. Although the sea was calm and several ships lay in close company, scarcely forty were saved out of the three hundred souls on board.

Numerous detailed and incompatible accounts of this disaster from its survivors and spectators have been given. Some extol the Duke of York's composure, his seamanship, his resolute efforts to save the vessel, and the discipline and devotion of the sailors, who, though about to drown, cheered as they watched him row away. Others dwell on the needless and fatal delays in abandoning the ship, on the confusion which prevailed, on the ugly rushes made for the only available boat, and finally portray James going off with his priests, his dogs, and a handful of close personal friends in the longboat, which "might well have held fifty," leaving the rest to perish miserably. Catholic and Tory writers, naturally enough, incline to the former version, and Protestants and Whigs to the latter. We have no concern with the merits of the controversy. What is important is Churchill's view of it. He, like Legge, was one of the favoured few invited into the boat by James, and to that he owed his life. One would therefore have expected that he would instinctively have taken the side of his master and, in a sense, rescuer, and would have judged his actions by the most lenient standards. Instead, he appears to have been the sternest critic. Sixty years later Sarah, in her illuminating comments on Lediard's history, writes as follows:

* Since my last account of Mr Lediard's Book, I have read the account of the shipwreck of the *Gloucester* (page 40). The Truth of which I had as soon as the Duke [of Marlborough] came to Scotland from his own Mouth: (for I was there) who blamed the Duke [of York] to me excessively for his Obstinacy and Cruelty. For if he would have been persuaded to go off himself at first, when it was certain the Ship could not be saved, the Duke of Marlborough was of the Opinion that there would not have been a Man lost. For tho' there was not Boats enough to carry them all away, all those he mentions that were drowned were lost by the Duke's obstinacy in not coming away sooner;

[1] In many histories these two shoals—the Lemon and Ower—are described as lying "off the Humber." They are actually thirty miles to the south of it.

And that was occasioned by a false courage to make it appear, as he thought he had what he had not; By which he was the occasion of losing so many Lives. But when his own was in danger, and there was no hope of saving any but those that were with Him, he gave the Duke of Marlborough his Sword to hinder Numbers of People that to save their own Lives would have jumped into the Boat, notwithstanding his Royal Highness was there, that would have sunk it. This was done, and the Duke went off safe; and all the rest in the Ship were lost, as Mr Lediard gives an account, except my Lord Griffin, who had served the Duke long, who, when the Ship was sinking, threw himself out of a Window, and saved himself by catching hold of a Hen Coop. . . . All that Lediard relates to filling the boat with the priests and the dogs is true. But I don't know who else went in the boat, or whether they were of the same religion.[1]

There can be no doubt that this is the real story which John told Sarah in the deepest secrecy as soon as he and the other woebegone survivors from the shipwreck arrived in Edinburgh. That no inkling of his servant's opinion ever came to James seems almost certain. We, however, in this afterlight can see quite plainly where the Churchills stood in relation to James. It is not merely want of sympathy, but deep disapproval. They served him because it was their duty and their livelihood. He retained them because better servants could not be found elsewhere. But all this lay far below the surface. The whole ducal household arrived at Whitehall, for good or ill, in the summer of 1682, and Churchill was rewarded on December 21, 1682, for his patient, astute diplomacy and invaluable services of the past three years with the barony of Churchill of Aymouth, in the peerage of Scotland,[2] and the command of the second troop of the Life Guards.

1 Spencer MSS.
2 Wolseley misdates this 1683. The patent is at Blenheim.

CHAPTER XI

THE PRINCESS ANNE

(1679–85)

FEW stories in our history are more politically instructive than the five years' pitiless duel between King Charles II and his ex-Minister Shaftesbury. The opposing forces were diversely composed, yet, as it proved, evenly balanced; the ground was varied and uncertain; the conditions of the combat were peculiarly English, the changes of fortune swift and unforeseeable, the issues profound and the stakes mortal. For the first three years Shaftesbury seemed to march with growing violence from strength to strength. Three separate Parliaments declared themselves with ever-rising spirit for his cause. London, its wealth, its magistrates, its juries, and its mob, were resolute behind him. Far and wide throughout the counties and towns of England the fear of "Popery and Slavery" dominated all other feelings and united under the leadership of the great Whig nobles almost all the sects and factions of the Centre and of the Left, as they had never been united even at the height of the Great Rebellion. Thus sustained, Shaftesbury set no limits to his aims or conduct. He exploited to the last ounce alike the treacheries of Montagu and the perjuries of Oates. He watched with ruthless eye a succession of innocent men, culminating in Lord Stafford, sent to their deaths on the scaffold or at Tyburn upon false testimony. He held high parley with the King, as if from power to power, demanded the handing over of Portsmouth and Hull to officers approved by Parliament, indicted the Duke of York before a London Grand Jury as a Popish recusant, threatened articles of impeachment against the Queen, and made every preparation in his power for an eventual resort to arms. This was the same Shaftesbury who, as a Minister in the Cabal, had acquiesced only four years

178

before in the general policy of the Secret Treaty of Dover, and only two years before had been a party to the Declaration of Indulgence and the acceptance of subsidies from France.

The King, on the other hand, seemed during the first three years to be almost defenceless. His weakness was visible to all. He was forced to leave Danby, his faithful agent, for whose actions he had assumed all possible responsibility, whom he had covered with his royal pardon, to languish for five years in the Tower. He dared not disown the suborned or perjured Crown witnesses brought forward in his name to prove a Popish plot, nor shield with his prerogative of mercy their doomed victims. He had to suffer the humiliation of banishing his brother and the insult of hearing his Queen accused of plotting his murder. He had to submit to, or perhaps even connive at his beloved son Monmouth joining the leaders of his foes.

All the while he lay in his voluptuous, glittering Court, with his expensive mistresses and anxious courtiers, dependent upon the dear-bought gold of France. And meanwhile behind the wrathful proceedings of justly offended faction-fanned Parliaments, Puritan England was scandalized, Cromwellians who had charged at Marston Moor or Naseby prayed that old days might come again, and the common people were taught to believe that the Great Plague and Fire had fallen upon the land as God's punishment for the wickedness of its ruler. Vulnerable in the last degree, conscious of his peril, and yet superb in patient courage, the profound, imperturbable, and crafty politician who wore the challenged crown endured the fury of the storm and awaited its climax. And in the end triumph! Triumph in a completeness and suddenness which seemed incredible to friends and enemies alike.

This was a civil war whose battles and sieges, whose stratagems and onfalls, were represented by State trials, constitutional deadlocks, and Parliamentary or municipal manœuvres. It was a war of and for public opinion, and as bitter and ferocious as many waged in the open field. Its events were the birth-throes of party government, whose sire was the Popish, and whose dam the Rye House, Plot. There had been *sides* in the Great Rebellion; henceforward there would be *parties*, less picturesque, but no less fierce. The three General Elections in succession required and evolved all those organizations—clubs, colours, and slogans—with which in later and gentler ages we are only too familiar. The mutual hatreds and injuries of the Whigs and Tories engraved their rival symbols for two hundred years on English life. In vain was Marlborough at the head of victorious armies to accuse "the detested names of Whig and Tory"; in vain would Chatham pronounce his majestic invocation, "Be one people!" The metals which were now molten were cast in moulds destined to decide the character and practical working of Parliamentary institutions not only in our island, but in every country where and while they have thrived.

The turning-point of the conflict was the King's sudden dissolution of the Parliament of 1680. After the third election both Houses were convened at Oxford in March 1681, to avoid the violent pressures which the citizens, apprentices, and the mass of London could exert. To this Parliament, the last of the reign, both factions resorted in the temper of civil war. It was "like a Polish Diet." The Whig chiefs arrived surrounded by their armed retainers, who eyed the King's guards with open menace. The new House of Commons seemed only to be set with more zealous purpose upon excluding James from the throne. Shaftesbury, after the Royal Speech, handed the King what was virtually an ultimatum in favour of the succession of Monmouth. "My lord, as I grow older I grow more steadfast," replied the King. Confronted with the attitude of the assembly, and finding that Oxford was a camp of armed bands whom a word might set at each other's throats, Charles proclaimed the dissolution, and lost no time in withdrawing under strong escort to Windsor. Shaftesbury made a resolute bid to keep both Houses in illegal session. But the sense of their corporate function had passed from the minds of the individual members. They who had seemed resolute to undertake all fell to pieces "as

THE FIRST EARL OF SHAFTESBURY
Sir Peter Lely
By permission of the Earl of Shaftesbury

180

LITTLE ROCK PUBLIC LIBRARY

if a gust of wind had suddenly scattered all the leaves from a tree."[1]

Stripped of their Parliamentary engines, the Whigs turned to conspiracy, and beneath conspiracy grew murder. Their declared purpose to exclude James from the succession broadened among many into naked republicanism. "Any design but a commonwealth," said Shaftesbury to Lord Howard, "would not go down with my supporters now."[2] There can be no doubt that schemes and even preparations for an armed national rising were afoot; nor that some of the greatest Parliamentary personages were active in them. Behind the machinations of the famous Whig leaders darker and even more violent forces stirred. Rumbold and other grim Cromwellian figures stalked the streets of London. A design to assassinate the King and the Duke where the road from Newmarket passed Rumbold's home, the Rye House, was discussed, and to some extent concerted, by a group of plotters in a London tavern. But while these projects, general and particular, germinated in the soil, the mood of the nation gradually but decisively changed; its anti-Catholic rage had exhausted itself in the shedding of innocent blood, and public sympathy gradually turned to the sufferers and against their loud-mouthed, hard-swearing, vainglorious, implacable pursuers.

Presently the King felt strong enough to prosecute Shaftesbury for high treason, and when the Grand Jury of Middlesex, elected by the City—"that republic by the King's side"— threw out the Bill, he turned his attention to the processes by which the London sheriffs were chosen. By a prolonged and elaborate series of political manœuvres, and with the assistance of a friendly Lord Mayor, Tory sheriffs were declared elected, and juries ardent for the Crown became available. Shaftesbury, as soon as he found himself undermined by such appointments, and perhaps alarmed by the whispers of murder plottings which reached his ears, fled to Holland, and died almost immediately in exile. The disclosure of the Rye House

1 Ranke, *History of England*, iv, 135.
2 James Ferguson, *Robert Ferguson the Plotter*, p. 72.

181

Plot, coming on so favourable a tide, aroused a volume of sympathy for the King which in its force and passion became almost a counterpart of the fears and angers created by the Popish Plot. From all parts of the country loyal addresses began to pour in. Many nobles and country gentlemen who had for long avoided the Court presented themselves dutifully at Whitehall. One by one the Rye House plotters, and even those who had been present when they plotted, were sent by the tribunals to the scaffold. Writs of *Quo warranto* impugned the authority of municipal corporations. In the blast of popular disapproval, and without any Parliament to focus their cause, the power of the Whigs collapsed and was for a time destroyed. The Tory reaction, blowing as savagely as the Whig aggressions that had called it forth, exacted innocent blood in its turn. Shaftesbury was already gone. Howard turned King's evidence. Russell and Algernon Sidney died on the scaffold, and Essex escaped it only by suicide in the Tower. These deaths were but the vicarious expiation of the shameful executions of the Popish Plot.

By 1683 the King was as safe on his throne as on the morrow of his coronation, nearly a quarter of a century before. He had come through an ordeal which few British sovereigns, certainly neither his father nor his brother, could have survived. For all his cynicism and apparent indolence and levity he had preserved the hereditary principle of the monarchy and its prerogative inviolate. He had successfully defended his brother's right to the throne; he had championed the honour of his Queen; he had obtained a more complete control of the national and municipal organs of government and of the judiciary than had existed since the days of his grandfather. He had never lost the support of the Episcopacy. He was poor, he was a pensioner of France, he was powerless on the Continent; but as long as he avoided the expenses of a foreign war he was master in his own house.

The next three years, 1683–85, form an interlude of peace and domestic sunshine in John Churchill's anxious, toilsome, exciting life. He was reabsorbed into the heart and centre of the Court he knew so well, and in which he had lived from childhood. He enjoyed the accustomed intimate favour of the King and the Duke. We read of his being one of Charles's two or three regular tennis partners [1]—with Godolphin and Feversham, "all so excellent players that if one beat the other 'tis alternatively"—and of accompanying the royal party on various progresses or excursions. He was promoted to the colonelcy of the King's Own regiment of Dragoons.[2] This improved the family income, but gave rise to jealous carpings.

> Let's cut our meat with spoons!
> The sense is as good
> As that Churchill should
> Be put to command the Dragoons.

The appointment was, however, not ill justified by events. Otherwise no important office or employment fell to his lot. It was perhaps the only easy, care-free time he ever had. No tortuous channels to thread, no intricate combinations to adjust, no doubtful, harassing, dire choices to take! Peace and, if not plenty, a competence. But as the dangers of the State and the need for action or manœuvre ceased, he subsided into the agreeable obscurities of home and social life. Charles seems to have regarded him as a well-liked courtier and companion whom he had long been used to have about him, as a military officer of a certain standing, as a discreet, attractive, experienced figure, a cherished piece of furniture in the royal household, but not at this time at all considered in the larger sphere of public affairs. Indeed, when he heard Churchill's name mentioned as one who might be Sunderland's Ministerial colleague the King said lightly that "he was not resolved to have two idle Secretaries of State."[3] The Court subsequently explained the rumour by cheerfully affirming that Churchill had lately been "learning to write." So all was calm and quiet, and far better than those wearing years of journeyings to and from The Hague or Edinburgh to London on errands of delicacy or distress.

1 Rutland Papers, *H.M.C.*, xii, Part II, 81.
2 The commission, dated November 19, 1683, is in the Blenheim MSS.
3 *H.M.C.*, vii, 362–363.

John could now live a great deal with his wife. He was even able upon the pay and perquisites of Colonel of the Dragoons and Colonel of a troop of Life Guards—the latter a lucrative appointment—to settle in the country. For the first time they had a home.

The Jennings family owned an old house and a few acres close to St Albans, on the opposite side of the town to their manor of Sandridge. It was called Holywell House on account of a well in which the nuns of Sopwell had softened their hard bread in bygone times. It stood on the road close to the bridge over the river Ver. About 1681 John seems to have bought out Frances' share in this small property, which, together with the manor of Sandridge, was then owned by the two sisters. Evidently Sarah was attached to her native town and family lands. Some time in 1684 she and her husband pulled down the old house, which was ill situated, and built themselves a modest dwelling in another part of the grounds, surrounded by well-laid-out gardens and furnished with a fine fishpond. The character and size of Holywell House can be judged from a contemporary sketch. Here was Marlborough's home for life. The pomp and magnificence of Blenheim Palace were for his posterity. Indeed, he seems to have been somewhat indifferent to the noble monument which the nation reared in honour of his victories. It was Holywell House that claimed his affections. Within it he gathered the pictures and treasures which he steadily collected, and upon its pediment in later life he portrayed the trophies of his battles. Here it was he lived with Sarah and his children whenever he could escape from Court or service. It was to this scene, as his letters show, with its ripening fruit and maturing trees, that his thoughts returned in the long campaigns, and here the main happiness of his life was enjoyed. Holywell House was pulled down in 1827. The elaborate prospectus of its sale contained no reference to its builder and first occupant. The river Ver has been canalized, and no recognizable trace remains.

Meanwhile their family grew. Poor "Hariote" was gone, but another daughter, Henrietta, born on July 19, 1681, survived the deadly perils of seventeenth-century infancy.

HOLYWELL HOUSE, ST ALBANS

Above, the front towards the road (the pediment contained military trophies in allusion
to the Duke's victories) ; below, the garden front.

By permission of Earl Spencer

184

At her christening we meet as a godmother an old acquaintance, Arabella. Her relations with the Duke had long ended. Provision had been made for "her train of bastards." The girls were in convents or being brought up as Catholics in France. Her son, a noble youth, in high favour, already showed the quality of the future Duke of Berwick. Arabella could now thankfully return to full respectability. Happily married to a Colonel Godfrey, she was to live to old age and be the witness of many surprising family events. John's third daughter, Anne—note the name—was born on February 27, 1684. She too thrived.

Although to outward appearance King Charles's Court was as brilliant and gay as ever, its inner life was seared by tragedy. The executions of great nobles whom everybody knew, like Stafford on the one side and Russell on the other; the ugly death in the Tower of Essex, so recently a trusted Minister, cast their shadows upon wide circles of relations and friends. Fear and grief lurked beneath the wigs and powder, ceremonies and masquerades. John Churchill seems at this time to have been most anxious to withdraw his wife altogether from the fevered scene, and to live with her in the country, riding to London only as required by his duties, which were also his livelihood. Sarah dutifully obeyed her husband's wish. But an event occurred which frustrated these modest ambitions.

Hitherto little has been said about the Princess Anne.[1] Henceforward she becomes the fulcrum of our tale. And here and now Sarah begins to play her commanding part. Her first contact with Anne had been in childhood. They had met in children's play at St James's when Sarah was ten and Princess Anne was only six. They were thrown together far more frequently when Sarah came to live in the palace, from 1673 onward. From the outset Anne became deeply attached to the brilliant, vivacious being who blossomed into womanhood before her childish eyes. The Princess was

---

[1] There is no very satisfactory biography of Queen Anne; that by Miss Anne Strickland in her *Lives of the Queens of England* (1841) has not been superseded, and is spoilt by its Jacobite partisanship. On the other hand, it is unfair to derive one's portrait of Anne from the writings of the Duchess of Marlborough.

fascinated by Sarah's knowledge, self-confidence, and strength of character. She was charmed by her care and devotion, and by all her resources of fun and comfort which so naturally and spontaneously came to her aid. Very early indeed in these young lives did those ties of love, kindling into passion on one side, and into affection and sincere friendship on the other, grow deep and strong, as yet unheeded by the bustling world. There was a romantic, indeed perfervid, element in Anne's love for Sarah to which the elder girl responded warmly several years before she realized the worldly importance of such a relationship. "The beginning of the Princess's kindness for me," wrote Sarah in after-days,

> had a much earlier date than my entrance into her service. My promotion to this honour was wholly owing to impressions she had before received to my advantage; we had used to play together when she was a child, and she even then expressed a particular fondness for me. This inclination increased with our years. I was often at Court, and the Princess always distinguished me by the pleasure she took to honour me, preferably to others, with her conversation and confidence. In all her parties for amusement I was sure by her choice to be one. . . .[1]

The passage of time gradually but swiftly effaced the difference in age, and Sarah as a married woman and mother at twenty-one exercised only a stronger spell upon the Princess of seventeen. "A friend," says Sarah,

> was what she most coveted, and for the sake of friendship which she did not disdain to have with me, she was fond even of that equality which she thought belonged to it. She grew uneasy to be treated by me with the form and ceremony due to her rank, nor could she bear from me the sound of words which implied in them distance and superiority. It was this turn of mind which made her one day propose to me, that whenever I should happen to be absent from her, we might in all our letters write ourselves by feigned names, such as would import nothing of distinction of rank between us. Morley and Freeman were the names her fancy hit upon, and she left me to choose by which of them I would be called. My frank, open temper naturally led me to pitch upon Freeman, and so the

[1] *Conduct*, pp. 9-10.

Princess took the other, and from this time Mrs Morley and Mrs Freeman began to converse as equals, made so by affection and friendship.

John Churchill's relations with the Princess, although on a different plane from those of Sarah, were nevertheless lighted by a growing personal attachment. His own interest in her fortunes is obvious; but upon this supervened as time passed that kind of respectful, yet sentimental devotion which Lord Melbourne showed to the young Queen Victoria. He regarded himself increasingly as Anne's protector and guide. He was her shield against the shocks and intrigues of politics and stood between her and the violent men of both parties. To secure her safety, her well-being, her peace of mind against all assaults, even in the end against Sarah herself, became the rule of his life. Never by word or action in the course of their long association, with all its historic stresses—not to the very end—not even in the bitter hour of dismissal—did he vary in his fidelity to Anne as Princess or Queen, nor in his chivalry to her as a woman.

Anne had but to reach maturity to become a factor of national consequence. Her marriage lay in the cold spheres of State policy. By King Charles's command, and with her father's acquiescence, she, like her elder sister, had been strictly bred a Protestant. Bishop Compton, a soldier before he was a priest—a very martinet of the Reformed religion—had been her preceptor. She had imbibed his teachings with simple, unquestioning, retentive faith. For her the Church of England was henceforward the one sure hope in this world and the next. The popularity of the union of William of Orange with Princess Mary in 1677 had already helped the King to hold his difficult balances at home and abroad. Here in days still critical was the opportunity for another royal Protestant alliance. Prince George of Hanover, afterwards King George I, was brought to England upon a plan of marrying the Princess, but he "left the British shores somewhat dishonourably without justifying the hopes he had excited."[1] International politics may have played

1 Mrs Thomson, *Sarah, Duchess of Marlborough*, i, 50.

their part in this defection, for Louis XIV was by no means unconcerned. Anne, though but fifteen at the time, was deeply offended, and ever afterwards nourished a prejudice against her eventual successor. Her sentimental flirtation with the Earl of Mulgrave—rides in Windsor Park, poems (he was a poet), and love-letters—was sternly suppressed by the royal authority. Lord Mulgrave, banished from the Court, found himself in a leaky frigate under orders for Tangier. It is even possible that Sarah was concerned in dispersing this fairyland aberration. Royal princesses have to take the rough with the smooth.

Charles now turned to a Danish prince, and this time his choice was not obnoxious to the French King. Indeed, Louis seems to have regarded the proceeding as a fair compromise. Although Prince George of Denmark was, of course, a Lutheran Protestant, he represented only a diminished Continental state, and the whole transaction seemed consigned to a modest plane. Prince George obeyed the command of his brother, the Danish King Christian V; and in July 1683 Colonel Churchill was sent to Denmark to conduct him to England to fall in love with the Princess Anne and marry her forthwith. George of Denmark was a fine-looking man, tall, blond, and good-natured. He had a reputation for personal courage, and by a cavalry charge had rescued his brother during a battle between the Danes and the Dutch in 1677. He was neither clever nor learned—a simple, normal man, without envy or ambition, and disposed by remarkable appetite and thirst for all the pleasures of the table. Charles's well-known verdict, "I have tried him drunk and I have tried him sober, but there is nothing in him," does not do justice to the homely virtues and unfailing good-humour of his staid and trustworthy character. It may well be that the Churchills had some part in arranging this marriage. Charles Churchill had been appointed ten years before a page of honour to King Christian. He had accompanied Prince George to England upon an earlier visit. We do not know what confidences may have been interchanged by these assistants, but at any rate Anne accepted with

PRINCE GEORGE OF DENMARK
Willem Wissing
By permission of Earl Spencer   188

LITTLE ROCK PUBLIC LIBRARY

complacency what fortune brought her. Her uncle the King had so decided; her father acquiesced; Louis XIV was content; and only William of Orange was displeased.

On July 28, 1683, the marriage was solemnized with royal pomp and popular approbation. Prince George derived a revenue of £10,000 a year from some small Danish islands. Parliament voted Anne £20,000 a year, and the King established the royal pair in their suite in a residence called the Cockpit, adjoining the Palace of Whitehall, standing where the Treasury Chambers are to-day.

This marriage of policy in which the feelings of the parties had been only formally consulted stood during twenty-four years every ordinary strain and almost unequalled family sorrows. Anne suffered either a miscarriage or a still-born baby with mechanical regularity year after year. Only one cherished son lived beyond his eleventh birthday. At forty-two she had buried sixteen children; and when so many hopes and grave issues hung upon her progeny, none survived her. Her life was repeatedly stabbed by pain, disappointment, and mourning, which her placid courage, strong, patient spirit, firm faith, and abiding sense of public duty enabled her to sustain. Her life, so largely that of an invalid, attached itself to grand simplicities—her religion, her husband, her country's welfare, her beloved friend and mentor, Sarah. These dominants for many years wrought the harmony of her circle, and their consequences adorned her name and reign with unfading glory. Her love for her husband was richly renewed, and she knew no bounds in her admiration of his capacities. The romantic side of her nature found its satisfactions in her strangely intense affection for Sarah. And behind, ever faithful in her service, lay the pervading genius of Marlborough with his enchanted sword.[1]

Anne lost no time in persuading her father to appoint Sarah one of her Ladies of the Bedchamber. The salary was not large (£200), but Sarah wished to serve the Princess. "The Duke," wrote Anne,[2] "had just come in when you were gone. He has given his consent for me to have you with me,

1 For a portrait of Anne see the plate facing p. 92.   2 Coxe, i, 27.

and I assure you it is a great pleasure to me. I should thank you for offering it, but I am not good at compliments." Cavillers have fastened upon the word 'offering'; but the relations of the two women were already such as to reduce the point to insignificance. It was a gracious turn of phrase in Anne to a friend whose society she desired, and not a condition in a diplomatic protocol. In a manuscript essay by Sarah, hitherto unpublished, copies of which are at Blenheim and Althorp, called *A Faithful Account of Many Things*, the following suggestive, impersonal, and of course retrospective account is given of their relations:

> * The Dutchess had address and accomplishments, sufficient to engage the affections and confidence of her Mistress without owing anything to the want of them in others. But yet this made room for her the sooner and gave her some advantage; and she now began to employ all Her wit and all Her vivacity and almost all Her time to divert, and entertain, and serve, the Princess; and to fix that favour, which now one might easily observe to be encreasing towards her every day. This favour quickly became a passion; and a Passion which possessed the Heart of the Princess too much to be hid. They were shut up together for many hours daily. Every moment of Absence was counted a sort of tedious, lifeless, state. To see the Duchess was a constant joy; and to part with her for never so short a time, a constant Uneasiness; As the Princess's own frequent expressions were. This worked even to the jealousy of a Lover. She used to say she desired to possess her wholly: and could hardly bear that she should ever escape, from this confinement, into other Company.

About 1712, Bishop Burnet compiled from Sarah's papers a substantial justification of her conduct towards Queen Anne. Two copies of this, one in the Bishop's own handwriting, have now been found at Blenheim. The Duchess was not satisfied with the production, and marked it "Not well done." Its introduction may, nevertheless, be of interest as an unpublished contemporary document.[1]

> * I came extream young into the Court and had the luck to be liked by manny in it, but by none more particularly than the

1 See Appendix, I.

Queen who took such pleasure in my company that as she had me much about her, so upon her marriage she prevailed with her Father that I should be a Lady of her Bedchamber. Her Court was so oddly composed that it was no extraordinary thing for me to be before them all in her favour, and confidence, this grew upon me to as high a degree, as was possible, *to all, that was passionately fond and tender*, nothing stood in my way, nothing was hard for me. I thought my Selfe, (all others thought it too) that I was as secure in a continuance of a high degree of favour, as ever any person was. I upon such an advancement considered what I ought to do in order to deserve and maintain it. The great principle I laid down in myself was to serve Her with an absolute fidelity and a constant zeal. But by fidelity I did not only mean not to betray her, not to discover [disclose] her secrets, and to be true to her in everything she trusted me with: but to avoid everything, that looked like dissimulation, and flattery, even tho I saw it might displease her; I was convinced that Princes were ruined by flatterers: I carried this so far as to think it was a part of flattery, not to tell her everything that was in any sort amisse in her. I saw poor K. James ruined by this that nobody would honestly tell him of his danger until it was past recovery: and that for fear of displeasing him. I therefore resolved to say everything that I thought concerned her to know, whom I served, with as much *affection*, as fidelity. . . .

As Sarah had to attend the Princess at Tunbridge Wells and elsewhere, and John himself still had to travel about with the Duke of York, the couple were occasionally separated, and there survive the following letters between them:[1]

John to Sarah   [1683–84]

* I had writ to you by the post, but that I was persuaded this would be with you sooner. You see I am very just [regular] in writing, and I hope I shall find by the daily receiving of yours that you are so. I hope in God you are out of all danger of miscarrying, for I swear to you I love you better than all the rest of the world put together, wherefore you ought to be so just as to make me a kind return, which will make me much happier

---

1 These letters, hitherto unpublished, are from the Blenheim MSS. The first letter can be dated roughly by the fact that Churchill's first surviving daughter, Henrietta, was born on July 19, 1681, and his second, Anne, on February 27, 1684.

than aught else in this world can do. If I can get a passage a Sunday I will come, but if I cannot I shall be with you a Monday morning by nine of the clock; for the Duke will leave this place by six. Pray [give] my most humble respects to your fair daughter, and believe me what I am with all my heart and soul,

Yours . . .

Pray tell Poidvine [his valet] I would have him wait upon Mr Legge for the note for the horses.

Friday night

[1684–85]

* I was in hopes to have found my dear soul here or at least a letter so that I might have known when you do come. There is no Gentleman of the Bedchamber here, so that I am forced to wait, which I hope will make you come before your clothes are made, and if you do not, as soon as I see a Gentleman of the Bedchamber's face, I will come away to you, for I long with all my heart and soul to be with you. Pray let me hear from you to-night if you do not come to-morrow.

For my Lady Churchill

[1684–85]

* I have not heard from you; however I will not forbear writing to let you know that your children are very well and that to-morrow we go to town and the next morning the Duke will be at Tunbridge, and I hope there will be room in the coach for me to come. The Duke will stay but one night, and if I come with him I must be forced to go back with him, so that I hope you will take it kindly my coming a hundred miles for the happiness of one night.

Monday
For my Lady Churchill at the Princess' at Tunbridge

[1685–86]

* I did yesterday receive two of yours, one of them having been forgot by a mistake of Sir John Worden's.[1] You do in one of them complain of my not writing. I do swear to you that I have not failed one day writing except yesterday and I had not then missed but that I was a-hacking with the King, and the post went just as we came home. So that you see how little reason

---

1 Or Werden's.

you have to be angry with me, and I do assure you if you do continue to be angry with me you are very unjust, for I do love you with all my heart and soul. Lady Anne asks for you very often so that I think you would do well if you wrote to her to thank her for her kindness in inquiring after your health. The pains which you complain on is certainly caused by your catching cold, so that if you have any kindness for me you will have a care of yourself, for your life is as dear to me as is my own. I have nothing more to add but that you and your children are the dearest things to me in this world.

Wednesday
For my Lady Churchill St James's

The closing years of Charles II were calm. In the wake of the passions of the Popish Plot and on the tide of Tory reaction the country regathered something of its poise. It seemed after a while as if the executions of the Popish and Rye House Plots had balanced each other, and a fresh start became possible. We observe the formation of a mass of central opinion, which, if it did not mitigate the strife of parties, could at least award the palm of success to the least culpable. This peculiarly English phenomenon could never henceforward be disregarded. Any party which ranged too far upon its own characteristic course was liable to offend a great body of men who, though perhaps marked by party labels, were by no means prepared to associate themselves with party extravagances.

At the end of the reign we see Charles working with several representatives of this moderate Tory view. Among these, opposed to Popery, opposed to France, mildly adverse to Dissent, content with peace, and respecting the government of King *and* Parliament, the famous Halifax was pre-eminent. His nature led him to turn against excess in any quarter; he swam instinctively against the stream. The taunt of "Trimmer" levelled at him by disappointed partisans has been accepted by history as the proof of his uprightness and sagacity. He compared himself with justice to the temperate zone which lies between "the regions in which men are frozen and the regions in which they are roasted."

He was the foremost statesman of these times; a love of moderation and sense of the practical seemed in him to emerge in bold rather than tepid courses. He could strike as hard for compromise as most leaders for victory. Memorable were the services which Halifax had rendered to the Crown and the Duke of York. His reasoned oratory, his biting sarcasm, his personal force and proud independence, had turned the scale against the first Exclusion Bill. His wise counsels had aided the King at crucial moments, and he himself often formed the rallying-point for men of goodwill. His greatest work for the nation and for modern times was yet to be done. Meanwhile he stood, a trusted Minister, at King Charles's side in the evening of a stormy day.

> Jotham of piercing wit and pregnant thought,
> Endued by nature and by learning taught
> To move assemblies, who but only tried
> The worse a while, then chose the better side;
> Nor chose alone, but turned the balance too,
> So much the weight of one brave man can do.[1]

Halifax must have represented Churchill's political views and temperament far more truly than any other statesman. Whether or not John learned war from Turenne, he certainly learned politics from Halifax. As we watch the Great Trimmer turning from side to side, from faction to faction, from Monmouth to William, or back again to James, yet always pursuing his aim of sobriety and appeasement at home and of marshalling all the best in England against Popery, autocracy, and France, we can almost see John's mind keeping pace and threading silently the labyrinths of intrigue in his footsteps. We are sure that when Halifax fought the Whigs against perjured testimony for the life of Stafford, and fought the Crown and the Tories against packed juries for the lives of Russell and Sidney, he carried with him the heartfelt sympathies of the Churchill who had resented the condemnation of Argyll, and whose humane conduct at the head of armies the histories of friend and foe were to proclaim.

In spite of their difference in age, rank, and authority a

---

[1] Dryden, *Absalom and Achitophel.*

THE MARQUIS OF HALIFAX

By permission of the Duke of Devonshire

194

considerable measure of friendship—respect in the younger, regard in the elder—already subsisted between the two men. We have printed what Halifax wrote to his brother, Henry Savile, about the possible vacancy in the Paris Embassy in 1680—words never meant for Churchill's eye and never seen by him. We know how ardently they both desired to wean James back to conformity with the Church of England in 1681. We shall see them marching—though at different speeds and in different guise—the same difficult, perilous roads in 1687 and 1688. And far on, in 1693, after they have both intrigued with the exiled Jacobite Court, it is the renowned Halifax who goes bail for Marlborough against the displeasure of King William, and is struck off the Privy Council for his pains. It was a long and honourable association, undisturbed by indescribable perplexities, of men who all their lives meant the same thing for England, and in the main achieved their purpose.

Another figure, at that time classed among the moderates, who had sat at the council board was Sir Edward Seymour. He was "the great Commoner" of those days. A fervent Tory of touchy, rancorous temper, of independent and undependable character, with great wealth and position, he marshalled a hundred members from the over-represented West Country. He could upon occasion have produced an army from the same regions for a national cause. He was the first Speaker of the House of Commons who was not a lawyer. His pride in his connexion with the Seymour of the Reformation and his intense hatred of Catholicism made him an inflexible opponent of James; but, on the other hand, the principle of Divine Right forbade him to vote for the Exclusion Bill. His pompous austerity was not proof against the rapid alternations of favour and neglect which marked his career. He was easily tamed by office, and as easily invigorated by the loss of it. He did not trouble to reconcile his words in Opposition with his deeds as a Minister; nor *vice versa*. He defended with vigour from the Government bench the abuses he had denounced as a private Member, and blithely renewed his virtue when deprived of power. On the whole, he was the most

195

magnificent, though by no means the most successful, place-hunter of his day. We shall meet him again, in 1688 and also later.

A third councillor, by hereditary distinction (for his father had been a trusted Lord Chancellor), Daniel Finch, Earl of Nottingham, was a devout Churchman, who, more than any other layman, could influence the bishops. Although he belonged to what would now be called the High Church party, he was so much alarmed at the intolerant processes of the Catholics in France and at the persecutions launched by Louis XIV that he tried to mitigate by every means the quarrel of the Episcopacy with the Dissenters, and to establish a general unity among all the Protestant bodies. His influence in the revolution of 1688 was to be profound.

But the daily work of administration was mainly in the hands of three men of more easy and practical temper, if of less solid political power. Laurence Hyde—now Earl of Rochester, "a Danby in a minor key"; the elusive, imponderable Sunderland; and always, "never in the way and never out of the way," Churchill's lifelong friend Godolphin. These were lightly called "the Chits." With all of them Churchill was intimate. The two last, and especially Godolphin, represented the nearest approach in those times to the high permanent civil servants of the present day. Well trained and deeply informed, smooth and competent in business, without marshalled interests behind them, or vehement party views, they adapted themselves readily to the royal will, and sought chiefly to give it a prudent and effective expression. They stood for less, but performed more than the more rugged political leaders.[1]

The King himself basked in the mellower light which had followed so much rough weather. He had overcome his enemies; and at whatever cost to his dignity or honour had restored peace at home and kept out of war abroad. He could afford to forgive Monmouth. He was strong enough to bring back James. He revolved with tolerant mind Halifax's desire to summon Parliament, and might well

---

[1] Cf. Feiling, *History of the Tory Party,* chapter vii.

expect that it would be loyal and serviceable. He still balanced and measured the grievous, insoluble problems with which he was oppressed: the ferocious divisions of his people, his want of money—that damnable thing—his dependence upon France, the odious state of Europe, the dangers of renewed Parliamentary strife, and, above all, the anxieties of the succession. For all his loves and troop of bastards, he had no legitimate heir. Strong and unswerving as he had been for the strict application of the principle of hereditary right, no one knew better than he the awful dangers which James's religion and character would bring upon the land. In spite of his own profound leanings to the old faith of Christendom, he had never lost contact with, and had in the main preserved the confidence of, the Church of England. He had used the laws of England and its Constitution as effective weapons in his warfare with the Whigs. He had never broken these laws in the process, nor trespassed beyond an arguable legality. He knew and loved his brother well, and foresaw how James's virtues and vices alike would embroil him with a nation as stubborn and resolute as he.

Yet where else to turn? How England would have rejoiced could he have but given her his handsome, gifted courageous by-blow—"our beloved Protestant Duke"! But never would he vitiate the lawful succession of the Crown, nor tolerate that picking and choosing between rival claims which would transform an hereditary into an elective monarchy. Had he not for this wrestled with his people and his Parliament? Was not the fate of Russell, of Sidney, of Essex, a proof of his invincible resolve?

Then there was William: the busy—nay, tireless—fiery but calculating, masterful and accepted ruler of Holland, and foremost champion of the Protestant world. The blood royal of England flowed in his veins, and Mary his wife was second heir-presumptive to the Crown. Here was a foreign sovereign, backed by a constitutional government and loyal fleets and armies, whose profound interest in the succession had never been disguised. How shrewd and patient William

197

had been; how skilfully he had steered a course through the English storms! Charles could admire kingcraft in another. William had in no way added to his difficulties; he had throughout professed a warm and dutiful affection for him. The Dutchman's personal relations with the leaders of both the English parties were widespread, direct, and close. He maintained an extensive correspondence across the North Sea, and was almost as closely immersed in English and Scottish affairs as in those of Holland. But he never committed himself to supporting the Exclusion Bills or any of the alternative projects for limiting the prerogatives of a Popish king. In vain did the Whigs appeal to him to declare himself in favour of the Exclusion Bill, saying in effect, "Of course, this will give you your chance." William knew better. He had seen clearly that, with James excluded, Monmouth would become a far more formidable rival. He saw his own chance would only come at a second remove. But he understood James thoroughly, and placed a steady confidence in his capacity to break his neck. The Prince of Orange was sure that James would never abandon the attempt to compel the English nation to submit to autocratic rule and Catholic conversion, and equally sure that the English nation would never submit to such designs. Hence in his farseeing way he did not wish James's powers to be specially limited by law. It was better for William that James should have a free hand, and if this led him to disaster, then at least his successor would not be a king with a mutilated prerogative.

Charles comprehended this situation with a nice taste; he knew all the moves upon the board. But what more could he do? At any rate, it seemed that time might be allowed to play its part. The King was only fifty-four; his health in general at this time seemed robust. To many intimates his life seemed as good as that of his brother. He could not measure the deep inroads which continuous sexual excitement had wrought upon his vigorous frame. Another ten years, to which he could reasonably look forward, might clarify the whole scene. So he returned with cordial acquiescence to the pleasures and amusements of his Court, toyed with Halifax's proposals for a new Parliament, rejoiced that the ship of State was for the moment on an even keel, and left the baffling problems of the future to solve themselves. They did so.

Meanwhile the Duke of York shared in the revivified popularity of the Crown. He became again in fact, if not in form, Lord High Admiral. The King, resting on his laurels, resigned much policy to his hand. He was looked upon as the leader of the extreme Tories. Had he not, it was said by persons who utterly misread the forces at work, been right all the time with his counsels of firmness? Had he not been skilful in managing the Scottish Parliament? Did not his sincere convictions and his bravery afloat and ashore deserve the highest respect? Versifiers wrote:[1]

> The glory of the British line,
> Old Jimmy's come again.

Indeed, the ardour of the Tory reaction began to cause some misgivings among the ablest counsellors of Charles II. Figures like Roger L'Estrange, long Charles's censor and pamphleteer, represented at the opposite end of the political scale opinions as dangerous and odious to the nation as those muttered by the Rye House conspirators. The lawyer Jeffreys, now the Tory Lord Chief Justice, whose brutal nature, savage partisanship, and high professional gifts made him a perfect instrument of judicial murder, ruled the Bench. Even those who most welcomed the turn of the tide were disquieted by its force, exclaiming as they shook their heads, "This is too good to last." But the Duke of York, now lord of the ascendant, held a different opinion.

Churchill was by this time in the middle thirties. He was in a position to judge men and affairs upon excellent information. It is only here and there that some record of his opinion exists. We can judge his politics chiefly by his friends. He was not accustomed to air his views upon grave matters, and such letters as have been preserved concern themselves only with private or family matters. We may be sure that he

[1] *Cit.* Feiling, p. 198.

thought deeply and clearly about the succession to the Crown, upon which such fateful issues hung. In the course of his service to James he had been brought into sharp antagonism with Monmouth and his party. Gone were the comradeships of Maestricht days. Churchill was definitely ranged and classed with the Tories—and with the high Tories—against all interference with his master's hereditary rights. He had the best opportunities of informing himself about the King's health; he had seen him a few years before smitten with a mysterious and alarming illness. It was now certain that if James were alive at the death of King Charles, he would ascend the throne, and Churchill had every reason but one to hope for the highest favour and advancement at his hands. Yet that one adverse reason was enough to undo all. The wise, observant soldier who had dwelt so long at or near the centre of power had no doubts whatever of the clash that must ensue between his devout, headstrong, bigoted, resolute patron and the whole resisting power of a Protestant nation. Here again his course was determined. In defence of the Protestant religion he would sever all loyalties, extinguish all gratitudes, and take all necessary measures. His wife's intimate, affectionate relations with the Princess Anne, her offer to undertake the office of her Lady of the Bedchamber, must have been in full accord with his wishes and designs. The influence, daily becoming decisive and dominant, which the Churchills exerted in the household of the Prince and Princess of Denmark was steadfastly used to strengthen and fortify its already marked Protestant character, and to link the young Princess with leading statesmen and divines who would confirm her vigorous faith.

The situation had, as we have seen, arisen naturally, by the invisible impulses of friendship and custom. It had now become a definite and primary factor in the Churchills' fortunes, as it was presently to be in those of the nation. From this time forward John and Sarah began to be increasingly detached from the Duke's circle, and noticeably associated—beyond the religious gulf—with his younger daughter. Indeed, during the reign of James II Churchill

LITTLE ROCK PUBLIC LIBRARY

was regarded by an informed foreign observer[1] as Princess Anne's friend and counsellor rather than the trusted servant of the new King. This in quiet times meant little, but a day was soon to come when it would mean everything. A connexion had been formed around the Protestant royal personage who stood third in the line of succession, cemented by a friendship and sympathy destined to withstand the shocks and trials of more than twenty years. This union of intense convictions, sentiments, habits, and interests was soon to be exposed to the sharpest and most violent tests, and to withstand them with the strength of solid rock.

The King seemed in his usual health at the beginning of 1685. After his dinner on the night of January 26 he sat, as was his custom, with the Duchess of Portsmouth and a small company of friends. Thomas Bruce, the Earl of Ailesbury, with whom Churchill's functions must often have brought him in friendly contact—to whom we owe most delightful, if sometimes untrustworthy, memoirs[2]—was on duty as Gentleman of the Bedchamber. He found the King "in the most charming humour possible." But

> when we came to the district of the bedchamber, I by my office was to light him to the bedchamber door, and giving the candle to the page of the backstairs, it went out, although a very large wax candle and without any wind. The page of the backstairs was more superstitious, for he looked on me, shaking his head.

The King chatted agreeably with his gentlemen as he undressed, and spoke about the repairing of Winchester Castle and the gardens he was making there. He said to Ailesbury, "I will order John" (a familiar word for the Earl of Bath, the Groom of the Stole, who was with the King when a boy) "to put you in waiting the first time I go thither, and although it be not your turn, to show you the place I delight so in, and shall be so happy this week as to have my house covered with lead." "And God knows," comments Ailesbury, "the Saturday following he was put in his coffin."

1 See below, pp. 237, 245–246.   2 *Memoirs,* pp. 85–87.

201

That night Ailesbury, lying in the next room, and "sleeping but indifferently, perceived that the King turned himself sometimes, not usual for him." The next morning he was "pale as ashes" and "could not or would not say one word." A violent fit of apoplexy supervened, and after gamely enduring prolonged torture at the hands of his distracted physicians Charles II breathed his last. All untimely, the long-dreaded event had come to pass. The interlude of peace was over, and King James II ruled the land.

CHAPTER XII

SEDGEMOOR

(1685)

FOR two years past James had played an active second part in the government of the kingdom, and once his brother's approaching end became certain, he concerned himself with every precaution necessary to ensure an unopposed succession. Indeed, it was not until after he had posted the Royal Guards at various important points, and had even obtained the dying King's signature to some measures of financial convenience, that, on the promptings of the Duchess of Portsmouth, he secured Charles's spiritual welfare by bringing a priest up the backstairs to receive him into the Church of Rome and give him extreme unction. Within a quarter of an hour of the King's death he met the Privy Council, whose duty it is to recognize the new sovereign. He laboured to contradict the belief that he was revengeful or inclined to arbitrary rule. He declared himself resolved to maintain both in State and Church a system of government established by law,

> for he recognized the members of the English Church as loyal subjects, he knew that the laws of England were sufficient to make the King a great monarch and that he would maintain the rights and prerogatives of the Crown, and would not invade any man's property.

It has even been asserted he went so far at this critical moment as to say that, "as regards his private religious opinions, no one should perceive that he entertained them," but that this sentence was deleted from the official report.[1]

These declarations were received by the dignitaries and magnates of the realm with profound relief and joy, and as the Royal Proclamation spread throughout the land it everywhere evoked expressions of gratitude and loyalty. Charles II

[1] Ranke, *History of England*, iv, 214–215.

had died at the moment when the Tory reaction was at its highest. The sentimental nature of the English people was stirred to its depth by the death of the King, who if he had tricked them often, had not, as they now felt, served them ill, and whose personal charm and human qualities and weaknesses were pervasively endearing. In the wave of grief and hope sweeping the nation the unbridgeable differences of faith, policy, and temper which separated a new prince and an old people were forgotten. James ascended the throne of his ancestors and predecessors with as fair a chance as ever monarch had.

The summoning of a Parliament, after a lapse of more than three years, was now indispensable. More than half the revenues of the State ceased upon the demise of the Crown. The need was otherwise unanswerable, and the hour could not be more propitious. On February 9 the writs were issued, and the general election of 1685 began. On the second Sunday after his accession, near noon, when the Court was thronged, King James and the Queen attended Mass and received the Sacrament in the Queen's chapel, the doors of which were thrown open for all to see. This act of high consequence dispelled the rosy hopes of the Protestant Court and aroused immediately the London clergy. But the Royal Proclamation, striking while the iron was hot, was not overtaken in those days of slow and imperfect news. The nation voted upon its first impulse and returned a Parliament which in quality and character represented all the strongest elements in the national life, and was in temper as loyal to the Crown as the Restoration Parliament of 1660. Not only embittered partisans, but cool observers were amazed by the change in the public mood. Four years after three successive annual Parliaments had ravened for the Bill to exclude him from the throne, James found himself in the presence of an ardent and devoted House of Commons. To this new Parliament he repeated his original declaration as amended. From it he received an enthusiastic response, and the revenues, grudged and meted to his brother, were to him voted in their amplitude for life. He had only to practise his religion for his conscience'

204

sake as a man, to observe the laws of the realm, and to keep
the promises he had made respecting them, in order to receive
and enjoy the faithful service of his subjects for all his days.
He began his reign with that same caution and moderation
which had marked his first government in Scotland, and he
reaped an immediate reward. Events were, however, at hand
which would impel and empower him to cast aside these wise
and vital restraints.

He ruled in the main with the later Ministers of Charles II, ✓
and such changes as he made in no way broke the continuity
of the Government. His brothers-in-law, the two Hydes,
Clarendon and Rochester, became Lord Privy Seal and Lord
Treasurer respectively. Halifax, who had sought the Treasury, and had been, but for King Charles's sudden death, on
the point of exposing Rochester's peculations, was constrained
to accept a so-called promotion to the Presidency of the Council. Godolphin continued Chamberlain to the Queen, and
Sunderland and Middleton were the Secretaries of State.
Churchill ranked below these leading figures. It may be that
his master was not unconscious of a fissure between them.
Yet he stood in good favour with the new régime. In the list
of the nine Lords of the Bedchamber his name was second
only to Peterborough's.[1] His colonelcy of the Dragoons was
confirmed; and he was immediately despatched on a mission
to Versailles, the ostensible object of which was to notify
Louis XIV of the accession, and its substantial purpose to
obtain an increased subsidy for the English Crown. For this
task his negotiations in 1679 and 1681 and his full knowledge
of the secret relations of the two Kings had well prepared him.
But Louis, taking time by the forelock, had forestalled the
request. Before Churchill could reach Paris Barillon had
waited upon James with an unsolicited gift of 500,000 livres,
and it was thought only becoming to express gratitude for this
modest favour before asking for the two or three millions a
year which the English King and Court regarded as desirable.

1 *Mémoire* of September [?], 1687 (*Correspondance politique, Angleterre*, t. 164,
f. 232). This same *Mémoire* says, "Mde De Chercheil est dame d'honn[eu]r
de la P[rinces]se de D[annemar]k qui l'aime tendrem[en]t. Elle a de l'esprit, et
l'on est persuadé que c'est elle qui contribue a éloigner cette P[rinces]se de la Cour,
de peur que le Roy son Père ne luy parle sur la religion."

Churchill was therefore overtaken by fresh instructions, and his mission was limited to ceremonies and thanks.[1] On this visit Churchill seems to have committed an unusual indiscretion. "The Earl of Galway," says Burnet,

> told me that when he [Churchill] came over [to France] in the first compliment upon the King's coming to the Crown, he said then to him that if the King was ever prevailed upon to alter our religion he would serve him no longer, but would withdraw from him.[2]

Charles James Fox comments:

> How little could Barillon guess that he [Louis XIV] was negotiating with one who was destined to be at the head of an Administration which in a few years would send the same Lord Churchill not to Paris to implore Louis for succour towards enslaving England or to thank him for pensions to her monarchs, but to combine all Europe against him in the cause of liberty![3]

That this proved to be Churchill's last visit to Paris was not, as will be shown in another volume, entirely his own fault. He returned to England at the beginning of April in time for the splendours of the coronation. An English peerage was conferred upon him, and he became Baron Churchill of Sandridge. Rougher work was soon at hand.

The news of King Charles's death fell like a thunderbolt on his well-loved, wayward bastard at The Hague. Monmouth by his natural vivacity had lent a fleeting gleam of gaiety to the dull, strait-laced routine of the Dutch Court. Politics apart, he had been received with genuine relish. But in the midst of dancing and ice-carnivals came the news that, instead of a father about to consummate an act of forgiveness, there ruled in England an uncle who had suffered insult and exile through his rivalry, whose last six years had been consumed in struggling against the party he led, and who hated him with all the hatred of intimacy, alike as Protestant and as Pretender.

Monmouth's mood of despair led him to seek in the

---

[1] Correspondence between Louis XIV and Barillon, *apud* C. J. Fox, *James II*, Appendix, pp. xxiv *seq.*
[2] Burnet, iii, 269.   [3] C. J. Fox, *James II*, p. 88.

companionship of his fond mistress, the beautiful Lady Wentworth, a shelter from the mischances of public life. He quitted The Hague at William's request within a few hours, and settled himself with his charming friend at Brussels. But more turbulent and daring spirits were not so agreeably soothed. Argyll—the "hunted partridge"—in his Dutch retreat brooded intently upon the sanctity of synodical as opposed to episcopal Christianity, and burned to be in the Highlands again at the head of his adoring clansmen. The plotter Ferguson, Lord Grey of Wark, Wade, and a dozen or more prominent men who had escaped from England and Scotland after the Rye House exposure, gripped Monmouth and bound him to a fatal design. Lady Wentworth herself, who loved him so well, loved also that he should be a king. She offered her jewels and wealth for his service. All these exiles had in their minds the picture of England in 1682. They saw again the fierce, eager, resolute forces—the great Whig lords, the House of Commons majorities, the City of London, the vindictive juries, the unrepresented Protestant masses—which had only yesterday seemed about to sweep their cause and themselves to triumph. They could not believe in the reality of a change of mood so swift and utter as had in fact occurred since then. Monmouth yielded against his better judgment to their importunities. It was agreed that Argyll should invade and rouse the Highlands and that Monmouth should land in England. Two tiny expeditions of three ships each, filled with munitions and bitter men of quality, were organized from slender resources, and three weeks after Argyll had set out for Kirkwall Monmouth sailed for the Channel.

It was curious that William should not be able to prevent these descents upon a friendly State. We are assured by the highest authorities that he did his utmost, that he advised Monmouth to offer his services to the Empire against the Turks, that he exerted his authority upon the Admiralty of Amsterdam to prevent these sailings. His conduct was impeccable. It was also ineffectual. The unhappy Stadtholder was compelled to remain an impotent spectator of an enterprise which, whatever might happen, must conduce enormously to his advantage. If by chance Monmouth succeeded, England would become his Protestant and martial ally against France and French Catholicism. If Monmouth failed, as seemed certain, the succession to the English crown would be remarkably simplified. The most successful statesmen are those who know how by their actions or inactions to reconcile self-interest with correctitude.

Monmouth tossed on the waves for nineteen days, driven hither and thither by the winds. He escaped the numerous English cruisers which watched the Straits of Dover, and on June 11 dropped anchor in that same Dorsetshire port of Lyme Regis in which, as the reader will recall, Eleanor Drake had formerly suffered the severities of a siege, and for which her son-in-law, Sir Winston Churchill, was now Member of Parliament. The Duke and his confederates, who had beguiled the anxious voyage with Cabinet-making, landed forthwith. Sword in hand, they repaired to the market-place, where they were received with rapture by the townsfolk, who, like themselves, were still living in the England of the Popish Plot, and looked back with reverence to the great days of Blake and Cromwell. Monmouth issued a proclamation, drawn up by Ferguson, accusing the King of having murdered Charles II, and of every other crime; affirming also that he himself was born in wedlock, and claiming to be the champion of the laws, liberty, and religion of the realm. The rush of adherents to enlist baffled the clerks who registered their names. Within twenty-four hours he was joined by fifteen hundred men.

Meanwhile messengers from the Mayor of Lyme, who abandoned the contumacious town, were riding as fast as relays of horses could carry them to London. On the morning of June 13 they broke in upon Sir Winston with the startling news that his constituency was in rebellion. He took them to the palace, and, summoning his son, was conducted to the King.

This must have been a great day for old Sir Winston, and one in which all the harmonies of his life seemed to merge.

Here was the King for whose sacred rights and line he had fought with sword and pen, for whom he had suffered so much, and who had done him the honour—no mere formality—of making him four times a grandfather, once more assaulted by rebellion. The same obstinate, traitorous forces —happily without votes—were again rampant in those same familiar scenes in which he had lived his life. The old cause was once more at stake in the old place; and here stood his son, Colonel of the Dragoons, the rising soldier of the day, high in the favour of the threatened monarch, long linked to his service—he it was who would march forward at the head of the Household troops, the *corps d'élite*, to lay the insolent usurper low. It was Sir Winston's apotheosis. There must have been a strong feeling of the continuity of history in this small group coincidence had brought together.

Instant resolves were taken. All available forces were ordered to Salisbury. That very night Churchill set out with four troops of the Blues and two of his own Dragoons—in all about three hundred horse—followed by Colonel Kirke with five companies of the Queen's Regiment.

Monmouth could scarcely have struck a more unlucky moment: Parliament was in session, the King's popularity was still at coronation height. An Act of Attainder against Monmouth was passed. The price of £5000 was set on his head. The Commons voted large, immediate supplies, and both Houses assured the King of their resolve to die in his defence. Moreover, the troops from Tangier had already landed. A prompt requisition was presented to William of Orange to send back, in accordance with the convention under which they served, the six English and Scottish regiments maintained in Dutch pay. William lost no time in complying. He had been unable to stop Monmouth's expedition from starting—it had got safely away; he could now make sure that it was destroyed. However painful it must have been to him on personal grounds to aid in the ruin of his inconvenient Protestant rival—so lately his attractive guest—he had to do his duty. The troops were dispatched forthwith; and William even offered to come over in person to take command of the royal army. This kindly proposal was declined.

Churchill marched south with great rapidity. He reached Bridport on June 17, having covered 120 miles in four days. The situation was even more serious than had been supposed when he left London. The nobility and gentry, whose influence had so long returned Sir Winston to the House of Commons, were loyal in the Cavalier tradition to the King. The people, countryfolk and townsmen alike, were for the Duke and Dissenting Protestantism. The militias of Dorset, Devon, and Somerset had been partially mobilized under the general direction of the Duke of Albemarle. Their training and discipline were weak, and their hearts were with "the Protestant Duke." Reinforcements of regular troops were imperative. From Bridport Churchill wrote to the King:

> I am sorry to send your Majesty this ill news; which is [that] unless speedy course be taken, we are like to lose this [part of the] country to the rebels; for we have those two [militia] regiments run away a second time . . . and it happened thus: The Duke of Albemarle sends to Sir E. Phellipps and Colonel Luttrell, that he would be at Axminster on such a day with some forces, and would have them meet him there; so away marched those two regiments, one out of Chard and the other out of Crewkern; and when they came to the top of the hill within half a quarter of a mile of the town, there came out some country people, and said the Duke of Monmouth was in the town; at that, one Captain Littleton cried out, We are all betrayed! so the soldiers immediately look[ed] one upon another, and threw down their arms, and fled, leaving their Officers and Colours behind; half, if not the greatest part, are gone to the rebels. I do humbly submit this to your Majesty's commands in what I shall do in it, for there is not any relying on these regiments that are left unless we had some of your Majesty's standing forces to lead them on and encourage them; for at this unfortunate news I never saw people so much daunted in my life.[1]

On the 18th Churchill was at Axminster, and on the 19th at Chard, in country which he knew so well (Ashe House was but eight miles away). Here his patrols came into contact

---

[1] Northumberland Papers, *H.M.C.*, iii, 99.

THE EARL OF MARLBOROUGH
John Closterman
National Portrait Gallery

210

with the hostile forces; and here also was a messenger from Monmouth reminding him of their old friendship and begging his aid. Churchill dismissed the messenger and sent the letter to the King.

Monmouth, at the head of some three thousand men and four guns, had entered Taunton on the 18th. Here he was received with royal state and lively affection. He was persuaded to proclaim himself King, thus confirming William in his sense of duty to James. The rebel numbers rose to above seven thousand, and he might have doubled them had he possessed the arms. His handful of cavalry, under Lord Grey of Wark, were mounted upon horses mostly untrained or even unbroken. His infantry were only partly armed with muskets, and for the rest depended upon scythes fastened on broomsticks. They had neither more nor less training than the militia, out of whom, indeed, they were largely composed. Nevertheless, in their zeal, in their comprehension of the quarrel, and in their stubborn courage, they were the ore from which the Ironsides had been forged.

We do not know what happened at Whitehall after Sir Winston went back to his dwelling, and John, appointed to the rank of Brigadier-General, set forth upon the Great West Road. He certainly hoped, and probably expected, that he would have the command of all the troops available; but in this he was disappointed. It may be that his old comradeship with Monmouth was counted against him. Certainly his own Protestantism and his close local association with the area affected by a Protestant movement might have caused misgivings in the Royal Council. At any rate, there were second thoughts. On June 19 Sunderland wrote to inform him that the Frenchman Feversham had been appointed Commander-in-Chief. This was a significant event; Feversham, though twelve years older, had never held Churchill's commands nor gained his distinction upon the Continent. Although present both at Maestricht and Enzheim and in several campaigns, Feversham had been only an observer. Churchill held an equal rank, and was an English-born soldier. He resented his supersession, and he knew it could only come from mistrust. The causes of his cleavage from his master, though deep, were latent and might never rise to the surface. He was still—even more than Feversham—to all eyes his faithful trusted agent and personal intimate. He had been for the last four years solidly and actively opposed to Monmouth. In James's cause he had countered him in the political negotiations and intrigue of the Exclusion Bills. His interests, whether as servant to James, as confidential adviser to Princess Anne, or even as a friend of William, were all equally opposed to this interloper in the lawful succession to the Crown. Here was a campaign begun which he had in his own hands, on which his heart was set, and which he knew himself more capable than anyone to direct. He did not entirely conceal his anger. "I see plainly," he wrote on July 4 to Clarendon,[1] "that I am to have the trouble, and that the honour will be another's." One of the remaining links which bound him to James's personal fortunes may well have broken here: nevertheless, with his customary self-control he subordinated his feelings to his duty and his policy, submitted himself with perfect propriety to Feversham, and directed his wrath solely upon the enemy.[2]

It is not our purpose to follow this strange small campaign in detail. Churchill, once in contact with the rebels, never let go. His well-trained force of regular cavalry, widely spread, enveloped and stabbed the flanks and rear of Monmouth's army. He followed them wherever they moved, changing from one flank to the other as occasion served, and always labouring to impress upon the enemy, and especially upon Monmouth, whose temperament he knew well, that they were aggressively opposed by the loyal regular forces of the Crown. At the same time he endeavoured to keep the militia out of danger, to have them concentrated and as far from the enemy as possible at points where he could, with his professional troops, ensure alike not only their lives but their fidelity.

1 Clarendon, *Correspondence and Diary,* i, 141.
2 He was promoted Major-General on July 3, possibly to soften his supersession by Feversham; but he knew nothing of this till after the battle.

Meanwhile such parts of the regular forces as could be spared from an agitated capital were approaching. Kirke, newly landed from Tangier, with his companies of the Queen's Regiment, joined Churchill at Chard on June 21. They had accomplished 140 miles in eight days—a fine feat for infantry, even with some help from horses. With this reinforcement Churchill revolved the chances of a decisive action. He wrote on June 21 to the Duke of Somerset, "I have forces enough not to apprehend [fear] the Duke of Monmouth, but on the contrary should be glad to meet with him and my men are in so good heart."[1] The quality and temper of the militia was, however, prohibitive; they were prone to join the rebels rather than fight them—in fact, they went over by whole companies. Churchill did not in this event feel strong enough to bar the way to Bristol, as was desired at Whitehall. No course was open to him but to await the arrival of the royal army, and meanwhile claw the enemy.

Monmouth's only chance was swiftness and audacity; without a wide, popular uprising he was doomed. The elements existed which might make him a King, but these elements were political rather than military. He must seize towns and cities and gain their arms and supplies before the royal troops arrived in strength. Bristol, the second city in the kingdom, was full of his partisans. Here was his first obvious objective. To gain the mastery of Bristol would be a formidable advantage. The distance from Lyme to Bristol is about seventy miles, and every risk should have been run to arrive there at the earliest moment. He had, of course, to organize his forces, and must spend some precious days in drilling his recruits. Moreover, most of his transport was drawn by oxen. He was received at Bridgwater with all the enthusiasm of Taunton. He was harried on his marches by Churchill, and hampered by want of trustworthy cavalry to drive him off. It was not until June 25, a fortnight after his landing, that, with forces now swollen to eight thousand foot and a thousand horse, he stood before the decayed ramparts of Bristol. He was too late. Feversham

1 Northumberland Papers, *H.M.C.*, iii, 98.

had entered the city on the 23rd with two hundred horse. The Duke of Beaufort held the hill where the castle had formerly stood, and thence intimidated the population. The royal army was already near Bath, and Churchill lay upon Monmouth's other flank. In these circumstances, only some of which were known to him, he abandoned his design; and with his turning back from Bristol his adventure became forlorn.

Churchill followed close at his heels, cutting off stragglers, hunting his patrols, and looking for a chance to strike. We must not omit to mention, since Wolseley is reproached with suppressing it, that on Friday, the 26th, a mile beyond the town of Pensford, Churchill halted his troops and hanged one "Jarvis the feltmaker," a prisoner who had been taken two days before; and that Jarvis died "obstinately and impenitently."

That same evening Churchill joined Feversham at Bath, where his brother, Charles Churchill, had also arrived, having escorted a train of artillery from Portsmouth. The next day Feversham advanced with the bulk of his forces to attack the rebels at Norton St Philip. The affair was ill-conducted. Five hundred of the royal foot, with some cavalry under the Duke of Grafton, involved themselves in a narrow lane, the hedgerows of which were lined by Monmouth's musketeers. These two by-blows of Charles II—bastard versus bastard—were locked in semi-fratricidal strife. Feversham and Churchill both arrived on the scene. The rebels fought stoutly, and the royal forces, drawing off with a loss of eighty men killed, retired to Bradford in some dissatisfaction. In spite of this incident, Monmouth's army began to melt. Two thousand men deserted. A convoy of arms and stores which was sorely needed was captured near Frome. Taunton, lately so ardent, sent a deputation to beseech him not to return to their town. Upon all this came the tidings that Argyll's revolt had been extinguished and that he and Rumbold had already been beheaded. Despondency and fear began to overspread not only Monmouth's troops, but all those friendly districts which had compromised themselves in his cause. Nowhere did they weigh more heavily than in his own heart.

214

THE CAMPAIGN OF SEDGEMOOR, 1685

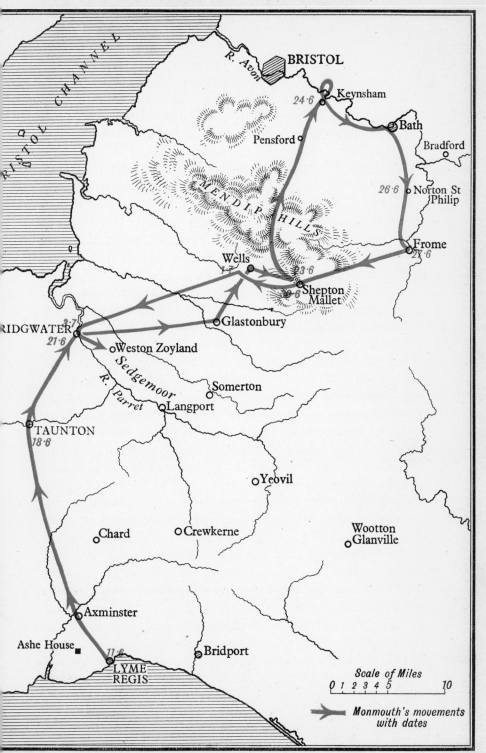

Scale of Miles

0 1 2 3 4 5   10

Monmouth's movements
with dates

On July 3 Monmouth in the deepest gloom re-entered Bridgwater, which he had left eleven days before. Not one man of note had joined him. His peasant army, officered by tradesmen, was wearied and perplexed by ceaseless marches and counter-marches in mud and rain, evidently to no purpose. But those fires still smouldered in their hearts which success would have fanned into flame and which in many only death could quench. On the 5th Feversham, with Churchill and all the royal forces in one body, came from Somerton and camped at Weston Zoyland. The energy of the campaign had sensibly relaxed since the new general had assumed command. Oppressed by the weather and only now provided with tents, he was content to leave the initiative to the rebels and settled himself in a good position facing the plain of Sedgemoor. A ditch, boggy in places, known locally as the Bussex Rhine, passable by cavalry only at two passages, or 'plungeons,' ran across his front and seemed to excuse him from the labour of entrenching. His cavalry billeted themselves in the village of Weston, on the right of his line; his artillery was on the opposite flank, a quarter of a mile farther off. The militia were left out of harm's way a good many miles behind. Not counting these auxiliaries, he mustered seven hundred horse, including the Household Cavalry and six battalions of infantry —in all, nearly three thousand regular troops with sixteen guns.

The two small armies were now scarcely three miles apart, and Monmouth must choose his course without delay. Should he assault the royal position? Should he defend himself in Bridgwater? Should he march once again northward on the Bristol road towards Gloucestershire, Cheshire, and the adherents who were believed to be assembling there? To attack the regulars in the open field was to court destruction. To be shut up in Bridgwater was only to postpone it. But the roads to the north were still open. He could certainly march past Feversham's right and cross the Avon at Keynsham before him. Though pursued, he would advance into a friendly region and a new scene. He chose the last alternative, and during the 4th and 5th disposed and prepared his forces with that intention. To deceive the enemy he employed the

215

inhabitants of Bridgwater ostentatiously upon the fortification of the town, and also issued orders for a retreat upon Taunton. Churchill, who digested every scrap of information, wrote on the 4th to Clarendon:

> I find by the enemy's warrant to the constables that they have more mind to get horses and saddles than anything else which looks as if he had a mind to break away with his horse to some other place and leave his foot entrenched at Bridgwater.

Monmouth, in fact, meant to march with all his force—at least, at the outset. But when, on the morning of the 5th, he quitted Bridgwater and was crossing the town bridge to join his men in the Castle Field, a local farm labourer[1] met him with intimate news of the royal army. It lay scattered in negligent fashion without entrenchment. The last night at Somerton no proper guards had been set; and it was said that laxity, drunkenness, and roystering prevailed. From the tower of Bridgwater Church the whole camp could be seen. Monmouth returned to the town, climbed the tower, saw for the first time the loosely spread camp, and took alike the most daring and the most prudent decision of his life—a night attack!

He called a council, and his supporters agreed. The farm labourer Godfrey, sent to make sure there were no entrenchments, confirmed his first report and undertook to guide the rebel column across the ground he knew well. The afternoon was spent in preparations and in prayer. Ferguson and the other preachers harangued the fanatical, homely bands. The plan was less simple than plans of war by night should be. The whole force would make a march of about six miles round Feversham's right. Grey's cavalry would branch off and, avoiding Chedzoy village, cross the Bussex Rhine at one of the plungeons to the east of the royal camp, surprise the Dragoons and Blues in Weston Zoyland, fire the village, and sweep round the rear upon the camp, the artillery, and the

1 He was not, as usually stated, a farmer, but a servant of a Mr Sparks, who lived in Chedzoy. Sparks had climbed the Chedzoy church tower in the morning and had watched the royal army encamping. To avoid compromising himself, he sent his man, who knew the country well, to tell the Duke what he had seen.

LITTLE ROCK PUBLIC LIBRARY

SEDGEMOOR

baggage at the same time that the infantry broke into the front of the position. It was a desperate cast; but Monmouth had about 3500 brave, determined men. In the night all cats are grey; and the confusion of a hand-to-hand grapple, with all its hopes of surprise and panic, was the best chance left. Indeed, it was a good chance; and but for this, that, and the other, no one knows what might have come of it. Accordingly, a little after eleven o'clock the rebels set forth along the Keynsham road, and after shuffling along for about two miles wheeled to the right into the mist of the moor.[1]

Serious charges have been levelled at Feversham by many historians. Burnet declares that Feversham "had no parties abroad, . . . got no intelligence, . . . and was abed without any care or order." It is certain he was asleep in bed when the musketry fire exploded all around. We have contemporary accounts of his heavy meals and lethargic habits. Although Churchill preserved his customary impeccable politeness, the royal officers spoke of their commander with contempt, mocking at his broken English and declaring that he only thought of eating and sleeping. Seven years before he had survived the operation, grievous in those days, of being trepanned after terrible injuries sustained in trying to limit the fire in Temple Lane by blowing up the houses. One record depicts him in the midst of the alarm methodically tying his cravat before the looking-glass of the farm in which he sheltered. In fact, however, though he omitted to post a guard on the plungeon beyond his right flank, he had not fallen far short of ordinary military routine. He had camped in a good position; he had posted at least five strong pickets of horse and one of foot on the approaches from the enemy; he had an inlying picket of a hundred men under arms, and he had sent Oglethorpe's troop of the Blues to patrol both of the roads from Bridgwater to the north, whither he, like Churchill, expected Monmouth to attempt escape. He visited his outposts in person and waited for some time

[1] Much the best account of Sedgemoor is written by Mr Maurice Page (Bridgwater Booklets, No. 4), who by minute searching of parish registers and local inquiries has corrected in numerous minor particulars the hitherto accepted versions; and who quotes for the first time the evidence of the Rector of Chedzoy and Mr Paschall.

217

for Oglethorpe's report. He went to bed just before one, after receiving a message from Oglethorpe that all was quiet. Though praised and rewarded at the time, Oglethorpe has also been blamed by the critics, especially by Lord Wolseley, the most competent of all. He proceeded with his troop for some distance upon the Bridgwater road, waited a long time on a hill close to the junction of the Bristol and Bath roads, and, finding nothing in the mysterious night, pushed on to the outskirts of the town. Here he learned that the rebel army had departed. Whither he could not tell!

Meanwhile Monmouth and his men plodded onward across the moor, with Grey, guided by Godfrey, in the van. The Black Ditch, one of the great drainage ditches called 'rhines,' had been successfully crossed. Grey, with his scraggy cavalry and part of the rebel foot, were already over the second (the Langmore Rhine), and the clock of Chedzoy Church had struck one, when suddenly a vedette of the Blues fired a pistol in alarm. Frantic excitement broke out. The assailants were now very near their still sleeping foes. Contrary to most accounts, the rebels knew about the Bussex Rhine, and Grey and his horsemen, improvidently leaving Godfrey behind, rode forward, looking for the plungeon. He struck the ditch at an impassable point. Instead of working to the left in harmony with his mission to turn the flank and rear, he swerved to his right with most of his men and rode along the edge across the front of Monmouth's infantry, whose rear was still scrambling across the Langmore Rhine in the darkness behind him. Meanwhile the royal trumpets sounded, the alarm was given, the drums beat, and the threatened camp sprang in an instant into fury and confusion. The startled Grey saw through the mist a small array of gleaming lights, and moved towards them. Some say he thought they were the lights of Weston. There was a different explanation. It had not yet been possible to rearm Dumbarton's regiment with flintlocks. The lights were their slow matches burning as the troops stood to arms. "Who are you for?" cried a voice from among the matchlocks. "The King."

218

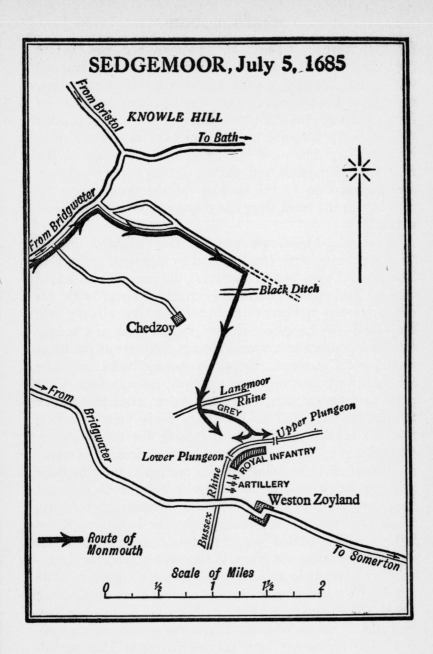

SEDGEMOOR, July 5, 1685

From Bristol

KNOWLE HILL

To Bath→

From Bridgwater

Black Ditch

Chedzoy

→From Bridgwater

Langmoor Rhine

GREY

Upper Plungeon

Lower Plungeon

ROYAL INFANTRY

Bussex Rhine

ARTILLERY

Weston Zoyland

Route of Monmouth

To Somerton

Scale of Miles

0   ½   1   1½   2

"Which King?" "King Monmouth, God with him!" "Take that with you," was the rejoinder, and a volley, followed at brief intervals by a second and a third as each platoon accomplished its ritual, crashed across the ditch. Grey or his untrained horses, or both, were stampeded, and scurried in complete disorder round the flanks of the infantry whom Monmouth was now leading up at the double, still in column of march. But the rest of the rebel cavalry had found the plungeon, and were only stopped at the last minute by Compton and a handful of the Blues from crossing by it.

Churchill, like Feversham, had had a long day, but he was awake, armed, equipped, and on the spot. In the absence of his chief he instantly took command. The rebels, who halted to deploy about eighty yards short of the rhine, began to fire wildly across it, while the royal regiments were rapidly forming. The danger of their bursting into the camp had been averted; but they outflanked the royal right, and when their three cannon, under a competent Dutch gunner, began to fire at a hundred yards into the masses of Dumbarton's regiment and the 1st Guards, men fell fast. Churchill therefore rearranged the infantry. He made the two left-hand battalions march behind the others to prolong his front to the right, and summoned the artillery. These were very slow; but the Bishop of Winchester, 'Old Patch,' who accompanied Feversham as spiritual guide, took the horses out of his coach, and by these six guns were dragged successively to the critical point. Feversham now appeared upon the scene. He approved Churchill's arrangements. He gave the extremely sensible order that the infantry were not to attempt to advance across the ditch till daylight, and rode to the left of his line.

Churchill felt the injury Monmouth's artillery was working at such close quarters upon the infantry. It was probably by his orders that Captain Littleton, of the Blues, who were spread about the front, passed the plungeon, formed up on the other side, and just as the sky was paling with the first light of dawn charged and captured the rebel guns. He did not, as is usually stated, lead the charge of this small body

himself. Some foot soldiers from the nearest battalion wad-
dled across and held what the cavalry had gained.

The firing had now lasted nearly three hours without the
two sides being able to come to grips, and, according to
Wolseley, the rebel ammunition was running short. Certainly
their wagons with the reserve of powder and ball, left two
miles behind, had been deserted by the teamsters in the panic
of Grey's horse. Day was breaking, and the royal artillery
had at length arrived. Drear and doom-like was the dawn
to Monmouth. He knew, as an officer experienced in Continental warfare, that his chance had failed and nothing
could now save his little army. It is amazing he did not
resolve to die on the field with all these earnest simples
he had drawn to their fate. But had he been capable of that,
he would have been capable of so much more that all our
tales would be different. Just as the full light grew upon the
plain he, with Grey, who had now rejoined him after his
excursion, and about fifty horsemen, rode from the field,
hoping to reach a port and seize a ship. On the rising ground
beyond the moor these fugitives and deserters drew rein.
There, still on the edge of the fatal ditch, stood the stubborn
remnants of the Noncomformist foot. The royal cavalry
enveloped them or pursued their routed comrades. Feversham's infantry, who were able to cross the ditch everywhere without apparent difficulty, advanced upon them at the
charge; but the valiant peasantry, miners, and weavers, small,
devout folk serving the Lord in humble station, with the butts
of their muskets and their scythes met the regulars breast to
breast, and closed their ranks with invincible behaviour. At
last the cannon came into action upon this lump of men. All
the sixteen guns had to fire for a considerable time before it
was torn to shreds and the scattered survivors fled, the prey
to a merciless pursuit. Of this tragedy Monmouth had but
one fleeting glance. He only knew that his followers were
still resisting when he quitted the field.

We must not be drawn too far from our particular theme.
Enough that the charming, handsome prince was caught—
drenched and starving—in a ditch; that, carried to London, he

grovelled in vain for life at the knees of his implacable uncle; that he repudiated the cause for which he had fought; that he offered to turn Catholic to save not his soul, but his life; and that finally, when these discordant sounds were ended, he died with perfect composure at the hands of a clumsy and demoralized executioner. The Lady Wentworth followed him a few months later, her heart being broken. Death can be kind.

By noon on the 6th Churchill was in Bridgwater with a thousand soldiers. Unhappy town, with its rank offences, its wounded, its mobs of prisoners or fugitives, its terrified inhabitants! Feversham followed more slowly. He had the Continental view of war. To him these English peasants and common folk were but an unsuccessful jacquerie. He had to festoon the trees with hanged men. With him was Kirke, who had the Tangier outlook, and whose soldiers, newly returned from the crusade against the Moors, bore the emblem of the Paschal Lamb. He and his Lambs showed no mercy except for cash. Worse still was to come.

It is pleasant to find that the foremost man in the fighting had no part in the aftermath of atrocities. Churchill seems to have disentangled himself from the tortured West Country with astonishing deftness. We think he hastened with the utmost speed to Sarah. There is a letter which he had written on June 30 to her at Holywell.

> I have received your picture which you sent by my Lord Colchester. I do assure you that it was very welcome to me, and will be when I am alone a great satisfaction to me, for the whole world put together I do not love so well as I do you, for I sweare to you I had much rather lose my own life than lose you. Therefore for my sake I recommend to you to have a care of yourself. We have had abundance of rain, which has very much tired our soldiers, which I think is ill, because it makes us not press the Duke of Monmouth so much as I think he should be, and that it will make me the longer from you, for I suppose until he be routed, I shall not have the happiness of being with you, which is most earnestly desired by me.

The rout having now been accomplished, he returned home. The royal rewards for the victory went to Feversham; he

THE DUKE OF MONMOUTH
Mary Beale
By permission of Lord Methuen 222

received the Garter and the command of the first and most lucrative troop of the Life Guards. But nothing could free the public mind from the impression that Churchill had saved and won the battle. The whole Army knew the facts. The officers included the Household troops, the Guards, and all the most fashionable soldiers about the Court. They said what they thought. Feversham's martial achievements became a laughing-stock, and the Duke of Buckingham wrote a farce about the general who gained a battle by lying in bed.[1] No doubt there was a strong prejudice against Feversham as a Frenchman; and it may well be, as many writers now contend, that he deserved more credit than he got from his contemporaries. The impression that this slothful foreigner was slumbering on his couch and that the vigilant Englishman saved the situation had more truth in it than the popular version of many historical events.

We must suppose in our attempt to revive from these fragments of history the personality of John Churchill that his treatment by James during and after the Sedgemoor campaign crystallized their private relations. John's sagacious eye weighed with precision his claims upon the royal favour. He must also have comprehended the King's point of view as fairly as he would have measured the virtues and weaknesses of any other adversary, once classed as such. But, apart from his own course and career, there were some matters which stirred his depths. To the butcheries of the Sedgemoor battlefield succeeded the horrors of the Bloody Assize. The Lord Chief Justice Jeffreys, quick to catch his master's mood and spurred by his own sadistic passions, wreaked vengeance upon Bridgwater, Taunton, and the guilty countryside. Nearly four hundred executions marked his progress. Twelve hundred rebels were sold as slaves for the

1 *The Battle of Sedgemoor,* Buckingham's *Works* (ed. 1775), ii, 117–124. Among other absurdities Feversham is made to say, "A pox take de Towna vid de hard Name: How you call de Towna, De Breeche? . . . Ay begarra, Breechwater; so Madama we have intelegenta dat de Rebel go to Breechwater; me say to my Mena, March you Rogua; so we marsha de greata Fielda, begar, de brava Contra where dey killa de Hare vid de Hawka, begar, de brav Sport in de Varld." The jargon shows the kind of prejudice felt by English society and the Army against foreigners, and the atmosphere around Feversham.

Trinidad and Barbados plantations. To this day in Trinidad there exists a colony of white men who, though they have not intermarried with the negroes, toil as equals at their side. They are called the 'red-legs.' They have lost all track of their origin or family trees. Their names have perished; and few there are who know that they include the rearguard of Monmouth's army, lagging a couple of centuries behind.

A squalid traffic in slaves and pardons became fashionable at Whitehall during the Bloody Assize. "Who has not heard," exclaims Ranke, "of the maids of Taunton?" These school-girls, marshalled by their teachers, had presented Monmouth with his embroidered banner. Their well-to-do families were forced to ransom their lives. It was very profitable for a courtier or a Lady of the Bedchamber to have a maid or two allotted to them.[1] This marketing of slaves became both an open scandal and a cause of broil. The Court felt that this booty was their due. The Lord Chief Justice resented such an inroad upon his perquisites, and while he sold pardons and mitigations almost at auction, he soon made it clear by some bloody examples upon those who sued for clemency through irregular channels, that he regarded the intercessions of Whitehall as intrusions upon the sacred pre-serves of the Judiciary. He affirmed a principle. The law, he felt, must in such matters be independent of the Executive. The whole episode was a cannibal outburst over which King James presided with spiritual exaltation.

We have a glimpse of John Churchill—and of his feelings

[1] Macaulay here fell comically into a ditch, and entirely through indulging those literary vices to which he was addicted. For one reason or another he had taken a dislike to William Penn, the Quaker leader. He treated him exactly as he treated Marlborough. By various deft turns he managed in his history to set him in an unpleasing light. He mentions, for instance, that he had attended two executions in a single day, one a hanging at Newgate and another a burning at Tyburn, and sug-gested that he had a taste for such spectacles; the fact being that Penn had solemnly promised both the victims to abide with them in their dying moments. The story of the Maids of Taunton seemed to furnish another opportunity for completing the portrait of William Penn in dark colours. A certain Penne had been forward in the dealings about their ransom. Macaulay lighted upon the name with glee. He speed-ily convinced himself it was William Penn, and wrote a scathing paragraph of his-tory upon the shameful fact. Unluckily for 'history,' however, it was a Penne—no connexion—whose Christian name was George who undoubtedly did the dirty work. The essay in which Paget exposes this blunder (which Macaulay tried to brazen out) is in itself a fitting punishment.

towards his master—in these times. There was the case of two youthful Baptists, the Hewlings.

Their sister, Hannah Hewling, presented a petition to the King in behalf of her brothers and was introduced for the purpose by Lord Churchill, afterwards Duke of Marlborough. While they waited in the antechamber for admittance, standing near the mantlepiece, Lord Churchill assured her of his most hearty wishes of success to her petition, "but, madam," said he, "I dare not flatter you with any such hopes, for that marble is as capable of feeling compassion as the King's heart."[1]

The result justified this severe opinion. Both the Hewlings were hanged.

1 W. Orme, *Remarkable Passages in the Life of William Kiffin*, p. 147.

CHAPTER XIII

THE ROYAL PLOT

(1685–87)

THE swift destruction of Monmouth and Argyll, the vengeance wreaked upon their adherents, the loyalty of Parliament and the fighting forces, combined to give the King a sense of sure and overwhelming power. He began forthwith to move forward along the path of his heart's desire. He would make England a Catholic country and himself an absolute monarch. The steps which he must take to these ends would, he knew, be many and hard. Only gradually and patiently could such great designs be accomplished; but he need no longer observe that caution or practise those deceits which had induced his accession promises. He had marched victorious through the ordeal of a double rebellion; he had proved by terrible examples his strength and his wrath. Who would now dare resist his sovereign will? No more for him the shifts and subterfuges to which his weak, indolent brother had been forced. Henceforward he would have Ministers who would be agents rather than counsellors; he would have compliant Parliaments or none at all; he would have judges who would set the royal authority above the law; he would have a strong, disciplined army devoted to his person; above all, he would suffer no longer that the true faith, which he himself embraced so dearly, should lie under the ban of penal laws. To free his Catholic subjects from their oppression and to raise them to offices of power and honour became for him a sacred duty.

As soon as Jeffreys' "campaign," as James called it, was ended he proposed to his Council the repeal of the Test Act and the Habeas Corpus Act, those two hated relics of Whig insurgency in the late reign. The measures taken to suppress the rebellion and the money supplied for that purpose by

LITTLE ROCK PUBLIC LIBRARY

Parliament furnished him with a large increase in his Army. Eight new regiments of cavalry and twelve of infantry were formed. The whole Tangier garrison was now at home. In the emergency many Catholics had been given commissions and commands. The King was determined to retain them, and to use them and other Catholic officers in the raising of the new regiments. He wished to see the Catholic peers resume their functions in the House of Lords. Halifax, as Lord President of the Council, resisted these departures and cited the statutes which they violated. Lord Keeper North warned his master against such courses. "Although the Duke of Monmouth was gone, yet there was a Prince of Orange on the other side of the water."[1] Halifax was removed not only from the Presidency of the Council, but from his other offices and from the Privy Council altogether; and when soon North died, Chief Justice Jeffreys, furious champion of the royal prerogative, fresh from the Bloody Assize, became Lord Chancellor in his stead. Sunderland later in the year added the vacant office of Lord President to that of Secretary of State, and became henceforward James's chief Minister.

Parliament met for its second session on November 9, and the King laid his immediate purpose before the Members. The lessons of the late rebellions showed, he declared with admitted reason, the uselessness of the militia. A strong standing army was indispensable to the peace and order of the realm, and Catholic officers were needed to maintain its efficiency. He had appointed such officers during the troubles; he would not dismiss them on the morrow of their faithful services. These two demands shook that friendly Parliament to its foundations. It was deeply and predominantly imbued with the Cavalier spirit. Its most hideous nightmare was a standing army; its dearest treasure the Established Church. Parliament was thus assaulted in both its secular and religious functions. Fear and perplexity disturbed all Members, and beneath their agitation anger smouldered.

Yet no one could accuse either House of turbulence or

1 R. North, *Lives of the Norths*, ii, 154.

precipitancy. The old loyalties, revived by recent dangers, still inspired the Tory nobles and country gentlemen. They disputed the failure of the militia, but they offered nevertheless £700,000 for the increase of the Army. Sir Winston in one of his last public appearances made a hearty appeal for such a grant. The House of Commons was even disposed to condone the breach of the Test Act committed by the Catholic officers and to remit their penalties. With profuse expressions of devotion, they asked only for reassurance that Acts of Parliament would not be permanently set aside by the prerogative, and for kind words about the security of their religion. The King answered their address sternly, and the Commons proceeded to consider the royal speech in detail. But even now when John Coke, Treasurer of the Queen Dowager's household, a man known for his loyalty, exclaimed, "We are all Englishmen and are not to be frighted out of our duty by a few high words," they clapped him in the Tower for his impropriety.

It was, indeed, the Upper House that renewed the solemn argument. They too sought to reopen debate on the King's speech, and here Devonshire, the hardy Whig; Halifax, the renowned ex-Minister; Bridgwater and Nottingham, actually members of the Privy Council; and, above all, Henry Compton, Bishop of London, asserted the rights of the nation. A day was fixed for the rediscussion of the Address, and the judges were invited to pronounce upon the lawfulness of the King's proceedings. James had not yet packed the Bench with his partisans. He saw plainly that the declaration which must now be expected from the judges and the House of Lords would constitute a massive obstacle to that very dispensing power upon which he intended to rely for the relief and preferment of the Catholics. He therefore, on November 20, suddenly appeared in the House of Lords, summoned the Commons to the Bar, and prorogued Parliament. It never met again while he was King.

Since Sedgemoor Churchill had watched impassively the King's proceedings. His position in the royal household precluded him from taking part in the debates of the Upper

House, in which he was but a newcomer. When the Duke of Albemarle had refused to serve under the discredited Feversham in the Army, Churchill had taken the vacant post. It was not until the trial of Lord Delamere in January 1686 for complicity in Monmouth's rebellion that he was compelled to set himself publicly in opposition to his master and benefactor. The King named Judge Jeffreys Lord High Steward, and Jeffreys appointed thirty peers as Triers. "All the thirty," writes Macaulay,[1]

> were in politics vehemently opposed to the prisoner. Fifteen of them were colonels of regiments, and might be removed from their lucrative commands at the pleasure of the King. . . . Every Trier, beginning from the lowest, had to rise separately and to give in his verdict, on his honour, before a great concourse. That verdict, accompanied by his name, would go to every part of the world, and would live in history.

Jeffreys, of course, acted like a prosecuting attorney rather than a judge. The chief witness for the Crown was a professional informer; but Delamere was certainly a dangerous Whig. The King took his seat in the House of Lords and glowered upon the scene. The Triers withdrew and consulted together for about half an hour. It fell to Churchill, as junior Baron among them, to speak first. He stood up, uncovered, and laying his hand upon his breast, answered, "Not guilty, upon my honour!"[2] The whole thirty peers followed him in acquittal. The King did not conceal his annoyance. The failure of the Crown to convict Delamere and the public relief which followed was the end of the vengeance for Monmouth's rebellion.

Freeing himself from Parliamentary opposition by repeated prorogations, King James proceeded throughout 1686 with the relief of his fellow-religionists. First he desired to dispense with the Test against Catholics in the Army. He consulted his judges on the means of achieving this. "Can I," he asked Judge Jones, who had accompanied Jeffreys on his campaign after Sedgemoor, "find twelve judges who will uphold my power to dispense with the laws?" "Your

[1] *History*, ii, 38.   [2] *State Trials*, ii, 593.

Majesty may find twelve judges to your mind, but hardly twelve lawyers." However, after various dismissals and appointments the Bench was packed, and a test case (the Colonel Hales case) arranged. The dispensing power was upheld by the court. Armed with this, James in May granted a dispensation to the curate of Putney, although he had become a Catholic, to continue in his benefice. At the same time Roman Catholic peers were admitted into the Privy Council. In January 1686 he set up an Ecclesiastical Commission, an instrument declared illegal by the Long Parliament, whose main function was to prevent Anglicans from preaching against Catholics. Bishop Compton had already been dismissed from the Privy Council. He was now suspended from his functions as Bishop of London.

By the end of the year James had driven away many of his most faithful friends and disquieted everybody. Halifax, who had saved him from the Exclusion Bill, was brooding in the country. Danby, only liberated from the Tower in 1684, had perforce abandoned his dream of Church and King. He saw it could never be realized with a Papist sovereign. Albemarle, son of the General Monk who had made the Restoration, had quitted the royal service in dudgeon. Bishop Compton, whose father, the Earl of Northampton, had fallen in the Civil War, who had himself been an officer of the Life Guards, was in strident opposition. The loyal Parliament which had rallied to James against Monmouth and Argyll could be brought together no more without the certainty of quarrel. Its lords and squires sat sullen and anxious in their homes amid their tenantry. The Church, the bulwark of Legitimacy, seethed with suppressed alarms, and only the powerful influence of Rochester upon the bishops and clergy prevented a vehement outburst. Soon the two Hydes, both Rochester and Clarendon, were to be chased from the King's side.

In those days the King was the actual head of the executive Government; he chose his own Ministers and settled his own policy. There was no recognized right of opposition to the Government. James had now made it clear that he would only be advised by Ministers who whole-heartedly accepted his view. If statesmen could not see their way to serve the King as he wished to be served, they had no expectation of ever being called again to public service. Indeed, the distinction was very nice between opposition and treason. What, then, was to be done? It was plain that the King, with all the downright resolution of his nature, was actively and of set purpose subverting the faith and Constitution of the country, contrary to all he had promised and to its inflexible resolve. For a space many endured in silence. The Whigs, though outraged, were in eclipse. The Tories, almost equally distressed, were wrapped up in the Church of England. One of the cardinal doctrines of that Church since the Restoration had been non-resistance to the royal power. With infinite imprudence the King wore away this security.

While, during the whole of 1686 and 1687, James held Parliament in abeyance, and used his dispensing power to introduce Roman Catholics into the various high offices, military and civil, Whigs and Tories drew closer together. The glaring differences which had sundered them in the last reign faded before their growing common peril. James could not fail to see that he was uniting the party that had challenged his brother and the party which had rallied so ardently to his brother's defence. He felt himself in presence of the silent hostility of all those forces which had brought about the Restoration and on which his own throne was based. He now embarked upon a political manœuvre which was at once audacious, crafty, and miscalculated. Hitherto he had striven only to relieve his Catholic subjects. He would now bid for the aid of the Dissenters, who lay equally under the ban of penal laws. He would unite the flanks of politics against the centre, and lead the old Roman Catholic nobility and gentry to make common cause with Puritans and Roundheads. All those who suffered for their faith through the hard laws demanded by the majority of the nation should band themselves together behind him in the name of religious toleration. The chapels and conventicles should find in him their champion against the Established Church. If Whigs

231

and Tories were combined, he would match them by a coalition of Papists and Nonconformists under the armed power of the Crown. Nay, he would not reject even the dim, stubborn masses who had swarmed to Monmouth's standards in the West, or had awaited him elsewhere, whose faith was the very antithesis of his own, and whose fathers had cut off his father's head. With these at his back, he would teach the Church of England, the Cavaliers, and those froward Whigs their duty. In William Penn, the Quaker courtier, influential in both this and the former reign, he found a powerful, skilful agent. Here, then, was the King of England breaking down the natural pillars of his throne and seeking to shore it up with novel, ill-assorted, inadequate props.

This strange departure produced its reaction upon foreign policy. James, although anxious for French money, was by no means disposed to be the vassal of the French King. He admired and wished to imitate the French systems of government both in Church and State, but he was resentful of any slur upon the independence of his realm. During 1685 and 1686 Louis XIV found serious cause for anxiety in the attitude of his royal brother. Although James enthusiastically hailed the revocation of the Edict of Nantes, he had protested against the persecution loosed upon the small principality of Orange, from which William had sprung. The prompt and loyal, if interested, assistance which William had rendered during Monmouth's rebellion had created a friendly feeling between the English and Dutch Courts. A cordial correspondence was maintained between James and his son-in-law. Now that he was relying upon the Nonconformists at home James was inclined to unite himself, for his supreme purpose of making England Catholic, with the champion of the Protestant faith abroad. William Penn was sent to Holland to help persuade the Prince of Orange to agree to a plan whereby England would support the Dutch against the French, if William of Orange would help James in carrying a Declaration of Indulgence for English Catholics and Dissenters.

These were the politics of paradox. They broke upon the

rock of William's farsighted self-interest. His connexions
with England were strengthened and multiplied every day.
His chest was filled with complaining letters from Whig and
Tory magnates. He knew what an improvident exchange
James was making in driving away the old traditional friends
of the English monarchy, and seeking in their stead to found
himself upon elements saturated with a conception of limited
monarchy then deemed republicanism. He would not try to
build upon a threatened authority. Vital to the Protestant
cause as was the alliance with England, William would not
seek it through such doubtful agency. He looked behind
the gimcrack politics of the King to the rising anger of the
nation, and kept the path clear for his own ambitions. He
therefore declined to support or approve the Declaration of
Indulgence.

William was already in close touch with Halifax. The
Great Trimmer felt intensely the new list of the ship, and
leaned all the weight of his sagacity and influence to counter
it. "I do not find the measures now taken." he wrote in a
letter of July 20, 1686,

> are such as would encourage a man to be a gamester, after he hath
> been turned out for a Wrangler; except one could divest oneself
> of those foolish things called principles, which I find the meaner
> sort of man uses like their clothes and make them willing to the
> fashion whatever it is; which is a pitch of understanding I am
> not yet come up to, and consequently am too dull to meddle with
> so nimble a trade as those whose politics grow of late in the world
> [a reference to Sunderland]. I am too slow a beast to keep pace
> with them now that they are upon the gallop. The four new
> Privy Councillors [all Catholics], the Commission of Supremacy
> [the Ecclesiastical Commission] and several other things set up
> included in them give a pretty fair prospect of what is reasonable
> to be expected.[1]

Thus Halifax!

In January 1687 came the fall of the Hydes. For a long
time both had been unhappy in their offices. Clarendon in
Ireland had been overawed by Tyrconnel; Rochester at

---

[1] Foxcroft, *Halifax*, i, 466.

Whitehall by Sunderland. In June 1686 Rochester had tried to wean James back to moderation through the influence of Catharine Sedley, the Duke of York's Protestant mistress in former days. For a space Catharine's influence seemed strong. She was created Countess of Dorchester. But the exertions of the King's confessor, and the just indignation of the Queen, soon recalled James to orthodox faith and marital propriety. Rochester bore the blame alike of the intrigue and of its failure. The reader will remember Hyde's attempts in 1681 to persuade James to conform to Protestantism. Now the rôles and objects were reversed. From October 1686 onwards James had been trying to convert his younger brother-in-law to the Roman faith. Rochester was very fond of office and made much money out of it. But at length he realized that the alternative before him was to quit the Treasurership or become a Catholic. Forthwith he set himself to make his case before the Anglican Church, so that all could see a public ground of quarrel. He consented to hear priestly arguments for his conversion to Rome, and after duly considering them announced that he was only the more confirmed in the Protestant faith. Indeed, he had been for some time so perturbed by the danger to Protestantism in Europe that, High Churchman as he was, he thought, like Halifax, that all the Protestant sects should now draw together for common defence.

Sunderland had expressed to the King his fears that Rochester would let himself be converted in order to cling to his office. The King knew better: but in the upshot he was no less vexed at Rochester's obduracy as a Protestant than pleased at getting rid of him as a Minister. On January 7, 1687, Rochester was dismissed from the Treasury, and three days later Clarendon in Ireland was replaced by Tyrconnel. The friend of the Hydes, Queensberry, had already been recalled from his Commissionership in Scotland, and was superseded by two Catholics, Perth and Melfort, of whom more later. These changes marked another definite stage in the reign of James II. The prorogation of Parliament at the end of 1685 had been the beginning of Cavalier and Anglican dis-

LITTLE ROCK PUBLIC LIBRARY

content against the Crown. With the dismissal of Rochester began the revolutionary conspiracy.

Meanwhile James was raising and preparing his army. Charles II's forces of about seven thousand men had cost £280,000 a year. Already James was spending £600,000 upon the upkeep of more than twenty thousand men. Three troops of Life Guards,[1] the Blues, ten regiments of horse or dragoons, two of foot-guards, and fifteen of the line, besides garrison troops, were under arms by February 1686. Every summer a great camp was formed at Hounslow to impress the Londoners. In August 1685 this contained about ten thousand men. A year later Feversham could assemble fifteen thousand men and twenty-eight guns. The King went often to the camp, seeking to make himself popular with the officers and all ranks. He had Mass celebrated in a wooden chapel borne on wheels and placed in the centre of the camp between the horse and foot. He watched the drill of the troops and dined with Feversham, Churchill, and other generals. He continued his infusion of Catholic officers and Irish recruits. He had a parson, Johnson, pilloried and whipped from Newgate to Tyburn for a seditious pamphlet addressed to Protestant soldiers. He comforted himself with the aspect of this formidable army, the like of which had not been seen since Cromwell, and against which nothing could be matched in England. He increasingly promoted Catholics to key posts. Arabella's son, the Duke of Berwick, now eighteen years old, was made governor of Portsmouth; and Catholics commanded at both Hull and Dover. At midsummer 1688 a Catholic admiral ruled the Channel Fleet.

Soon after the dismissal of the Hydes William sent over to England a trusted envoy. Dykevelt, a Dutchman of the highest character and standing, arrived in London partly to exhibit the Prince of Orange as pleading with James to moderate his measures, and partly to enter into communication with the Opposition leaders. Dykevelt warned James almost as an ultimatum that neither William nor Mary, should they succeed to the Crown, would maintain any of his

---

[1] Each equal almost to a regiment.

Romanizing policy. Even if the Test Act were repealed they would re-enact it, and would reign in association with the Church of England and the Parliamentary system. The King, in his irritation at this interference in his affairs, may have overlooked the fact that the Prince of Orange was at the same time presenting a rival political programme to his subjects. Dykevelt saw all the statesmen opposed to the Court; he received their views and assurances, and at the same time made it clear that they could count upon William and Mary for support in their struggle and protection in their distress.

For some months past the King and the Catholic party had been toying with a plan for declaring Princess Anne next in succession to the Crown, on condition that she would turn Catholic. Such designs, if they were ever seriously intended, or their mere rumour, threw the Cockpit into the most violent internal commotion. Here the Protestant circle had become close and tight. Princess Anne was convulsed with fear and anger at the suggestion that her faith would be tampered with, and roused herself quite sincerely to a mood of martyrdom. Taught and fortified by Bishop Compton, dwelling in intense intimacy with her beloved Sarah, guided through her as well as directly by John Churchill, she now embarked with her husband upon real antagonism to her father.

As early as December 29, 1686, before Dykevelt's arrival, she had written to her sister Mary about her friend Lord Churchill. "I believe," she said, "that he will always obey the King in all things that are consistent with religion—yet rather than change that, I daresay he will lose all his places and all that he has." In February she sought, no doubt upon the advice of the Churchills, permission to visit her sister at The Hague. Barillon was much concerned at this suggestion, the objections to which he readily perceived. "The Princess Anne has strongly pressed the King to allow her to go, but he has bluntly refused!" On March 14 he reports that Anne

has been worked up with the plan of going to Holland under the pretext of meeting her sister. Once she was there she would have been prevented from coming back and the Protestant party would have been fortified by the union of these two princesses, the lawful heirs to the Crown, who could have made declarations and protestations against the whole Catholic movement. King James was not without suspicion that Churchill had his share in proposing such a journey and that his wife, the Princess Anne's favourite, had awakened her ambition.[1]

Even Rochester and his wife were suspected of being favourable. "There could be no doubt that Dykevelt had encouraged the Protestant cabals." "The Bishop of Wells had preached against the Government in Anne's presence." And again on April 3: "Princess Anne openly shows her zeal for the Protestant religion and has been *incognita* to various churches to hear popular preachers. The King still hopes to convert her to Catholicism."

A letter of Anne's to her sister Mary reveals her position with startling clarity. Dalrymple has printed it in an abridged and mutilated form from the Carte manuscripts. He omits three interesting passages and misdates it by a year, thereby misleading the whole string of historians who have transcribed him unquestioningly. The Spencer Papers contain a copy which, since it illuminates the position of Anne and the Churchills, deserves to be printed here, for the first time, in its integrity.[2]

YE COCKPIT
March 13th [1687]

This letter going by sure hands I will now venture to write my mind very freely to you, and in the first place must tell you, that the satisfaction I proposed to myself of seeing you this spring has been denied me, which has been no small trouble to me as you may easily imagine: and the disappointment has been the greater because the King gave me leave when I first asked it; for the night I came from Richmond, I desired him to give the Prince leave to go into Denmark, and me to go into Holland, which he granted immediately without any difficulty, but in a few days after, he told me I must not go. So that 'tis plain he has spoke of it to some body that persuaded him against it, and 'tis as certain that that body was Lord Sunderland, for the King trusts him with everything;

---

[1] *Correspondance politique, Angleterre,* t. 161, f. 172.
[2] The passages omitted by Dalrymple are printed in italics.

*and he going on so fiercely for the interest of the Papists, is afraid
you should be told a true character of him and this I really believe
is the reason why I was refus'd coming to you, tho' may be, he
and the Priests together give other reasons to the King therefore
since I am not to see my dear Sister. . . .*

You may remember I have once before ventured to tell you,
that I thought Lord Sunderland a very ill man, and I am more
confirmed every day in that opinion. Everybody knows how often
this man turned backwards and forwards in the late King's time;
and now, to complete all his virtues, he is working with all his
might to bring in Popery. He is perpetually with the priests, and
stirs up the King to do things faster than I believe he would
of himself. Things are come to that pass now, that, if they go
on so much longer, I believe in a little while, no Protestant will
be able to live here.

The King has never said a word to me about religion since the
time I told you of; but I expect it every minute, and am resolved
to undergo anything rather than change my religion. Nay, if it
should come to such extremities, I will chuse to live on alms
rather than change.

This worthy Lord does not go publicly to mass, but hears it
privately at a priest's chamber, and never lets anybody be there,
but a servant of his.

His lady too, is as extraordinary in her kind; for she is a flattering, dissembling, false woman; but she has so fawning and
endearing a way, that she will deceive any body at first, and it is
not possible to find out all her ways in a little time. She cares
not at what rate she lives, but never pays any body. She will
cheat, though it be for a little. Then she has had her gallants,
though may be not so many as some ladies here; and with all
these good qualities she is a constant church woman; so that to
outward appearance one would take her for a saint, and to hear
her talk, you would think she was a very good Protestant; but
she is as much one as the other; for it is certain that her Lord
does nothing without her.

*By what I have said you may judge what good hands the King
and Kingdom are in, and what an uneasy thing it is to all good
honest people, that they must seem to live civilly with this Lord
and his Lady. I had not your letter by Mr Dykevelt till last week,
but I have never ventured to speak to him, because I am not used
to speak to people about business and this Lord is so much upon
the watch that I am afraid of him. So I have desired Lord*

Churchill (who is one that I can trust, and I am sure is a very honest man and a good Protestant) to speak to Mr Dykevelt for me, to know what it is he has to say to me, and by the next opportunity I will answer it, for one dares not write anything by the post!

One thing there is, which I forgot to tell you, about this noble Lord [Sunderland] which is, that it is thought, if every thing does not go as he would have it, that he will pick a quarrel with the court, and so retire, and by that means it is possible he will think he makes his court to you.[1]

There is one thing about yourself which I cannot help giving my opinion in, which is, that if the King should desire you and the Prince of Orange to come over to make him a visit, I think it would be better (if you can make any handsome excuse) not to do it; for though I dare swear the King could have no thought against either of you, yet since people can say one thing, and do another, one cannot help being afraid; if either of you should come, I should be very glad to see you; but really if you or the Prince should come, I should be frightened out of my wits for fear any harm should happen to either of you!

Pray don't let any body see this, nor don't speak of it: pray let me desire you not to take notice of what I have said to any body except the Prince of Orange; for 'tis all treason that I have spoke, and the King commanded me not to say [to] any that I once thought of coming into Holland; and I fear if he should know that it was no secret, he would be angry with me, therefore as soon as you have read this, pray burn it: for I would not that anybody but the Prince of Orange; and yourself should know what I have said. When I have another opportunity 'tis possible that I may have more to say, but for this time having writ so much already, I hope you will forgive me for saying no more now, but that no tongue can ever express how much my heart is yours.

We can see plainly from this letter the deadly breach which had already opened between Anne and her father. Though she rejects, after raising it, the idea that James would be a party to assassination, she warns her sister of the risks which William would incur by paying a visit to the English Court. She believes Sunderland capable of any villainy. There is no doubt that, with her simple faith and courage, she would have let herself be led to death rather than to Rome. In

1 This prediction should not pass unnoticed as the story unfolds.

239

many humbler homes such fears and resolves now dominated daily life.

At Anne's desire Churchill held his conversation on her behalf with Dykevelt. He is not responsible for her vapourings to her sister, but the letter which he wrote to William eight days after the envoy's departure represented, even at this early date, a final decision. It could not well have been expressed in plainer terms.

May 17, 1687

The Princess of Denmark having ordered me to discourse with Monsieur Dykevelt, and to let him know her resolutions, so that he might let your highness and the princess her sister know that she was resolved, by the assistance of God, to suffer all extremities, even to death itself, rather than be brought to change her religion, I thought it my duty to your highness and the princess royal, by this opportunity of Monsieur Dykevelt, to give you assurances under my own hand, that my places and the King's favour I set at nought, in comparison of being true to my religion. In all things but this the King may command me; and I call God to witness, that even with joy I should expose my life for his service, so sensible am I of his favours. I know the troubling you, sir, with thus much of myself, I being of so little use to your highness, is very impertinent, but I think it may be a great ease to your highness and the princess to be satisfied that the Princess of Denmark is safe in the trusting of me; I being resolved, although I cannot live the life of a saint, if there be ever occasion for it, to show the resolution of a martyr.

Dykevelt received similar assurances from Danby, Nottingham, Halifax, Devonshire, Russell, and others. He saw at the same time that there was no danger of the King spoiling William's chances by mending his ways. He returned to The Hague and told his many tales to William. The future Bishop Burnet, once intimate in the councils of the English Court, was already there, independently confirming Dykevelt's accounts. From this time forward our domestic tension was definitely connected with William of Orange, and he, in fact, became the head of the revolution plot.

CHAPTER XIV

THE NATIONAL COUNTER-PLOT

(1687–88)

IN the autumn of 1687 the King made a royal progress in the West of England. Churchill accompanied him. They traversed many of the districts which two years before had been aflame for Monmouth. But the resolve of the King to extend liberty of conscience to the Nonconformists, although it was but a help for his Catholic policy, had raised hopes which for the moment almost effaced the memories of the Bloody Assize. The Catholic King received a passable welcome from the ultra-Protestants whose relations he had lately slaughtered or sold into slavery. 'Liberty of conscience' and the removal of the penal laws were war-cries which drowned even the screams and lamentations of the hideous yesterday. James felt that, with his Army dominated by Irish soldiers and Catholic officers and allied to the Dissenting masses of the Cromwellian tradition, he could afford to brave the wrath of the old, devoted friends of his house, of his line, of his person. Vain hope! Frightful miscalculation! At the best a desperate enterprise! At the least the lists were set for a destructive civil war. But was it not his duty, if need be, to tear his realm to pieces for his soul's salvation and the glory of God? Thus this melancholy zealot persevered along the road to his own ruin.

On this same progress in the West the King touched about five thousand people for the King's Evil, and at Winchester was attended in the ceremony by Catholic priests. The anonymous author of *The Lives of the Two Illustrious Generals* reports at length the conversation between Churchill and the King on this occasion. This book is our only authority, but it is the earliest of all Churchill's biographies and has been accepted by most historians. The colloquy has obviously been embroidered; it was almost certainly not invented.

In the Deanery garden at Winchester before dinner the King asked Churchill what people thought "about the method I have taken of performing the ceremony of touching in their churches." "Why, truly," he replied, "they show very little liking to it; and it is the general voice of your people that your Majesty is paving the way for the introduction of Popery." "How!" exclaimed the King, in anger. "Have I not given them my royal word, and will they not believe their King? I have given liberty of conscience to others; I was always of the opinion that toleration was necessary for all Christian people, and most certainly I will not be abridged of that liberty myself, nor suffer those of my own religion to be deprived of paying their devotions to God in their own way." "What I spoke, sir," said Churchill, "proceeded purely from my zeal for your Majesty's service, which I prefer above all things next to that of God, and I humbly beseech your Majesty to believe no subject in all your three kingdoms would venture further than I would to purchase your favour and good liking; but I have been bred a Protestant, and intend to live and die in that communion; above nine parts in ten of the whole people are of the same persuasion, and I fear (which excess of duty makes me say) from the genius of the English nation, and their natural aversion to the Roman Catholic worship, some consequences which I dare not so much as name, and which it creates in me a horror to think of." The King listened attentively to what, from anyone else, he would have warmly resented, and then said deliberately, "I tell you, Churchill, I will exercise my own religion in such a manner as I shall think fitting. I will show favour to my Catholic subjects, and be a common father to all my Protestants of what religion soever: but I am to remember that I am King, and to be obeyed by them. As for the consequences, I shall leave them to Providence, and make use of the power God has put in my hands to prevent anything that shall be injurious to my honour, or derogatory to the duty that is owing to me." The King then turned away with a stern look and would speak to Churchill no more that night. "He went to dinner, during which his discourse to the Dean of Winchester, Dr Maggot, who stood next to his chair, was altogether about Passive Obedience. I myself," says the author, "was a stander by and heard it; without knowing the occasion of it at that time, till the Lord Churchill told me what words had happened between the King and him."[1]

The provocations of the royal policy constantly increased. The publication of Dryden's *The Hind and the Panther* offers their poetical justification. In April 1687 the King, dispensing with the law by his prerogative, issued his first Declaration of Indulgence. The spring saw his attempt to force a Catholic President upon Magdalen College, Oxford, and the expulsion of the Fellows for their resistance. In July James planned the public reception of the Papal nuncio, d'Adda. The Duke of Somerset when commanded to conduct the ceremonial objected on the ground that the recognition of Papal officials had been declared illegal at the Reformation. "I am above the law," said James. "Your Majesty is so," was the reply, "but I am not." He was at once dismissed from all his offices.

The King had, in modern parlance and now familiar style, set up his political platform. The second step was to create a party machine, and the third to secure by its agency a Parliament with a mandate for the repeal of the Tests. The narrow franchise could be manipulated to a very large extent by the Lord-Lieutenants of counties, by the magistrates, and in the towns and cities by the corporations. Upon these, therefore, the royal energies were now directed. The Lord-Lieutenants, including many of the greatest territorial magnates, who refused to help pack a favourable Parliament, were dismissed, and Catholics or faithful nominees of the Court installed in their place. The municipal corporations and the benches of magistrates were drastically remodelled so as to secure the fullest representation, or even the preponderance,

1 *The Lives of the Two Illustrious Generals*, pp. 19–21. The conversation has been changed from reported into direct speech.

of Papists and Dissenters. The Government tried to extort from all candidates a pledge to vote for the King's policy.

These measures implied a complete political and social transformation. The nobility and the country gentlemen were outraged by being either turned out of their local dignitaries or made to receive representatives of the hitherto depressed classes as colleagues. The quarter-sessions and the municipal corporations were the only forms of local government which the people knew. The Lord-Lieutenants were the visible executive instruments of the royal authority. In every one of these bodies and functions the ferment and irritation of change grew. The process of setting Papists and Dissenters over, or in place of, Anglicans and Cavaliers must rupture and recast the whole social structure of English life. The purpose, character, and scope of these measures were profoundly comprehended in that incredibly rigid society from the proudest, wealthiest nobles down to the mass of the common people in town and village. The simples, like the gentles, feared the Pope, hated the French, and pitied the Huguenot refugees. They too, though voteless, counted. Their superiors could not be insensible to an atmosphere of ardour and goodwill around them. The spirit of the people found its own paths of influence. Psychic forces do not require the ballot-box. A recent Catholic writer[1] has portrayed the opposition to James as the resistance of the rich and powerful. This is true. It was successful because the rich and powerful championed the causes and prejudices which the masses espoused, but without superior leadership were unable to defend.

The six English and Scots regiments in Dutch pay and service which had been sent over to resist Monmouth had all returned to Holland. James and his Ministers became apprehensive lest this fine body of men should some day pay them another and less friendly visit. For some months in 1687 James and Louis were trying to arrange for the transfer of these regiments from the Dutch service to the French. Churchill seems to have used all his personal influence—such

1 Mr Hilaire Belloc, *James II* (1928).

as it then was—with James to prevent their departure from Holland, and to obtain the command of them in Holland for himself. Sunderland told Barillon on November 3, 1687:

> I believe this proposal will be accepted and that it would have been done already had not Lord Churchill taken great trouble for a long time to represent to His Majesty how advantageous it would be to him to have a body of his subjects maintained in Holland. Lord Churchill's aim was to be in command of this force. But he will find himself disappointed as this regiment [*sic*] is already destined for the Duke of Berwick, and in any case a Catholic commander would have been appointed, an officer of experience with the title of Colonel. . . .[1]

Churchill's desire for the appointment, the significance of which is apparent, was, as Sunderland foresaw, frustrated. But the troops stayed in Holland. William and the States-General, for reasons becoming increasingly obvious, refused point-blank to let them go. An acute tension arose between the two Governments. Their fundamental differences were exposed, and for the first time war was felt to be in the air.

Among the notables who now fell under the royal displeasure was Lord Scarsdale, the Lord-Lieutenant of Derbyshire. As First Gentleman-in-Waiting to Prince George of Denmark, he was one of the Cockpit group. He refused to obey the King's orders to rig the impending election, and the Prince and Princess sent Churchill to ask the King what he wished them to do in the matter. James preferred not to give them any instructions. "I leave the decision," he said, "to your sense of duty." On this they did nothing, and the King was then prevailed upon by his Ministers to order them to dismiss Scarsdale. They refused to do so. The Churchills went to the country to avoid becoming embroiled in so delicate a dispute among their superiors, and being held responsible for the conduct of Princess Anne, who ruled her husband as completely as she herself was guided by Sarah. Barillon notes upon this incident that Lord Churchill seemed to be losing favour every day. He added

[1] *Correspondance politique, Angleterre*, t. 162, ff. 267 verso, 268.

that Churchill had hoped to get the command of the regiment which was to be maintained—and here his notes were surely only partly correct—*by the French*,[1] as he had thought "that employment would be very useful," besides believing that by it he "would get out of the constant difficulties he was in at home." Churchill, he said, had not been informed of the definite agreement about the regiment.[2]

An order of the Duke of Berwick that thirty Irish Catholics should be enlisted in the 8th Regiment of the Line provoked mutinous complaint. The Lieutenant-Colonel and five captains protested. They declared that they had raised the regiment at their own charges to defend the Crown in time of danger. They had no difficulty in maintaining its strength with English recruits. They threatened to lay down their commissions if these "strangers" were forced upon them. Tried by a council of war, they were cashiered. Clarke's *Life of King James II* says that "Churchill moved the court to sentence the six officers to death." Macaulay could not attempt to make his readers swallow this. Such a punishment was, in any case, beyond the competence of a court-martial in time of peace. Had he endorsed the story he would have been exposed at once. He therefore decided, after his usual method, to make it serve as a proof of his impartiality and love of truth, and thereby to lay the foundations of some more damaging and less easily disprovable libel later on. In recording this story he describes it as "one of the thousand fictions invented at Saint-Germains for the purpose of blackening a character which was black enough without such daubing." This once more reveals his principle: in blackening this man there must be no daubing. The purpose was meritorious, but the execution must be artistic.

The defenders of James's conduct are concerned to exaggerate the number of English Catholics. It is even claimed that one-eighth of the population still adhered, in spite of generations of persecutions, to the Old Faith. Accord-

[1] Author's italics.
[2] *Correspondance politique, Angleterre*, t. 162, ff. 335 *seq.*

ing to a return of 1689, there were then only 13,856 Catholics in the whole country, or less than one in four hundred of the people.[1] The royal attempt to make a remarkable political spectacle of these few thousands of Papists, advanced to the headship of local and national affairs, even though supported by the Dissenters, was bound to range all the dominant national forces, incomparably stronger, against the Crown. The Pope, in accordance with the policy of the Holy See, which the next chapter will explain, deprecated James's excessive zeal, and his legate in England urged caution and prudence. The old Catholic families in England, apart from individuals advanced to high office, were, as Ailesbury's *Memoirs* show, deeply apprehensive of the headlong adventure upon which the King was launching them. They felt this sudden disproportionate favour was far from being in their true interests, and would only bring upon them the wrath and frightful passions which were being raised all about them. Still the King hardened his heart and strengthened his Army.

The most continuous chronicle of these days is found in Barillon's despatches to Louis XIV.[2] The experienced Ambassador who had long lain in the centre of fashion and affairs and had been confidant and paymaster of the King, the Court, and most of the leading politicians, had unmatched opportunities of knowing and judging the British scene. As early as December 24, 1685, he reports that James is expected to abandon the Episcopal for the Nonconformist party. On January 7 he conveys to Louis James's reaction upon the revocation of the Edict of Nantes. "The King of England realizes to his core that nothing is so great or so salutary as the task which your Majesty has undertaken." On the 14th, "The King has prorogued Parliament and hopes to dissolve it and obtain a Parliament of Nonconformists." On the 21st he writes of the Catharine Sedley intrigue, "She has been given a title and Duchess of Portsmouth's appointments. In London this is taken as anti-Catholic demonstration."

1 Dalrymple, ii, 2, 41–42.
2 *Correspondance politique, Angleterre*, t. 161–165, *passim*.

By the 25th the King has been brought back to the fold. "The King," says the Ambassador, "promises he will not see Sedley again. He loves his wife. *Elle est Italienne et fort glorieuse!*" On the 28th he observes, "Liberty of conscience can only be established by a Nonconformist Parliament. In conjunction with this an Irish army will play its part. It is being filled with Catholic officers." On February 19, "Permission has been given for Catholic books to be printed. The King is holding to his course in spite of a Court cabal which urges him to summon Parliament." On March 25:

> The King has spoken to me with great confidence of all his designs which are directed principally to the advantage of the Catholic religion which he believes your Majesty has equally at heart, having worked with so much success for the destruction of heresy in France.

"And," he adds, "The Catholic party is on top." May 27: "The troops are in camp at Hounslow." June 21: James has told him that things are not going as well as he hoped. There is a cabal against him. Murray, the Scottish Commissioner, has found proofs of a secret correspondence between the Prince of Orange and the Scots. June 24: "The King is anxious to punish anti-Catholic preachers and for this purpose has set up an Ecclesiastical Commission." August 12: "The Bishop of London refuses to recognize this jurisdiction." On September 13, "It is decided not to call Parliament until the following year." October 13: "James has sent priests to Jersey and Guernsey to convert the Protestants." December 23: "Rochester prefers to quit the Treasury rather than become a Catholic." December 30: "The King has told the Ambassador that the Treasurer must be a man in sympathy with his own ideals, and as Rochester was not, the Treasury would be put in commission." James tells the Ambassador that "Rochester favoured Calvinists." But he reports on January 13, 1687, that " Rochester's dismissal causes great consternation at Court: all fear for their posts." In February comes his first mention of Dykevelt's visit. Dykevelt is expected to concert *avec les Milords Pro-*

LITTLE ROCK PUBLIC LIBRARY

testants. It would be difficult to rival this continuous selection of significant events. Well may Charles James Fox call Barillon's letters "worth their weight in gold."

For many months, however, there was still parley. The parsons preached against Popery. Statesmen and divines exerted themselves by the dispersal of pamphlets throughout the country to offset James's attempt to rally the Nonconformists. Halifax issued his cogent *Letter to a Dissenter.* Burnet wrote from The Hague appealing to the Anglicans to stand steadfastly against the King's policy, despite their doctrine of non-resistance; and Fagel, the Dutch greffier,[1] sent a letter, widely circulated in England, which was understood to represent the similar sentiments of William of Orange.

Churchill had, as we have seen, entered fully into all the movements of protest against the royal policy. In December 1686 Anne had written to Mary assuring her of the strong Anglicanism of the Churchills. Her letter, already noticed, in the spring of 1687 had followed. In March Churchill had conversed with Dykevelt. In May he wrote to William. In September took place his remarkable conversation with James at Winchester. In November he tried to get the command of the English regiments in the Dutch service, and so escape from the net which was closing round him at home. In December he supported and animated Anne in her endeavour to retain in her service Lord Scarsdale despite his refusal, as Lord-Lieutenant of Derbyshire, to obey James's orders. Finally, in January 1688 Churchill told James directly that he would not himself support the repeal of the penal Tests. A contemporary letter of January 12 states, "Lord Churchill swears he will not do what the King requires of him."[2]

No man in all the stately company that represented the national character in these crucial days had made his opinion more plain, but James continued to rely on the intimacies and fidelities of twenty years of service on one hand and his benefactions on the other. He could not realize the truth that personal gratitude could never weigh in any great mind

1 A high Dutch office corresponding to our Clerk of Parliaments.
2 Johnstone's letters, *cit.* J. Mackintosh, *History of the Revolution,* pp. 197-198.

249

against the issues now presented to Englishmen. He knew Churchill loathed his policy, but fondly believed he loved his person more. At the crunch he was sure he could count on his influence, his diplomacy, and his sword. Meanwhile master and servant dwelt in all their old familiarity, and Churchill was constantly at the King's side in his bedroom, at his toilet, behind his chair at meals, and on horseback beside his carriage, just as he had been since he was a page.

How did this prolonged situation, with its many delicate, repugnant, and irreconcilable features, affect his inner mind? Was he distressed or was he indifferent about his personal relations with the King? On the surface he showed no trace of embarrassment. He possessed to a degree almost sublime the prosaic gift of common sense. His sure judgment and serene, dispassionate nature enabled him, amid the most baffling problems of interest and duty, to dwell inwardly and secretly at peace with his gravely taken decisions; and, of course, without further self-questionings to take in due season all measures necessary to render them effectual. The personalities which warm our hearts often cast much away from sentiment or compunction. Not so this man. He made up his mind with cold, humane sagacity, and a profound weighing of all the largest and smallest circumstances: and thenceforward he faced obloquy, if it were inevitable, as calmly as the ordinary chances of battle, after all had been done to prepare victory with the least loss of life. From the beginning of 1686 onward he was resolved to resist his master's designs. He saw in the Prince of Orange the agent who alone could bring in the indispensable armed power. He made his choice, if the worst should happen, to quit James and join William. He saw that the importance of his part in such a conflict would be measured by his influence over the Princess Anne and by his authority in the Army. If the hour of action should strike, he meant to use both potent factors to achieve, as smoothly and reasonably as possible, the public purpose and success of the course he had chosen.

In modern times such decisions would not be required.

An officer or a courtier could resign his employments, retire to the country, and await events or the process of public reaction to his sacrifices. But for Churchill to leave the Court, to resign his command in the Army, would not merely have meant exclusion from all forms of public service and from all share in the impending crisis. No one who had been so close to the sovereign could, while he was in the full flush of manly activity and acquainted with so many secrets, retire without incurring the gravest suspicions. Instead of dwelling at Holywell with his family, he would probably have found himself in the Tower. He could, no doubt, have attempted to leave the kingdom and follow the long string of refugees and exiles who gathered in the Netherlands. But a simple flight like this would have been only to abandon simultaneously his King and his country; at once to desert the cause of Protestantism and to leave the Princess Anne, who had hitherto followed his guidance and depended so much upon him, in complete isolation.

He had certainly made two definite attempts to quit the Court under conditions which would not have entirely divested him of power, and thus to end a personal connexion with James already become false and painful. If Princess Anne had been allowed to go to The Hague, as he had planned, he and Sarah would certainly have gone with her. If he had obtained command of the British troops in Holland he would have been at William's side and in a position to exert an influence upon events. These courses had been barred: and, apart from reducing himself to a cipher and destroying all his means of service to causes which profoundly stirred him, there was nothing left but to remain and face all the dangers and peculiar reproaches of his station. All he could give the King was the faithful declaration of his opinion, and this on many occasions he made abundantly clear. If James, knowing his mind, employed him, it was at his own risk.

It was remarkable, indeed, that the King still kept Churchill about him. He made it plain to all his intimates that those who sought his favour, or still more his friendship, must embrace his faith. Many of his personal attendants yielded to the glamour of the royal smile or the fear of the royal frown. Salisbury, Melfort, Lorne, and many others thought that office was well worth a Mass. And no one needed official employment more than Churchill. He had no spacious estates in which to dwell, he lived only in the Court, at the head of his regiment, or with the prince he served; but to all attempts upon his faith he remained obdurate. He watched with silent disgust Sunderland, with whom he had many relationships and was to have more, take the plunge. The chief Minister of England, with all his wealth and high birth, bare-headed and bare-footed, knelt in his shirt and knocked humbly at the door of the confessional. Churchill had only to imitate him to be the King's right arm, captain of his host, his long-cherished friend.

He never seems to have had the slightest trouble in rejecting such possibilities. Of course, he was a devout and lifelong Anglican Protestant. Even Macaulay is forced to admit that "he believed implicitly in the religion he had learned as a boy." But we doubt if his choice, as his apologists contend, was made only upon religious grounds. He had a political opinion too. He knew England, and measured with superior accuracy the force of the passions now rising throughout the land. All the great men whose friendship he enjoyed, Halifax, Shrewsbury, Rochester, were moving in the one direction. On that same course he had launched the Princess Anne. Never mind the army at Hounslow! There would—at the worst—be two opposite factions there, and beyond the seas there was the Prince of Orange with trustworthy troops. But suppose it was the French who landed, instead of the Dutch! Still, he had chosen the part he would play.

The phrases 'religious toleration' and 'liberty of conscience' command spontaneous approval in modern times. The penal laws against Catholics and Dissenters were harsh and bitter. To create an England in which all men could seek God as they pleased and dwell in peace with their fellows was indeed a noble aim for a King. But it was not the aim of King James the Second; he sought the conversion of

England to the Roman Catholic faith. The first step to that end was to win toleration for his Catholic subjects. As a make-weight only, he reluctantly but resolutely extended his programme to cover and enlist the Nonconformists. "The King," wrote Barillon, "desires intensely [*avoit fort envie*] that Catholics and Catholics alone should have freedom to practise their religion."[1] Once his first step had been achieved, no one could doubt that Catholic toleration would give place to Catholic ascendancy, and after Catholic ascendancy was securely established Catholic uniformity would have become the goal in England as in France. Everything recorded about James, from his earliest conversion to Rome, proves that he acknowledged no bounds, except those enforced by circumstances, either to his religious zeal or to the compulsions necessary to satisfy it. He admired and applauded the intolerance of Louis XIV; he rejoiced intensely at the revocation of the Edict of Nantes; he longed to use against the heresy in which his kingdom was sunk the secular terrors and torments which his brother sovereign could so happily apply.

Our ancestors saw, with the uncanny shrewdness which long, slow, increasing peril engenders, an endless vista of oppression and persecution, decked in a tinsel of fair-seeming toleration. They saw daily landing on their shores the miserable victims of Catholic 'toleration' as practised in France by the most powerful sovereign in the world. They knew the close sympathy and co-operation of the French and English Governments: they saw all that they cared for in this world and the next threatened, and if they failed to defend their rights and freedom, there might soon be no refuge open to them in any part of the globe. They therefore entered, not without many scruples and hesitations, but with inexorable resolve, upon the paths of conspiracy and rebellion.

If appeal is made to present-day opinion, the tribunal, while it acclaims 'religious toleration,' will at the same time inquire whether the conspiracy was only upon one side. Must the whole British nation submit, as the French people had been forced to do, to the religious convictions—whatever they

1 Letter dated April 19/29, 1686.

might be or might become—of their anointed King? Was
that King to be absolved from all reproach if night and day
he concerted his plans, marshalled his adherents, trained his
armies, in order to change the whole life, laws, and beliefs of
his people? Was he entitled to break the solemn promises
he had made, to practise every deceit and manœuvre which
served his purpose, to use all the pressures of force and favour
to compel obedience? Was he not guilty in his turn of conspiring against the people over whom he ruled? Was he not
in rebellion against all that was most sacred, most precious,
to the hearts of millions? Surely, then, it was a double
conspiracy that was afoot, and must now on both sides go
forward to an issue.

CHAPTER XV

DRAGONNADE

(1678–88)

URING the ten years which followed the Peace of Nimwegen Louis XIV reached the zenith of his power. England, rent by her domestic quarrels, had ceased to be a factor in European affairs. The Empire was equally paralysed for action in the West. Its whole resources were required to meet the Ottoman invasions. In the same period the Hungarian national movement produced fierce secondary revolts, and the Emperor and his generals could not turn their eyes from the east and from the south. The coalition which had imposed some check upon the aggressions of France in 1668 and 1678 had fallen to pieces. Louis, conscious of his dominating power, gave full play to his ambitions. He sought to revive on a scale more vast the empire of Charlemagne. He contemplated himself as a candidate for the Imperial throne. He was deep in schemes which would secure the reversion of Spain and her New World empire to a French prince. His inroads upon his neighbours were unceasing. He kept England divided by bribery and intrigue. He encouraged the Turks and the Magyars in their assaults upon the Hapsburg monarchy, and thus stabbed the Empire in the back at the same time as his forward pressure upon its western frontiers grew. In 1681 he swooped across the Rhine, and, alleging the doctrine of the reunion of ancient seigneurial domains, occupied the independent Protestant town of Strasburg, as he had already absorbed the greater part of the Spanish province of Franche-Comté. He also seized Casale, and made further expansions on the north-eastern frontiers of France. In some cases a judicial investigation preceded the seizure, but Strasburg was occupied "without the formality of justice."

255

In the spring of 1683 the Sultan assembled at Adrianople an army—prodigious for those days—of a quarter of a million men, and marched through Belgrade upon Vienna. The Emperor appealed to Christendom for succour. The Pope raised the standard of a Holy War on his behalf. Louis was content to remark with chilling indifference that the days of the Crusades were over. John Sobieski, King of Poland, with forty thousand men came to the rescue. In September a Christian army including Sobieski and his Poles and the Austrians under Charles of Lorraine, together with Saxons and Bavarians, defeated the Turks under the walls of Vienna in an eight-hours battle. The victors bound themselves in an alliance, to which Venice also adhered, for a continuous war against the Turks.

These conditions favoured the designs of France, and seemed to secure her recent encroachments along the Rhine and elsewhere. In 1684 a renewed expansionist movement was launched in all directions. Louis bombarded Genoa, besieged Luxembourg, massed troops upon the Spanish frontier, and, the hereditary House of the Palatinate having failed, laid claim through his sister-in-law to large territorial compensations in north-west Germany. The rest of Europe was unable to unite for resistance. In August Louis found himself strong enough to impose upon both branches of the Hapsburgs, in the Empire and in Spain, the twenty-years truce of Ratisbon, which forced them to accept and recognize all his acquisitions. His neighbours cowered beneath his unrelenting scourge in pain and fear.

While these sombre developments filled the secular sphere the Great King's designs against Protestantism became fully manifest. In the course of a very partial education two important principles had been instilled into Louis: the theory of Divine Right and the wickedness of Protestantism. As he grew older he became especially troubled that anyone should not be *de la religion du roi*, and maintained that Protestantism was the harbinger of *le mauvais exemple de la liberté*.[1] From

[1] Cf. E. Lavisse, *Histoire de France*, t. 7; D. Ogg, *Europe in the Seventeenth Century*, chapter vii.

LOUIS XIV
By permission of the Duke of Marlborough

1661 to 1679, however, he had been contented with endeavouring to convert the Huguenots in his realm by propaganda, and with irritating them by unfavourable interpretations of their charter of existence, the Edict of Nantes. A bureau was set up to encourage reversions to Catholicism by paying 12s. 6d. for each convert. To this bureau the King contributed generously. But such persuasions did not procure widespread or genuine conversions, and sterner measures were considered necessary. In 1680 a Colonel Marillac was despatched to Poitou with a regiment of dragoons. Here they were billeted on rich Huguenots, whom they proceeded to eat out of house and home. In the course of their duties they also forcibly dragged women, old men, and children to the churches, where they were sprinkled with holy water and declared Catholics. Other Protestants were tortured, whipped, or raped, and the total result was thirty thousand conversions in this district. The dragonnades had begun. 'Dragonnade' summed up the whole policy of France to Europe.

Madame de Maintenon, now the mistress of the King's pieties and secretly his wife, was dubious about the sincerity of these conversions, and deprecated the more violent forms of persecution; but the King regarded himself as an apostle, although, observes Saint-Simon, his methods of evangelization diverged somewhat from those of the original Twelve. All this was but preliminary to the crowning act of intolerance. In 1685 the Edict of Nantes was revoked. Throughout all the expanding dominions of France Protestantism became a crime. Expropriation, imprisonment, and death were the penalties by which this policy—terrible to hundreds of thousands of loyal, industrious Frenchmen—was enforced; and by a frightful provision flight from tyranny across the frontiers was forbidden, as it is at the present time from Russia. Thus our ancestors saw the all-powerful, all-grasping military monarch become also the avowed, implacable foe of Protestantism, and, indeed, of political freedom of every kind throughout Europe; and the aggressions of Louis were simultaneously launched upon the hearths and upon the souls of all mankind within his reach.

We have no patience with the lackey pens which have sought to invest this long, hateful process with the appearances of dignity and honour. During the whole of his life Louis XIV was the curse and pest of Europe. No worse enemy of human freedom has ever appeared in the trappings of polite civilization. Insatiable appetite, cold, calculating ruthlessness, monumental conceit, presented themselves armed with fire and sword. The veneer of culture and good manners, of brilliant ceremonies and elaborate etiquette, only adds a heightening effect to the villainy of his life's story. Better the barbarian conquerors of antiquity, primordial figures of the abyss, than this high-heeled, beperiwigged dandy, strutting amid the bows and scrapes of mistresses and confessors to the torment of his age. Petty and mediocre in all except his lusts and power, the Sun King disturbed and harried mankind during more than fifty years of arrogant pomp.

When the amusement of wars was temporarily suspended, his building extravagances maintained the ceaseless depletion of the wealth of France. Thousands of his soldiers and workmen perished in a futile attempt to bring the waters of the Eure to make his fountains play at Versailles. The French nobility, invited or summoned from their estates, were housed in one teeming hotbed of subservience, scandal, and intrigue in the royal palace. Thus they lost all contact with their tenantry and all influence upon political affairs, and the French Crown was deprived of the strength of a patriarchate to unite it with the people. All was sacrificed to the worship of a single man. The past of France and its future, its revenues and its manhood, alike were squandered for his personal pride. He never dared in all his wars to lead his armies in a battle. He preened himself under obsequious flattery, and read aloud or recited, with tears coursing down his cheeks, the poems and inscriptions which dutiful men of letters composed in his honour. By a life more narrowly personal even than that of Napoleon he blindly prepared the guillotines which after a hundred years had passed slew his blameless descendant, and destroyed not only the dynasty, but the system of society which was his supreme ideal.

It was fortunate indeed that Louis's aggressions were universal. During the same years when his flail fell so cruelly upon the Huguenots and when he saw himself the heaven-appointed champion of the Old Faith, he engaged in a most grievous quarrel with the Papacy. Like Henry VIII of England, the Grand Monarch was "a good Catholic who wanted to be his own Pope." All in France must bow to his will. "He found it insufferable," says Ranke in his massive work,[1] "that the Roman See should pursue a policy not only independent of, but also frequently in direct opposition to his own." He marshalled and disciplined the French clergy with the same thoroughness as his armies. He grasped with arrogant hand all ecclesiastical revenues and patronage. He claimed not only temporal, but in many directions spiritual control. The Gallican Church yielded themselves with patriotic adulation to his commands. They vied with the courtiers, poets, and dramatists of Versailles in enthusiastic servility. All who diverged from the line of march fell under the same blighting hand which had destroyed the Hugenots.

But outside France Louis in this sphere encountered a resolute resistance. In that long line of men, often remarkable, who have occupied the Papal throne Innocent XI holds one of the foremost places. The virtues of this eminently practical and competent saint, who began life as a soldier, shine with a modern glow across the generations. How he practised humility and self-denial in all that concerned himself; how he eschewed nepotism and luxury; how he forced the economies in the Vatican budget which enabled him at once to restore its own solvency and to relieve its debtors; how he purified every department of Papal administration—all has been faithfully and deservedly set forth. In manner gentle, in temper tolerant, in mood humane, in outlook broad and comprehending, he nevertheless possessed and exercised an inflexible will and an imperturbable daring. He used his spiritual weapons with the address of an accomplished duellist, and he understood the

1 *History of the Popes*, vol. iii, Book VIII, § 16.

political balances of Europe as well as any statesman then alive. Such was the Pope who withstood Louis XIV with the skill and patience of William of Orange, and defeated him as decisively as did Marlborough.

The head of the Catholic faith disapproved of French persecution of the Protestants. He condemned conversions effected by such means. Christ had not used armed apostles. "Men must be led to the temple, not dragged into it." Louis organized the Gallican Church against the Holy See. He sent his Ambassador to Rome with a heavy escort of cavalry —a diplomatic dragonnade. "They come with horses and chariots," said Innocent, "but we will walk in the name of the Lord." He withdrew all spiritual authority from the French episcopacy. He pronounced decrees of interdict and excommunication; and what was perhaps of no less immediate importance, he wove himself into the whole European combination against the predominance of France. Across the gulf of the Reformation and the Inquisition he weighted the swords of Protestant armies. He comforted the Catholic Emperor. He consorted with the Calvinist Prince of Orange. To him more than to any other individual we owe the fact that the wars of William and, after Innocent's death, of Marlborough were, for Europe at large, secular struggles for worldly dominion, and that the lines of battle were no longer, as in preceding generations, the lines of faith. In the armies of the Grand Alliance Catholic and Protestant troops fought in unquestioning comradeship. The Mass and the Anglican Communion were celebrated side by side in camp and field, while hard by Dutch Calvinists, English Puritans, and Scottish Presbyterians raised their psalms and prayers before—all together—falling, united in hearty zest, upon the common foe.

> Shall I ask the brave soldier who fights by my side
> In the cause of mankind, if our creeds agree?
> Shall I give up the friend I have valued and tried,
> If he kneel not before the same altar with me?[1]

Thus was the age of religious toleration opened by the sword,

---

[1] Thomas Moore, *Come send round the Wine.*

and thus, amid Catholic divisions, did the Protestant states preserve their souls alive.

Meanwhile throughout Europe the aggrandizement of France and the persecution of the Huguenots were witnessed with dismay or despair. Upon the Great Elector the effect of the revocation of the Edict of Nantes, following the accession of a Catholic King in England, was decisive. All his balancings between France and the Empire disappeared, and he extended the hand of friendship to Vienna. By the Edict of Potsdam he welcomed to Prussia the Huguenot refugees now fleeing at the peril of their lives from the oppression of their sovereign. Some of the greatest warriors of France quitted their native land for ever. The renowned Huguenot marshal Schomberg took service with the Great Elector, and eventually became the trusted lieutenant of William of Orange. Henri de Massue, second Marquis de Ruvigny, was so distinguished in war and diplomacy that Louis offered him special exemption from the consequences of the revocation. Ruvigny refused, and made his way to England. As Earl of Galway he became later on one of Marlborough's leading generals in the War of the Spanish Succession. "The whole of Europe," wrote a Dutch statesman, "is inundated with enemies of Louis XIV since the expulsion of the Huguenots."[1] Not only the Protestants, but nearly all the members of the Holy Roman Empire, especially those in southern and western Germany, now drew together for mutual protection. In July 1686 the League of Augsburg came into being. This treaty, though ostensibly defensive and to maintain the *status quo*— including the humbling Truce of Ratisbon—was also a military convention against France of detailed, strict, and far-reaching obligation. Neither Holland, which sought to go farther, nor England, which was pressed against her will towards the opposite side, was as yet enlisted.

Nevertheless, throughout all classes in England a deep fear and loathing of France began to spread. Not only were the ruling classes, in spite of their fierce divisions, profoundly affected, but the mass of the nation was stirred to its depths.

1 *Cit.* Noorden, *Europäische Geschichte,* p. 30.

In that sultry summer of 1685 Edmund Verney voiced the savage hatred of Louis XIV among the English squires: "I heare he stinckes alive and his cankers will stinck worse when he is dead, and so will his memory to all eternity."[1] In the ale-houses or upon the village greens ballads and songs expressed the popular sentiment against the French. In the parish churches collections were made to aid the Huguenots. The refugees now beginning to stream into England in considerable numbers, bringing their arts and crafts with them, were received with sympathy and hospitality from every class. French weavers, silk-workers, and paper-makers were welcomed not as aliens but as brothers by the English working-folk, and the foundations of important future industries were laid by their skill and trade-secrets. Acute observers in France like Vauban and, later, Fénelon watched with sorrow, as their writings record, the fundamental enmity growing between the French and all their neighbours, or measured with alarm the increasing strain and injury which its gigantic military burden cast upon their own country. Thus slowly, fitfully, but none the less surely, the sense of a common cause grew across the barriers of class, race, creed, and interest in the hearts of millions of men.

All moved to climax in the fateful year 1688. The Grand Monarch's quarrel with the Papacy was at its height. To disputes about pontifical authority and 'extra-territoriality' was added the conflict for the Electorate of Cologne. There were associated in those days with the Archbishopric of Cologne the sees of Munster and Liége. Thus the realm of Cologne comprised the long belt of land on the very marches which divided France from Germany and Holland, including the control of all the principal bridgeheads on the main rivers. A vacancy in the Archbishopric now occurred. Louis chose the one man of all others who was most hateful and dangerous to the Protestant Powers, and who was at the same time specially obnoxious to the Pope. Cardinal Fürstenberg, Bishop of Strasburg, was a German ecclesiastic who for more than thirty years had been a French tool. He had, in fact,

1 Cf. *Memoirs of the Verney Family during the Seventeenth Century.*

become the supreme manager of the French diplomatic missions in Germany. The occupation of Cologne by French troops followed the election of Fürstenberg. These events showed that not only the Palatinate but the Electorate of Cologne was about to be effectively incorporated in the French system. Against this Holland, Prussia, the Germanic Princes, the Emperor Leopold, and the Papacy were united in common interest and equal danger. Meanwhile the Turkish pressure upon the Empire was decisively relieved. The great battle of Mohacs, won so surprisingly against orders by an Imperialist commander of rising fame, Prince Eugene, broke for a time the Ottoman offensive power. Large Austrian armies were liberated for the west. Only the weight of Protestant England was wanting to create in its fullest extent the Grand Alliance against France. But England was in the grip of James II.

CHAPTER XVI

THE PROTESTANT WIND

(1688, *Autumn*)

THE lines of battle were now slowly yet remorselessly
drawing up in our island. Everything pointed, as in
1642, to the outbreak of civil war; but now the grouping
of the forces was far different from the days when Charles I
had unfurled his standard at Nottingham. The King had
a large, well-equipped regular army, with a powerful artillery. He believed himself master of the best, if not at the
moment the largest, navy afloat. He could call for powerful
armed aid from Ireland and from France. He held the
principal sea-ports and arsenals under trusty Catholic governors. He enjoyed substantial revenues. He had on his side
his Catholic co-religionists, all the personal following which
the Government and the Court could command, and, strangely assorted with these, a very considerable concourse of
Dissenters and traditional Roundheads. He assumed that the
Church of England was paralysed by its doctrine of non-
resistance, and he had been careful not to allow any Parliament to assemble for collective action.

Ranged against him were not only the Whigs, but almost
all the old friends of the Crown. The men who had made
the Restoration, the sons of the men who had fought and
died for his father at Marston Moor and Naseby, the Church
whose bishops and ministers had so long faced persecution
for the principle of Divine Right, the universities who had
melted their plate for King Charles's coffers and sent their
young scholars to his armies, the nobility and landed gentry
whose interests had seemed so bound up with the monarchy:
all, with bent heads and burning hearts, must now prepare
themselves to outface their King in arms.

It would indeed have been a strange war in which the sons

of Puritans, Roundheads, and regicides would have marched for a Catholic and catholicizing King against Churchmen and Cavaliers, while the mass of the people remained helpless, passionate, terrified spectators. It would have been a war of the extremes against the means; a war of a heterogeneous coalition against the central body of English wealth, rank, and grit. Few there were who could truly measure the value of all these various elements and the force of their harmonious combination, should it occur. And above and beyond all lay the incalculable hazards and accidents of the battlefield.

Very fearsome and dubious must the prospect have seemed to the nobility, gentry, and clergy who embodied the life and meaning of the England that we still know. They had no army; they had no lawful means of resistance, expression, or debate. They could not appeal to the unenfranchised millions of peasants and townsmen. They saw in mental eye the King in martial panoply advancing upon them with all that royal power in whose sanctity they themselves were the chief believers, with French troops ready to descend at any moment upon their shores to quell rebellion, with the children of the Ironsides hand in hand with Jesuit priests. Never did the aristocracy or the Established Church face a sterner test or serve the nation better than in 1688. They never flinched; they never doubted. They comprehended and embodied "the genius of the English nation,"[1] they faced this hideous, fraudulent, damnable hotch-potch of anti-national designs without a tremor, and they conquered without a blow. Why they conquered and, above all, why they conquered bloodlessly, turned upon the action of no more than as many men and women as can be counted upon one's fingers.

Nearly all the preliminaries of the struggle in England were concerned with public opinion. The King could give his orders to the land and sea forces, and to all his great officers and adherents. He possessed a complete executive machine which, if it worked, was probably irresistible. But the nobility, the parsons, squires, and merchants who formed the

1 See Churchill's conversation with the King at Winchester (pp. 242–243).

conscious entity of England, were divided by the recent feuds of Whig and Tory and by many gradations of unorganized thought and temper. Their salvation depended upon their cohesion, and that cohesion could only be achieved by spontaneous action arising in a hundred loosely connected centres. Here lay the main risk. Unless their leaders could act together, each playing his part in his own station, their chances were precarious. Together they had to wait for indefinite and uncertain periods, together they must strike with the hour. Yet to concert action was treason.

In so wide and secret a confederacy, with scanty means of council and communication, every divergence, personal or local, was pregnant with disaster. Two main divisions of policy persisted almost to the end; each had massive arguments. The moderates, led by Halifax and Nottingham, urged caution and delay. The Ministry, they pleaded, was breaking up. Sunderland, Godolphin, Dartmouth were now striving to restrain the headstrong King. Alternatively, "Let him have rope enough!" Either things would get better or an overwhelming case would be presented upon which all could unite. No case had yet arisen to warrant actual treason. Nothing was more imprudent than a premature resort to arms. Remember Sedgemoor only three years ago, and how a standing army rallies to its duty once fighting has begun, and the soldiers see an enemy before them. "All is going well, if you do not spoil it."

On the other hand stood the party of action, headed by Danby. Danby was the stalwart. He was the first man of great position who definitely set himself to bring William and a foreign army into England. With Danby were the Whig leaders—Shrewsbury, Devonshire, and some others. These men urged that the danger was growing each day; that the King was bringing over Irish troops, that the Catholic grip upon the Army was strengthening, that the House of Lords could be watered and the House of Commons packed, and above all that no reform or mitigation could be trusted from such a bigot. The only hope lay in a disciplined Protestant army. As early as the spring of 1688 they took

266

LITTLE ROCK PUBLIC LIBRARY

a most audacious decision. They invited William to invade England; and William replied that if he received at the right moment a formal request from leading English statesmen he would come, and that he would be ready by September. What followed played into the hands of these resolute men.

From April onward the party of action made good preparations. They took others into their confidence in proportion to what they needed to know. Trusty persons were informed, and their duties allotted. Efforts were made to draw in the moderates. The whole design was laid before Nottingham. At first he agreed, and then, upon misgivings in which cowardice played no part, he retracted his promise. How deadly the conspiracy had become can be judged from the story that his fellow-statesmen, leaders of a great party, Shrewsbury at their head, determined to ensure his silence by shooting him. He admitted to them that it was their right.[1] Eventually, and with justice, they trusted to his oath. A nation-wide conspiracy was on foot by the end of May. Detailed plans were made, and a great many personal contacts established. The land was full of whisperings and of mysterious comings and goings. Sunderland, elusive, baffling to his enemies, incomprehensible to posterity, heard and understood much, not all of which was imparted to his master. Barillon knew less, but reported all he knew to both the Kings whose interests he served. Louis took a grave view. James shut his ears, pursued his course, and reviewed his troops.

Upon the troops much, though not all, depended. If the Army obeyed its orders and fought for the King, England would be torn by a civil war the end of which no man could foresee. But if the Army refused to fight or was prevented from fighting by any means, then the great issues at stake would be settled bloodlessly. It seems certain, though there is no actual proof, that the general revolutionary conspiracy had a definite military core; and that this formed itself in the Army, or at least among the high officers of the Army, step by step with the designs of the statesmen. The supreme object of all the conspirators, civil or military, was to coerce

1 Foxcroft, *Supplement to Burnet's History*, pp. 290–291.

267

the King without using physical force. We cannot doubt that this was Churchill's long-formed intention. It is reasonable to assume that in this resolve he took every measure in his power; and, of course, these measures contemplated, if the need arose, treason and mutiny as known to the law, and personal treachery to his master. With him in secret consultation were the colonels of the two Tangier regiments, Kirke and Trelawny, the Duke of Grafton, commanding the Guards, the Duke of Ormonde, and a number of other officers.

Bishop Burnet has summed up the case very fairly. Of the military conspiracy he wrote in 1691:

> The chief officers of the army were tried [approached]; Churchill, Kirk, and Trelawny went into it; and Trelawny got his brother that was bishop of Bristol to join in it. Churchill did likewise undertake for Prince George and the Princess Anne; and those officers said they durst answer for the much greatest part of the army, and promised to do their utmost endeavours to bring as many as possibly they could into it. Churchill has been much censured; for as he had risen in the king's service through several degrees up to be a favourite, so a kindness which had begun upon the king's commerce with his sister was now so well fixed, that no man had more of personal favour and had found greater effects of it than he had. His coming into this design had the appearance of treachery and ingratitude, which has brought him under much reproach. But as he never betrayed any of the king's secrets to the prince, so he never set the king on violent measures, but, on the contrary, as oft as he spake to him of his affairs (which was indeed but seldom), he gave him always moderate counsels.[1]

Bishops, generals, Jesuits, and Nonconformist leaders eyed each other in a sinister silence as spring blossomed into summer. And now events struck their hammer-blows. At the end of April James issued a second and more far-reaching Declaration of Indulgence. In a reasoned manifesto he bid for the whole-hearted support of all—and they were many— who suffered—and they suffered grievously—from the penal laws. He ordered that the Declaration should be read in all the churches. On May 18 the Seven Bishops, headed by the

[1] Foxcroft, *Supplement to Burnet's History*, pp. 291–292.

Primate, the venerable Sancroft, protested against this use of the dispensing power. The clergy obeyed their ecclesiastical superiors, and from few pulpits throughout the country was the Declaration read. James, furious at disobedience and apparently scandalized at this departure, by the Church he was seeking to undermine, from its doctrine of non-resistance, demanded that the Bishops should be put on trial for seditious libel. Sunderland, now definitely alarmed, endeavoured to dissuade the King from this extreme step. He saw the spark which would fire the mine on which he knew himself to dwell. Even Lord Chancellor Jeffreys told Clarendon that the King was going too far, and had also the impudence to observe, "As to the judges, they are most of them rogues."[1] The King persisted: the trial was ordered, and the Bishops, all of whom refused the proffered bail, were committed to the Tower.

On June 10, while the trial was still pending, the Queen gave birth to a son. This prodigious event produced general consternation. Until then every one might hope that the stresses which racked English society would die with the death of the King. Till then the accession of either Mary, the heir presumptive, or Anne, the next in order, promised an end to the struggle between a Catholic monarch and a Protestant people. Peaceable folk could therefore be patient until the tyranny was past. But here was the succession assured in the male line to an indefinite series of Catholic princes. It was unendurable.

The conveyance of the Bishops to the Tower, their two days' trial, and their acquittal on June 30 by a Middlesex jury, were occasions of passionate outbursts in their favour by all classes in the capital. Enormous crowds thronged the river-banks to watch the barges carry the prisoners to and fro, or knelt in the streets in the hopes of being blessed by them. The humblest citizens were swayed by the same emotions which convulsed the rank and fashion of London. The troops at Hounslow joined in the rejoicings of the people. "What is that clamour?" asked the King, as he was leaving the camp

1 Clarendon, *Correspondence and Diary*, ii, 179.

after a visit. "Sire, it is nothing; the soldiers are glad that the Bishops are acquitted." "Do you call that nothing?" said James. These manifestations were repeated as the news spread throughout the country.

On that same night, while cannon and tumults proclaimed the public joy, the seven leaders of the party of action met at Shrewsbury's town house, and there and then signed and dispatched their famous letter to William. The signatories were Shrewsbury, Danby, Russell, Bishop Compton, Devonshire, Henry Sidney, and Lumley. Of these seven Compton had long been in the closest touch with Churchill at the Cockpit, yet he did not know how far Churchill was engaged, nor exactly what he knew. Shrewsbury and Russell were Churchill's intimate friends. Though not always colleagues in office, all three acted in concert for many years.

The letter, in the sure hands of Admiral Herbert, disguised as a common sailor, sped to The Hague, and its authors dispersed throughout the island for the purpose of levying war upon the King. Shrewsbury, though brought up a Catholic, had become a Protestant in the storms of 1681. He never detached himself from his new faith. Now, after mortgaging his estates to raise £40,000, he crossed the sea to join William and thenceforward stood at his side. Danby undertook to raise Yorkshire; Compton toured the North "to see his sisters." Devonshire, who had been condemned to an enormous fine for assaulting a Court partisan in the royal palace and had lain since 1685 in rebellious obscurity at Chatsworth, raised a regiment of horse from his tenantry. William, stricken in his ambition by the birth of a male heir, exclaimed, "Now or never!" and began the preparation of his expedition.

Churchill was not of sufficient political rank or territorial influence to be a signatory. Whether, if asked, he would have signed is unknown; but there is little doubt he would have deemed it an honour. Though of secondary importance, he lay more in the centre of the web and held more threads than the larger figures. Day by day he waited on the King, and watched the temper of the troops. Night by night he sat in the narrow, devoted cluster at the Cockpit. If he was in touch with Shrewsbury and Russell and their party of action, he was also intimate with Sunderland, the chief Minister, and with Halifax, the outstanding moderate. His countenance was inscrutable, his manner bland, his discretion unfailing.

The birth of the baby Prince who set so many ponderous wheels in motion was received with general incredulity, sincere or studiously affected. From the beginning doubts had been thrown upon the belated pregnancy of the Queen. The prayers and intercessions in which the Catholics had indulged, and their confident predictions that a son would be born as the result, led to a widespread conviction that a trick had been practised. The legend that a supposititious child had been smuggled into St James's Palace in a warming-pan was rife before the ashes of the official bonfires had vanished from the streets. By a strange imprudence of the King's the majority of persons present at the birth were Papists, the wives of Papists, or foreigners. The Archbishop was absent: he had that day been conducted to the Tower. Neither of the Hydes had been summoned, though as Privy Councillors, brothers-in-law of the King, and uncles of the two Princesses whose rights to the Crown were affected, their presence would have been natural. The Dutch Ambassador, who had a special duty to William, was not invited. More important perhaps than all, Princess Anne was not there. She was at Bath. The Churchills were with her, and Sarah no doubt received an authentic account from the still beautiful Frances, now Duchess of Tyrconnel, who was on the spot.

It has been suggested that Anne had kept deliberately out of the way at the far-seeing suggestion of her favourites. How they could foretell the swift and premature accouchement, of which but twelve hours' notice was given, or imagine the controversies that would arise about it, is not explained. Nevertheless, the fact that Anne was absent enabled her to adopt a placid but unshakable scepticism upon the event which barred her succession to the Crown. "I shall never now be satisfied," she wrote suavely to Mary, "whether

271

the child be true or false. Maybe 'tis our brother. . . . Where one believes it, a thousand do not. For my part unless they do give a very plain demonstration . . . I shall ever be of the number of unbelievers." When the Privy Council waited on her to present depositions affirming the reality of the birth, Anne took refuge in the pious observation that the King's word was far more to her than any deposition. William, who had incautiously authorized a thanksgiving service when the news was received, made haste to align himself and his consort with the highly convenient and popular conviction. It was vital to the nation to establish the doctrine that the child was an impostor. Sincerely attached to the principle of legitimacy, confronted with the appearance of a Papist heir, the English Protestants had no other means of escape from the intolerable admission. With the characteristic instinct and ingenuity of the English people for reconciling facts, law, and propriety with public interests and their own desires, they enshrined the legend of the warming-pan as a fundamental article of political faith. It was not dispensed with until after some eventful years, and when the question had ceased to have any practical importance.

Churchill now, as the days of action drew near, renewed his pledge given fifteen months before, and wrote to William:

August 4, 1688

Mr Sydney will let you know how I intend to behave myself: I think it is what I owe to God and my country. My honour I take leave to put into your royal highness's hands, in which I think it safe. If you think there is anything else that I ought to do, you have but to command me, and I shall pay an entire obedience to it, being resolved to die in that religion that it has pleased God to give you both the will and power to protect.[1]

Such a letter written by a serving officer, at a time when conspiracy was rife and invasion imminent, was a deadly guarantee. Its capture or betrayal would justly involve the

1 The original letter has recently been acquired by Professor Trevelyan, and his courtesy has allowed its reproduction here in facsimile.

yr

mr Sidney will lett you know how I intend
to behave my selfe; I think itt is what
I owe to god and my Contry; my honor g
take leave to put into your Royalle
hineßes hands, in which I think itt safe;
if you think ther is anny thing else
that I aught to doe, you have but to comand
mee and I shall pay an intier obedience to itt,
being resolued to dye in that Relidgion,
that it has pleased god to give you, both the
will and power to protect; I am with all
respect,   yr   your Royalle hineße
                                        obedient sarvant
                                        Churchill

MARLBOROUGH TO WILLIAM OF ORANGE (AUGUST 1688)

By permission of Professor G. M. Trevelyan

forfeit of his life at the hands of either a civil or a military tribunal. The invitation of the seven notables had been sent in the precautions of cipher. But Churchill's letter, which survives to this day, is in his own handwriting, signed with his name. He seems to have wished to share in a special degree the risks which his friends the signatories had incurred.

William could claim the fulfilment of such a gage at sight. If events had been different, if the great enterprise had never been undertaken, still it would have remained in his chest or in that of his successor, whoever he might be; and at any time, in conditions which had no relation to the issues of that day, it might be produced. If James II had made peace with his people and had reigned for the whole span of his life, this letter was a weapon of blackmail which a Dutch Ambassador could use upon Churchill for persuasion or revenge. Hardly ever in his life of reticence, diplomacy, and precaution had he given such a hostage. "Churchill," says Macaulay,

in a letter written with a certain elevation of language, which was the sure mark that he was going to commit a baseness, declared that he was determined to perform his duty to heaven and to his country, and that he put his honour absolutely into the hands of the Prince of Orange. William doubtless read these words with one of those bitter and cynical smiles which gave his face its least pleasing expression. It was not his business to take care of the honour of other men; nor had the most rigid casuists pronounced it unlawful in a general to invite, to use, and to reward the services of deserters whom he could not but despise.[1]

Thus we see that the elevation of language is an aggravation of the offence, that a declaration by a man in a delicate position that, when the time comes, he can be counted upon to run all risks for a worthy public cause is made more despicable because it is well written. The simple dignity of the language could not easily be excelled; and we do not think that William read it with "one of those bitter and cynical smiles which gave his face its least pleasing expression." He was appealing to Englishmen to give him just such guarantees.

1 *History*, ii, 443.

We know that at this time he liked and admired Churchill, that they looked at European political and religious problems through the same eyes, that they had talked long together ten years before; that they both saw the domination of France as the danger and the marshalling of Protestantism as the only means of countering it. We remember how keenly William had desired Churchill to be the English Ambassador at The Hague. We have seen how Churchill would have liked to have the command of the British contingent in the Dutch pay. There are no grounds, there is no warrant, except Macaulay's spiteful imagination, for assuming that William's features lost their more pleasing expression in a bitter and cynical smile. If he was the master-statesman Macaulay has depicted, he must have realized that this was a practical and binding pledge from a remarkable man in a desperate hour. We shall recur to this incident when dealing with Marlborough's alleged correspondence with King James.

The time has now come to consider the part played by Sunderland. He was the son of a pure Cavalier, Henry Spencer, killed at Newbury. His mother, Dorothy Sidney, a gifted, brilliant woman, belonged to one of the most famous families on the opposite side. Thus the best Cavalier and Puritan blood flowed in his veins. He had married Anne Digby, of a Parliamentary stock. He seemed to be born into the very heart and centre of social and political England, and he was connected with both parties by ties of blood. He never made speeches; but he had a vast familiarity with leading figures in every camp and throughout the aristocracy. He knew better than any other man the politics and inclination of the different noble families; and he had access to all. Hence his knowledge and opinions were invaluable to a succession of sovereigns. He had voted for the Exclusion Bill, but was soon back in Charles's Cabinet, and acquired the highest favour under James. He had ousted the Hydes by outbidding them in favouring James's autocratic and Papist designs. To ingratiate himself with the King he had become a Papist. He was now virtually Prime Minister. He had encouraged the King on the course

THE SECOND EARL OF SUNDERLAND
Sir Peter Lely
By permission of Earl Spencer

274

which led to his ruin. We find him later, only two years after the Revolution, taking his place as the trusted confidant of William III, and during practically the whole of William's reign he was the power behind the making of Cabinets. An astounding record, outstripping the fiercest hatreds and mounting upon every form of error, treachery, and disaster!

By the autumn of 1688 Sunderland was in full retreat. He had protested to James against the second Declaration of Indulgence and the trial of the Bishops. He laboured, on the other hand, to restrain Churchill from taking premature decisions. He was, he hinted, about to make an eleventh-hour effort to save the situation. The King would call a free Parliament; patience! and all would be well. While he had helped the King upon his fatal courses, and profited by so doing, he nevertheless dissuaded him from bringing in the French troops and accepting the fleet which Louis XIV so earnestly proffered. While he pocketed the money of which he was in constant need from France, he was also in touch with William. Thus it has been said that he lured his master to his follies and his fate, turned away from him at the end, and at the same time procured his rejection of the French aid which might have saved him. Indeed, so strange was his nature and conduct that coherence has been found in the explanation that all his actions were from the beginning part of a plot to destroy James, or at least that he had by now joined the great conspiracy.

Those who hold this opinion point to the disloyal letters written by his wife to her alleged lover, Henry Sidney, plotting at The Hague, while Sunderland was the chief responsible Minister of the Crown. Certainly no man played a greater part in the downfall of King James, except King James himself. When the crash came in October Sunderland fled to Holland, and was by no means ill received. The whole series of his actions from 1685 to 1690, when he was welcomed back to high office by William III, points to his having been in cordial relations with William at least throughout the whole of 1688. If we reject this theory of a plot, it is not because it does not fit the facts. Such complicated and largely purposeless treachery at the cost of so many toils and dangers, while other more profitable and attractive courses were open, cannot be reconciled with design or pattern in any form. Sunderland was during the reigns of Charles and James, in the aspect of a competent official, one of those dangerous beings who, with many gifts of mind, have no principle of action; who do not care what is done, so long as they are in the centre of it; to whom bustle, excitement, intrigue, are the breath of life; and whose dance from one delirium to another seems almost necessary to their sanity. The alarming experiences of 1688 and the advance of old age broke his nerve; and we shall see him under King William a discreet, timid, wise counsellor, wondering with all the world how he could have escaped so well the consequences of his violent days.

All this impending struggle, so ominous for our island people, so decisive upon their destiny, was, as the last chapter has shown, one factor, but a vital factor, in the world war now about to begin. Across the sea, watching with strained vigilance the assembling armies of France, lay William of Orange with the troops and fleet of Holland. England, in her griefs and rages, was the decisive piece on the Continental board. Profoundly Protestant, vehemently anti-French, was she, with all her resources, to be cast upon the side of Gallican intolerance and French aggrandisement? Was she so to be committed, probably with fatal effect, against the whole instinct and interest of her people by the perverse obstinacy of a single man? Protestant Europe and Protestant England alike looked to William, as the champion of freedom against the many-sided tyrannies of Louis, to break the accursed spell. William accepted the dangerous duty. In the terse words of Halifax, "he took England on the way to France."

Before the Prince of Orange could invade England he had not only to prepare and assemble his troops and ships, but to obtain freedom to use them for such a purpose. At a moment when the whole of the French Army was massed and ready for immediate advance, it was not easy to persuade the threatened princes of Germany or the anxious burghers of

Holland that their best chance of safety lay in sending the Dutch Army into England upon an expedition so full of uncertainty. The Great Elector was dead, but Frederick III, who had succeeded him in April, was resolute for war and, like his father, convinced that England must be gained. He even lent William a contingent of Prussian troops under the command of Marshal Schomberg. The other German princes acquiesced in the Prussian view. Most Catholic Spain set political above religious considerations, and made no bones about an expedition to dethrone a Catholic king. The Emperor alone demurred. Although dethronement was not suggested, his religious scruples were aroused. Lulled by communications from the Vatican at William's instance, he eventually agreed to an expedition to restore harmony in England and detach her from France. Only a dominating sense of common danger could have united these diverse interests and creeds upon a strategy so farseeing and broad-minded.

William had next to convince the States-General: they had agreed to an enormous expenditure during the last two years upon the Dutch armaments; their land forces were upon a war footing, their fleet decisively stronger than the English. But the decision of the Dutch, and their ruler also, must be governed by the action of France. If the French armies marched against Holland the whole Dutch strength would be needed to meet the invader, and England must perforce be left to her fate. If, on the other hand, Louis struck upon the Rhine at Prussia and Germany, then the enterprise on which the Stadtholder's heart was set could go forward. All therefore hung in suspense. Meanwhile a great fleet of transports, with all the necessary supplies, had gathered in the Texel under the protection of the Dutch Navy, and the expeditionary force lay concentrated close at hand.

Louis XIV, with whom the initiative rested, delayed his choice till the last moment. He was ready to come to James's aid if James would definitely throw England on to the French side in the impending European struggle. All through July and August he offered him money, an army of thirty thousand men, and the French fleet. The French troops would enforce discipline and loyalty upon the English Army, and together they could certainly crush all resistance to the royal will. James, partly from patriotic pride in the independence of his country, partly from fear of the resentment which a French alliance would arouse among his subjects, and under the advice of Sunderland, made light of his own dangers and dallied with the French offers. He was still absorbed in his electioneering plans to produce by hook or by crook a House of Commons favourable to the repeal of the Test Act. All prospect of this would be swept away by an outbreak of war, the announcement of a French alliance or the arrival of French troops. On September 2 Louis, with large armies straining at the leash, and compelled by the military situation, resolved to bring matters to a head. He delivered through his Ambassador at The Hague an ultimatum to the Dutch Republic. It was declared that William's military preparations were a menace to England: that "friendship and alliance" existed between England and France, and that any enterprise undertaken by the Dutch against England would involve an immediate French declaration of war on Holland.

This violent step defeated its own object in both the countries affected. The States-General were enraged by the menace. James, in the utmost embarrassment at the declaration, publicly repudiated all idea of an alliance. The rejection of his aid not only offended Louis; it aroused his suspicions. It was so contrary to James's vital interests that it seemed explicable only by some secret arrangement between James and William, or between Sunderland and the States-General. The irresolute, shifting policy of the English Government lent colour to the belief in Holland that it was tied to France, and in France that it was tied to Holland. At any rate, the die was cast. Louis abandoned the hope of procuring England as an ally; he must be content with seeing her, as he believed and trusted, torn by a savage civil war in which William would be involved, and during which the island kingdom could play no part in Europe. On September 25 all the French armies were set in motion, not against the Dutch frontier, but towards the middle Rhine. From the moment that this movement became certain the States-General eagerly granted William permission for his English descent, and James's hour was come.

As the autumn weeks slipped by, excitement and tension grew throughout the island, and the vast conspiracy which now comprised the main strength of the nation heaved beneath the surface of affairs. The King's attempt to bring in some of the regiments of Irish Roman Catholics which Tyrconnel had raised for him produced symptoms so menacing that the process was abandoned. The hatred and fears of all classes found expression in an insulting, derisive ballad against the Irish and the Papists. *Lilliburlero*, like *Tipperary* in our own times, was on all lips, in all ears, and carried a cryptic message of war to all hearts. "Lilliburlero" and "Bullen-a-lah" had been the passwords of the Irish in their massacres of Protestants in 1641. The doggerel lines, written by Lord Wharton with deep knowledge of the common folk and their modes of thought and expression, had no provable relation to William—nor to invasion or revolt. But the jingle of the chorus made an impression upon the Army "that cannot be imagined by those that saw it not. The whole army, and at last the people, both in city and country, were singing it perpetually. And perhaps never had so slight a thing so great an effect."[1] Every one watched the weathercock. All turned on the wind. Rumour ran riot. The Irish were coming. The French were coming. The Papists were planning a general massacre of Protestants. The kingdom was sold to Louis. Nothing was safe, and no one could be trusted. The laws, the Constitution, the Church—all were in jeopardy. But a deliverer would appear. He would come clad with power from over the seas to rescue England from Popery and slavery—if only the wind would blow from the east. And here one of Wharton's couplets, which nominally

1 Burnet, iii, 19.

applied to Tyrconnel, gained a new and, indeed, an opposite significance.

> O, why does he stay so long behind?
> Ho! by my shoul, 'tis a Protestant wind.

The Protestant wind was blowing in the hearts of men, rising in fierce gusts to gale fury. Soon it would blow across the North Sea!

> "Lero, lero, lilliburlero!
> Lilliburlero, bullen-a-lah!"

sang the soldiers and peasants of England in endless repetition through those days, "singing," as its author afterwards claimed, "a deluded prince out of three kingdoms."

Sunderland and Jeffreys were at this moment in chief control of the Cabinet. The magnitude of William's preparations and the alarming state of feeling throughout England produced a complete change in their attitude. Confronted by impending invasion from abroad and by imminent revolt at home, these two Ministers, recently so pliable and so reckless, strenuously advised the King to reverse his whole policy. They abandoned at one stroke all the meticulous efforts to pack a Nonconformist House of Commons upon which infinite labour had been spent, and by which widespread irritation had been caused. Parliament must indeed be called without delay, and the King and his Government must face the fact that it would be Episcopalian in character. All further aggressive Catholic measures must be stopped, and a reconciliation made with the Church of England. The fact that this advice came from the two Ministers who had hitherto been the most hardy, and who were both, it seemed, committed beyond forgiveness to the royal policy and all the hatreds it had roused, was staggering. They must indeed have swept the King off his feet by their outburst of warning. He crumpled under their pressure and panic. Within a week he was persuaded that he could not make head against William of Orange without the support of the Church of England. To gain this support he must negotiate with the bishops. He must stoop to conquer—or even to escape.

LITTLE ROCK PUBLIC LIBRARY

THE PROTESTANT WIND

On October 3, in a conference at which the Primate and
most of the bishops were present, he agreed to abolish the
Ecclesiastical Commission, to close the Roman Catholic
schools, to restore the Protestant Fellows of Magdalen College, to put the Act of Uniformity into force against Catholics
and Dissenters. Action was taken accordingly with the utmost
speed. The Lord-Lieutenants who had been dismissed were
invited to resume their functions. Their charters were
restored to the recalcitrant municipalities. The bishops were
begged to let bygones be bygones. The Tory squires were
urged to take their old places in the magistracy. Too late!
The adverse movement had slowly but at length gathered
a momentum which was uncontrollable even by those who
had started it. Moreover, Englishmen in those days were
obstinate and tough. As the old Tory squire John Bramston
observed when asked to return to the place from which he
had been ejected, "Some would think one kick of the breech
is enough for a gentleman."[1] Although many expressions
of gratitude and loyalty were tendered by the leading persons
affected by these concessions, there was not time for them to
change the currents of public opinion, which flowed with
increasing force. It was evident that this sudden, belated
repentance was a proof only of the weakness of the Government in the presence of approaching peril.

Now the unhappy King began to realize that by his folly
and Sunderland's advice he had lost all. At the end of
October he dismissed his Minister for vacillation and lack of
firmness in counsel. James had drawn upon himself the
evils of all courses and gained the benefit of none. He had
alienated his friends; he had united all his enemies. William
was about to invade him. Louis had abandoned him. The
Pope, for the sake of whose faith he had hazarded all, in
aversion to whom his subjects were in revolt, was working
with his enemies. Outside France he had not a friend or sym-
pathizer in Europe; and France was marching away from him
upon Germany. At home he had centered upon himself the
anger of almost all the wealth and power and learning of the

[1] *Autobiography of Sir John Bramston* (Camden Society, 1845), p. 326.

nation without winning support from the popular masses. He had wounded Cavaliers without gaining Roundheads. He had estranged the Church without rallying the Chapel. Although Penn and the Nonconformist organizations had naturally supported his attempt to remove the penal laws, the great bulk of their followers remained vehemently hostile to Popery, and would rather endure maltreatment themselves than join in a Catholic crusade. The Catholic gentry whose wrongs had stirred his heart were now panicstricken by the plight into which he had led them. He was not even destined to go down fighting for the cause in which he so fervently believed. In the last few months of his reign he was compelled to desert the standard he had himself set up, and to try in vain to placate the furies he had aroused, by the sacrifice of all the objectives in whose pursuit he had aroused them.

Nor has the passage of generations vindicated his efforts for Catholic toleration. Had he joined the Catholic Hapsburgs and the Protestant princes in their war against the domination of France, he would have established with his own subjects a confidence and comradeship which might well have enabled him, if not to remove, at least gradually to neglect the enforcement of the Tests. Had he allowed the incomparable soldier whose gifts he had himself so long discerned to gain for him Protestant battles upon the Continent, the English people, relieved from their fear, might well have been generous to the co-religionists of the victorious prince who had served them well. So supple a part was beyond him, and, indeed, beneath him. Instead, he set in train a movement of events which made anti-Popery and a warming-pan the foundation of a dynasty, and riveted upon the English Catholics for more than a hundred and fifty years the shackles of the penal laws.

CHAPTER XVII

THE INVASION

(1688, *November*)

HITHERTO these chapters have usually dealt with several years; but now the pace of events is such that two chapters can cover little more than a month. On October 19 William set out upon the seas. He had taken leave of the States-General in a speech that moved even the Amsterdammers to tears.

> He took God to witness that since he had been entrusted with the affairs of their commonwealth, he had never entertained a wish that was contrary to its interest. If he had erred, he erred as a man, his heart was not to blame. In his present enterprise he trusted to Providence; but if anything fatal should happen to him, to them he recommended his memory, their common country and the Princess his wife, who loved that country as she did her own. His last thoughts should be upon them and upon her.[1]

His small army was a microcosm of Protestant Europe— Dutch, Swedes, Danes, Prussians, English, and Scottish, together with a forlorn, devoted band of French Huguenots who had no longer any country of their own. They were embarked upon about five hundred vessels escorted by sixty warships—almost the entire Dutch fleet. The English Rear-Admiral Herbert led the van, and the Prince of Orange hoisted, together with his own arms, the flag of England, on which was embroidered his motto, "I will maintain," with the addition, "the Protestant religion and the liberties of England"; all of which was made good. Dalrymple has written of the feelings of the Dutch as they watched this impressive concourse of vessels quitting their shores:

> . . . some flattered with the grandeur of their republic, others reflecting with anxiety that their frontier on one side was in the

1 Dalrymple, ii, Part II, 188.

hands of the ancient tyrants, and on the other, exposed to an army of foreign mercenaries, all the artillery of their towns carried off, only a few ships of war left in their harbours, and the whole strength of the republic sent, during the rigours of Winter, to depend upon the hazards of winds and seas, and the fortune of war.[1]

A violent gale scattered the fleet and cast it back upon the ports of Holland. One vessel, upon which no fewer than four companies of infantry were embarked, was driven on to the English coast and captured. The numbers of troops on this single vessel, together with the size of the fleet, gave the idea that William's army was four times as large as it was. But, anyhow, it had been driven back and ruined by the storms. James saw the finger of God. "It is not to be wondered at," he said, when he received the news at dinner, "for the Host has been exposed these several days." Convinced that the divine power and Holy Church had given him his son, he thought that they would also destroy his foes; and he dismissed Sunderland from his office as First Minister for being a faint-heart. But the new Secretary of State, Preston, a Protestant, renewed to him the advice of the fallen Minister. He must call a Parliament without manipulation and without delay.

Now this was a deadly matter for the King. No such Parliament could assemble in such a situation without calling in question not only the whole prerogative of the Crown, but, far graver, the *bona fides* of his son's birth. And here, by the mercy of God, was the hostile fleet scattered. Of course he refused. On this the Lord Chancellor Jeffreys abandoned himself to despair. "It is all naught," he exclaimed, with his customary profanity. "The Virgin Mary is to do all."

The reader will remember Churchill's friend and cousin George Legge, now Lord Dartmouth. When a Catholic admiral had brought the fleet to the verge of flagrant mutiny by celebrating High Mass upon his flagship, Dartmouth, a Protestant personally devoted to the King, had been placed in command to restore discipline. Dartmouth lay in the

1 Dalrymple, ii, Part II, 190.

WILLIAM III
By permission of Earl Spencer

mouth of the Thames with a naval force which, though not capable of fighting a pitched battle with the Dutch fleet, could easily, if the occasion had served, have played havoc with that fleet, encumbered with its convoy. William's plans and, to a large extent, the fate of England depended on the wind. All preparations had been made by Danby, Devonshire, and Delamere for armed revolt in Yorkshire and Cheshire, and throughout the North men were being mustered, drilled, and as far as possible armed. It was believed that William would strive to land in the North, and thither considerable bodies of the royal troops were proceeding. But the winds decided otherwise, and William ran south under full sail. On November 3 he anchored, so as to regather his whole fleet, in the Straits of Dover, in full view of the crowded coasts of England and France. The same wind that carried him here prevented Dartmouth from coming out of the Thames in any formation fit for battle, even if the loyalty of his captains and their seamen would have undertaken it. When to doubt, disinclination, and inferior strength are added adverse weather conditions, the inaction of naval forces is to be expected. The English fleet followed tardily behind the invader, and the same Protestant wind which blew him back to Torbay when he had overshot it forced the pursuers, who had got as far as Portland, to take shelter at Spithead. On November 5 William landed at Torbay, on the coast of Devon. Carstares, the Scottish divine, who had endured the boot and the thumb-screw before escaping to Holland, reminded him that this was the joyous anniversary, long celebrated by the common people of England, of the detection of the Gunpowder Plot; and William said to Burnet, ever at his side, "What do you think of Predestination now?"

James was not at first unduly alarmed at the news. It was better that the invasion should have fallen on the Western counties than upon Yorkshire. He hoped to pen William in the West, and to hamper his communications by sea. The troops which had been sent to Yorkshire were recalled to the South, and Salisbury was fixed as the point of assembly for the royal army. Meanwhile William established himself at

Exeter and awaited the arrival of adherents. For ten days none came. Danby had expected him in Yorkshire. The West had learned its lesson after Sedgemoor, and no preparations for a rebellion had been made. William was disconcerted by this apparent apathy, and thought at first he was betrayed. However, gradually some notables arrived, and Sir Edward Seymour formed an association in his support. Most of the grievances set out in William's proclamation before he sailed had been redressed by James by the time he landed, and the issue appeared to narrow itself to the sole demand for a free Parliament. James declared that he could not call a Parliament while a hostile foreign army was in the country in the control of "a hundred voices"; and he left London for Windsor in order to avoid the pressure which the population of the capital endeavoured to exert upon him. In this lull the King still looked with confidence upon his Army, and it is thither we must turn for the next event.

Some confusion of thought is evident in the searing reproaches with which both parties and successive generations have disfigured Churchill's reputation and have singled him out to bear whatever there was of shame in the wonderful deliverance of which all stood sorely in need. No one has impugned the sincerity of his religious convictions or the wisdom of his political view. No one can dispute the proofs of his long attachment to both, or of the repeated declarations by which his position became well known to all whom it concerned. Few will urge that personal indebtedness to a prince requires behaviour contrary to a man's conscience and to the interests of his native land. Every one will repudiate the idea that Churchill—a fervent Protestant, a resolved opponent of French domination in Europe, and an adherent of our laws and Constitution as then known—should have lent his gifts and sword to the bloody task of forcibly converting his fellow-countrymen to Popery, and of setting up in England a despotism on the French model, by French arms and in French interests.

It follows, therefore, that Churchill was right to abandon

LITTLE ROCK PUBLIC LIBRARY

King James. The only questions open are When? and How? Ought he to have quitted the King when he wrote his first letter of May 1687 to William of Orange? Surely not: the circumstances in question might never have come to pass. The King might yield to the increasing pressure brought upon him from all sides. He might reverse his policy. He did, in fact, reverse it. Was it, then, when he wrote his second letter to William, in August 1688, that he should have deserted James? But by this time he knew from Sunderland of the intended change of policy which even the most hard-bitten, self-seeking Ministers resolved to press upon their master, and of the probable summoning of a new Parliament chosen in the old way. Ought he, then, to have left the King's service, given up his commissions and appointments, and gone to his home or, if need be, to a prison, when James dismissed Sunderland at the end of October and withdrew the writs for a free Parliament? But by now William was on the seas. Trusting in the solemn written promises of leading Englishmen—among which Churchill's undertakings were the most explicit—he had launched out upon the hazardous enterprise to which they had called him. Ought Churchill, then, in November 1688 to have extinguished himself as a factor in the momentous events actually impending, and left William to look for his pledged aid in vain? Surely there is more shame in a breach of faith contrary to convictions than in a severance of loyalty in harmony with them. A flight from responsibility was only treachery in another and an abject form.

It was a hideous situation into which he had been drawn by no fault of his own, by no unwise or wrongful action, by no failure of service, by no abandonment of principle. But it was a situation which had to be faced and dealt with calmly and sensibly in the manner most likely to minimize the public dangers and sufferings, and to procure a good result for his country and for himself. Moreover, in conspiracies and rebellions the penalties for failure are rightly so severe that all who are unluckily drawn into them have not only a vital need for themselves, but also a duty to others associated with them and to the cause at stake, to ensure success, and above all bloodless success, by forethought and every well-concerted measure. To lure, like Monmouth, associates and humble followers on fools' errands to their doom can find no defenders. Thus Churchill had to go through with his undertakings, and by such steps as were likely to win.

This was a dangerous time for James to have at the head of the host the Frenchman, Feversham, who had been so harshly lampooned round London and in all the garrisons after Sedgemoor. There was at the King's disposal Feversham's brother, the competent French general Roye. He certainly thought of offering the chief command to him. Roye, who had learned since his arrival of the intense feeling in the Army against France and French patronage, was well enough informed to put the suggestion aside. He could not, he said, command an army not one word of whose language he could speak. So Feversham remained Commander-in-Chief. All the more necessary was it to have Churchill almost on any terms at the royal headquarters. In the opinion of those rather loosely disciplined professional soldiers, with their brave and haughty society officers, he was without equal or rival the leading English general. The habit of soldiers to fix upon a leader who embodies to them a martial ideal and to obey him in a crisis has often been proved. Here was an hour when everything hung upon the temper of the troops. The only hope of inducing the army, and especially its officers, to fight for the King was to give the impression that the best fighting man of English blood would give or be associated with the orders they received. The misgivings which James had owned when he superseded Churchill before Sedgemoor must have recurred to his mind in an aggravated form at this juncture. But what else was there to do? Accordingly on November 7 Churchill was promoted Lieutenant-General with the command of a brigade, or, as we should now call it, a division, of the army concentrating at Salisbury.

Churchill could not consider this advancement as a mark of favour. It was, in fact, the hopeful appropriation of his military prestige to the royal cause at a moment when all title-deeds were called in question. Acceptance involved no

'BLIC LIBRARY

assumption of new obligations on his part. In this important but subordinate position he had a seat at the councils of war and a voice in their decisions. He was not, however, in either nominal command or actual control of the army. His opinion was invited; his influence and authority were invoked. He was saddled before the nation with the responsibility. But the King really leaned upon the two Frenchmen. They were immune from the passions which shook England. He could count on their fidelity however his own subjects might behave. Thus Churchill was at the same moment made to fill the public eye and kept under supervision and control. In the circumstances this was probably the best course open to the King.

During these heart-shaking days many alternative solutions of the nation's problem presented themselves. When the royal headquarters arrived at Salisbury, it might well be found that the mood of the troops was such that no battle could be fought; but that, on the other hand, a negotiation would be entered into, as afterwards happened, with the Prince of Orange and his invading army. At that time none of the English conspirators had contemplated the dethronement of the King, and William had carefully dissembled his ambitions. His small, solid army was only the steel tip of the spear of a British resolve. He could not conquer six million English with fifteen thousand men. The constable had arrived upon the scene of disorder. He was helpless without the support of public opinion and of sturdy, well-disposed citizens. It might well be that a parley between the chiefs on both sides would result in an agreement. James might become a limited monarch, permitted to exercise his personal religion in private, but compelled to govern with Parliamentary institutions, to preserve the Protestant character of England, and, as part of the League of Augsburg, to make war upon France. He might even be compelled to choose between having his son excluded from the succession or brought up a Protestant. Again, there might be a regency, with William as Mayor of the Palace, with James as a powerless but much respected Merovingian king, the succession at his death assured to his daughters, the Protestants Mary and Anne. All these possibilities were still open when James left London.

The King had barely arrived at Windsor when disconcerting news was received. Lord Cornbury, eldest son of Lord Clarendon, an officer of the Life Guards, found himself for a few hours in command of the troops assembling at Salisbury. Declaring that he had received orders for an immediate raid on one of William's advanced detachments, he set off with three regiments of horse, and marched them sixty miles to Axminster, whence after a brief halt he proceeded towards Honiton, professing to be about to attack the enemy. Young Berwick, who was going from Portsmouth to Salisbury to join the army, filled with suspicion by this departure, set out immediately after Cornbury with other troops—an action of singular quality when he was only eighteen. Cornbury intended to carry the whole three regiments into the Prince's army. William, duly apprised, had set superior forces in motion to surround them, and the troops would certainly have been disarmed or, if possible, incorporated. But the officers were puzzled by the length of the marches and the obvious imprudence of the operation. They demanded the production of the orders. Cornbury, seeing himself detected, rode over to William with about two hundred men, while the rest of the brigade only extricated themselves with difficulty from the trap into which they were being led.

Cornbury's desertion was the first of the successive blows by which James was to learn that he could not trust his Army. Nevertheless, the incident cut both ways. Though Cornbury had deserted, the officers and soldiers had given a signal proof of their vigilant loyalty, and this military treason had miscarried. It was impossible to tell who among the officers of the Army could be trusted. It seemed certain that if they could all be trusted the Army would fight, and if it fought it would probably win.

The fact that Cornbury was intimate with his cousin the Princess Anne and was constantly at the Cockpit; the fact that the military arrangements had been so cast as to leave this young officer in chief command at Salisbury for some critical hours, and that he should have taken such audacious action, all pointed to a plot in which the superior chiefs of the Army, and Churchill above all, were engaged. There is no proof; but it may well be so. Certainly Churchill was trying to bring about the predominance of William without the fighting of a battle, and this would well have served for a preliminary move.

On the 18th Princess Anne sent to William a letter the outline of which had been evidently prepared beforehand.[1]

THE COCKPIT
November 18

Having on all occasions given you and my sister all imaginable assurances of the real friendship and kindness I have for you both, I hope it is not necessary for me to repeat any thing of that kind; and on the subject you have now wrote to me, I shall not trouble you with many compliments, only in short assure you, that you have my wishes for your good success in this so just an undertaking; and I hope the Prince [*i.e.*, her husband, Prince George of Denmark] will soon be with you, to let you see his readiness to join with you, who I am sure will do you all the service that lies in his power. He went yesterday with the King towards Salisbury, intending to go from thence to you as soon as his friends thought it proper. I am not yet certain if I shall continue here, or remove into the City; that shall depend on the advice my friends will give me; but wherever I am, I shall be ready to shew you how very much I am your humble servant.

On November 17 the King set out from Windsor to join the army at Salisbury. It was a strange party that fared with him to the wars. More than half were resolved, and most of these already pledged, to abandon him. Some had been for months actively conspiring with the invader. His own son-in-law, Prince George of Denmark, had actually agreed to the arrangement by which the Princess Anne should at the chosen moment leave London for William's camp. His own Household troops were honeycombed with disloyalty. His nephew, the Duke of Grafton, and nearly all his most capable officers, the leaders of many of his trusted regiments, were merely

---

1 Dalrymple, ii, Part II, 249.

awaiting an opportunity to transfer their services to the enemy. Every decision, except those of hour and method, had been taken. Apart from his own Catholic communion and the French agents, there was no one upon whom he could depend. Even his fiercest partisans of Sedgemoor three short years before, men like Kirke and Trelawny, were now his foes. On all sides salutes and ceremony, unaffected respect and reverence for his person, and yet on all sides implacable treason, indistinguishable from public duty.

Among these men rode Churchill. None was more sure of himself than the newly promoted Lieutenant-General. His mind had long been made up, his pledge given, and his plans laid. Indeed, these evidences of design are the ground upon which censure has specially fastened. The elaborate, smooth-working preparations which are admired when they produce the march to Blenheim are repellent, though not less necessary, in a conspiracy. In London Sarah had her instructions about the Princess Anne, which she would fulfil with sure punctuality. Afloat, his brother George was working, with an ever-growing crowd of sea officers, to gain the fleet, and was himself about to carry his ship, the *Newcastle*, to William. Churchill himself was united in resolve and confederation with the principal nobles and functionaries. All—each playing his part wherever stationed—were taking day by day the steps which, should their designs miscarry, would cost them hearth and home and life itself. Ruin, exile, the scaffold— these were the stakes to which the compulsory game of politics had risen. They were already cast upon the board; there could be no withdrawal of them. Irrevocable! All grim, cold, doom-laden!

LITTLE ROCK PUBLIC LIBRARY

CHAPTER XVIII

THE REVOLUTION

(1688, *November*)

AT this crisis in his fortunes King James could marshal as
large an army as Oliver Cromwell at his height. Nearly
forty thousand regular soldiers were in the royal pay and
moving at the royal command towards Salisbury and the
Dutch invader. But the Scottish troops, about four thousand
strong, had only reached Carlisle, the bulk of the three
thousand Irish were still beyond Chester, and at least seven
thousand men must be left to hold down London. Still,
twenty-five thousand men, or double the number of William's
expedition, were around Salisbury when the King arrived on
November 19. Here was the largest concentration of trained
full-time troops which England had ever seen. What would
they do?

This was the question which dominated the thoughts of all
the leading figures who composed the King's headquarters
or held the commands. There had been several vexatious
delays and hitches in the assembly of the troops. The
Secretary at War, Mr Blathwayt, is suspected by modern
writers of obstruction. The Irish Catholic regiments, who
were specially important, seemed to lag upon the road, and
only came in one by one. The King and Churchill eyed each
other, the sovereign in mute appeal, the servant in grave
reserve: and both sought to penetrate by every channel
open to them the secret of the Army. To the King, with his
two French generals and the French Ambassador ever at his
side, the aspect was obscure and dubious. To Churchill and
the commanders banded with him it was highly disconcerting. Most of the officers were no doubt thoroughly dis-
affected. The Protestant regimental officers were divided
and in evident distress. But the Papist officers and their men

293

were ardent in their loyalty, and no one could be sure that the Protestant rank and file, if strongly gripped, were not capable of being led against the foreign foe or foreign deliverers. The least trustworthy regiments at James's disposal were those upon whom he should have been able to count the most. The Guards, the Dragoons and Cavalry, those officers and men who habitually surrounded the Court, who had felt the mood of London, and were aware of the political issues at stake, were known to use mutinous language. But the main body of the Line at this juncture, though Protestant in sentiment, were still governed by their discipline and their uniforms.

Four anxious and oppressive days of reviews, inspections, and conferences followed. On November 21 the King proposed to visit his advanced covering troops, cavalry and infantry, who lay under Kirke about Warminster. The stresses through which he was passing induced in the unhappy monarch an obstinate bleeding of the nose. He was unable to ride forth. In after-days he regarded this affliction as a special interposition of Providence which alone saved him from being delivered by Churchill and Kirke into the hands of William. Berwick repeats this allegation in his *Memoirs,* and calls it "a pretty remarkable circumstance."[1] Jacobite scribes and pamphleteers have expanded it into a plot by Churchill and Kirke to murder the King, Churchill himself, they assure us, having undertaken to stab him in his coach.

Whatever may be charged against Churchill's morals, no one has impugned his sagacity, especially where his own interests were concerned. If he had murdered King James, William would have been able to reach the throne after enforcing merciless execution upon the criminals who had slain his beloved father-in-law. The greater the severity with which he treated them, the more becoming the auspices under which he would have succeeded. Indeed, it would be vital to him to avenge by every terror known to the law a crime by which he would himself have profited so highly. This accusation, which even Macaulay does not adopt, may be

1 *Memoirs,* i, 31.

rebutted on these low but solid grounds and consigned to the rubbish heap of Jacobite mendacity.

We may dismiss also as an unwarrantable suspicion Churchill's alleged scheme to deliver the King into the hands of William. In dealing with these calumnies one after the other it is best to use the arguments which would most have appealed to those who bring them forth. The last thing that William desired was to have James on his hands. Nothing would have repelled the sympathy and public acceptance on which he counted more than the news that he had captured or stolen the King and was keeping him prisoner. All those forces that were demanding a free Parliament would have also demanded a free King. William, the adroit, masterly statesman, moving in an atmosphere which he and his English supporters understood, would never have made such a mistake, and Churchill, who knew the situation even better than William, was the last man to commit such a silly act.

It must be added that Churchill himself repudiated this charge as soon as he heard of it. Clarendon's diary[1] states:

> *December* 3, 1688. In the dining room [at Berwick, near Hindon[2]] I met my Lord Churchill. I told him what the King had told the Lords of his Lordship's design to deliver His Majesty to the Prince of Orange, if he had gone to Warminster. He denied it with many protestations, saying, that he would venture his life in defence of his person; that he would never be ungrateful to the King; and that he had never left him, but that he saw our religion and country were in danger of being destroyed.

It is natural that such charges should be made after the event about a man who had deserted his sovereign and benefactor by those who had suffered so woefully from his action.

Only in one respect does Churchill appear to have been curiously imprudent. He seems to have abandoned his usual reserved manner. The inscrutable dissembler, according

1 Clarendon, *Correspondence and Diary,* ii, 211, 214.
2 This was a house belonging to Bishop Burnet in Wiltshire.

to the Jacobite gossip, for once was indiscreet. An air of recklessness, of insolence, of flippancy even—so far as we know, unexampled in the rest of his life—is attached to his demeanour and procedure. He had, they tell us, "lolled out his tongue" at the Hyde Park review of the Army and "openly laughed" at the whole affair.[1] This behaviour had been seen and reported. He, Sunderland, and Godolphin, when the news of Lord Cornbury's desertion was received at Windsor, had been seen *unawares* "going hand in hand along the gallery in the greatest transports of joy imaginable."[2] At supper on the 20th he, with the Dukes of Grafton and Ormonde and others, had urged the newly arrived colonel of the Royal Irish Regiment and the Duke of Northumberland, of the Household Cavalry, to join the revolutionary party, heedless of the fact that, unless they were gained, as they were not, the conversation would be reported, as indeed it was. At the meeting of superior officers James appealed to their loyalty. Churchill and others repeated their usual assurances, but a deputation was sent immediately afterwards to Feversham to inform him that, however devoted they were to his Majesty's service, they could not in conscience fight against a prince who was coming over with no other design than to "protect the calling of a free Parliament for the security of their religion and liberties." The Jacobite writers declare that Churchill was the first to swear that he would "shed his last drop of blood" in the King's defence. This phrase finds confirmation in his own letters and conversations: but these also make it clear that he meant in defence of the King's person; not of his power, nor still less of his policy. Such equivocations were inevitable and common. They were the symptoms of violent times. A vast repudiation of allegiance united Englishmen of every rank and party. Those who, like Churchill, stood nearest the King until they quitted him had no other choice. But not often was treason less deceitfully veiled. It was in its last phase more like a political breach between Ministers than a plot against a sovereign.

[1] Ailesbury, *Memoirs,* pp. 184–185.   [2] Clarke, *Life of James II,* ii, 218.

It is recorded that at this same meeting the King ended his appeal to his officers by offering to allow any who could not serve him faithfully to go freely.

> He which hath no stomach to this fight,
> Let him depart; his passport shall be made
> And crowns for convoy put into his purse.

But this could be no real offer. Can anyone suppose that if Churchill or any other had risen from the council board and said, "I accept Your Majesty's offer, and am now going home, or, if I choose, to join the army of the Prince of Orange," he would have been suffered to leave the royal presence free or without a clash of arms? There are some offers which authority can make and may be wise to make, but which are in the nature of things utterly valueless to the weaker side. Here was no way out.

James, warned from many quarters, meditated Churchill's arrest. Feversham on his knees demanded it, declaring his disaffection patent. Churchill's incarceration at Portsmouth was debated. This was not a light matter to decide. His appointment had been advertised to the troops. The news of his arrest would have been not less injurious than his desertion. The shock to the Army would have been as great. So many were involved, so near, so intimate, so long-trusted and proved so faithful, that the unhappy sovereign knew not where to begin, nor, if he began, where to stop. On all sides his narrow circle of Papists, Irish, and Frenchmen encountered whisperings, averted eyes, or even cold shoulders and hostile looks. The King hesitated, delayed, put the matter off until the morrow.

We need not delve into a painful analysis of Churchill's feelings at this juncture. Lord Wolseley has drawn for us a harrowing picture of the moral and sentimental stresses through which his hero is supposed to have passed on the night of November 23, when he is represented as finally making up his mind to desert James, and how he must have balanced his duty and gratitude to his master and patron on the one hand against the Protestant cause upon the other. These well-meant efforts of a friendly biographer have certainly no foundation. All had, as we have shown, been settled long before. There never had been any process of weighing and balancing which side to take. The only difficulty had been to judge a ceaselessly shifting situation. But now all was simple. Policy and plans were settled; the last preparations had been made. The hour of action was always, to him, the least arduous of trials. That hour had now come.

A council of war was held on the evening of November 23. Churchill, supported by Grafton, when asked his opinion, advised an advance towards the enemy, while Feversham and Roye were for retreat. The King accepted Feversham's opinion. Macaulay's account reads as if irritation at having his advice rejected, and the knowledge that this could only arise from distrust of his intentions, determined Churchill's course. This cannot be so. His may well have been the right advice to give on military grounds. There is a curious symmetry about his actions on many occasions which seems to range a correctness and justice of view on the event of the moment with his general designs. But it is equally arguable that he gave the right advice either because he knew the opposite course would be adopted, or because, if he had been taken at his word, that would have been convenient to his resolves. Every forward march would carry him nearer to William, would enable the two women for whose safety he was concerned, his wife and the Princess Anne, to make their escape more easily, and even his own decisive ride would be shorter. Once the Army was dispersed in its retreat, and the loyal were separated from the disloyal regiments, his arrest would be easy. All these matters are covered by the general relationship in which the chief actors stood to one another and by judgment upon the main issues.

We believe that Churchill stayed with the Army till the very last moment that he dared—and he dared much. By the end of the council on the 23rd he had convinced himself that the military plot had failed; that there was no prospect that the English commanders would be able to go to the King and say in the name of the Army, "You must open negotiations with William, and you must call a free Parliament."

They had used, so far as it was possible, all their influence upon the troops without decisive results, and brought themselves into extreme peril thereby. Nothing remained but to escape with their immediate retinues and followers.

Therefore, on this same night Churchill, the Duke of Grafton, and Colonel Berkeley, with about four hundred officers and troopers, mounted their horses and rode forth from their camp by Salisbury. Some time during the 24th they arrived at Crewkerne, about twelve miles from William's headquarters at Axminster, after a march of nearly fifty miles.[1] Churchill left the following letter to the King behind him:

SIR,

Since men are seldom suspected of sincerity, when they act contrary to their interests, and though my dutiful behaviour to Your Majesty in the worst of times (for which I acknowledge my poor service is much overpaid) may not be sufficient to incline you to a charitable interpretation of my actions, yet I hope the great advantage I enjoy under Your Majesty, *which I own I can never expect in any other change of government,*[2] may reasonably convince Your Majesty and the world that I am actuated by a higher principle, when I offer that violence to my inclination and interest as to desert Your Majesty at a time when your affairs seem to challenge the strictest obedience from all your subjects, much more from one who lies under the greatest personal obligations to Your Majesty. This, sir, could proceed from nothing but the inviolable dictates of my conscience, and a necessary concern for my religion (which no good man can oppose), and with which I am instructed nothing can come in competition. Heaven knows with what partiality my dutiful opinion of Your Majesty has hitherto represented those unhappy designs which inconsiderate and self-interested men have framed against Your Majesty's true interest and the Protestant religion; but as I can no longer join with such to give a pretence by conquest to bring them to effect, so I

---

1 All historical and biographical authorities have hitherto stated that Churchill was only accompanied by a handful of adherents. The following letter of William's seems to show that he took a considerable body of officers with him.

William to Bentinck (*November 24/December 4, 1688*)

"A gentleman has just arrived to convey me Lord Bristol's respects, who said that in passing through Crochorn [Crewkerne], he found there Lord Churchill with about four hundred horses [? horse], all officers who are coming to join us." (*Correspondence of William and Portland,* i, 61.)

2 Author's italics.

will alway with the hazard of my life and fortune (so much Your
Majesty's due) endeavour to preserve your royal person and
lawful rights, with all the tender concerns and dutiful respect
that becomes, sir, Your Majesty's most dutiful and most obliged
subject and servant,

CHURCHILL[1]

In the records at Blenheim a copy of this letter was found
wrapped in another written by Prince George of Denmark,
no doubt at the same time and under Churchill's advice. But
the Prince, who, with Ormonde, deserted his father-in-law
the next day, takes a view which extends beyond the island
that had become his home; and for the first time we see how
large a part the Protestant coalition against France played
in the councils of the Cockpit.

"Whilst the restless spirits of the enemies of the reformed
religion," wrote the Prince,

backed by the cruel zeal and prevailing power of France justly
alarm and unite all the Protestant princes of Christendom and
engage them in so vast an expense for the support of it, can I
act so degenerate and mean a part as to deny my concurrence to
such worthy endeavours for disabusing of your Majesty by the
reinforcement of those laws and establishment of that government on which alone depends the well-being of your Majesty and
of the Protestant religion in Europe.

We have no doubt that these words expressed the deepest
convictions of Churchill as well as those of the honest Prince
who wrote them. James's ideal of England redeemed to the
true faith, dwelling in definitely established absolute monarchy, advancing independently, but in royal alliance with the
great King of France to the extirpation of Protestantism in
Europe, shone for him clear and bright. In the mind of his
servant there arose perhaps another picture more practical, not
less dire, not less majestic. John Churchill saw the rise of
Britain to the summit of Europe, curbing and breaking with
the aid of William of Orange the overweening power of
France. He saw himself, with the Dutchman if need be, or
under England's Protestant Princess, advancing at the head

1 Printed from the copy among the Blenheim MSS.

of armies to the destruction of that proud dominion. He may even have seen at this early time the building up upon the ruins of the French splendour of a British greatness which should spread far and wide throughout the world and set its stamp upon the future.

To William, Churchill's arrival at Axminster was an enormous relief. Next to defeat his deadliest danger was victory. (To avoid bloodshed, to avoid beating with foreign troops a British army in the field, was essential to his aim of securing the throne.) He welcomed his new adherent with formal ceremony, and used his services to the best advantage.

It is said in the *Life of James II* that when Churchill arrived at William's headquarters Marshal Schomberg greeted him with the remark "that he was the first Lieutenant-General he had ever heard that had deserted from his colours." But William's manifesto to the British Army had said:

> We hope likewise that you will not suffer yourselves to be abused by a false Notion of Honour, but that you will in the first place consider what you owe to Almighty God and your Religion, to your Country, to your selves, and to your Posterity, which you, as Men of Honour, ought to prefer to all private Considerations and Engagements whatsoever.

We can well understand the Jacobite exiles putting such a taunt in the mouth of Schomberg, but it seems unlikely that William's confidant and second-in-command should at this critical juncture have indulged in such an ill-timed and inconsistent affront. After all, Schomberg himself had, on this same cause of Protestantism, changed sides not as a Lieutenant-General, but as a Marshal of France, and no man lay more exposed than he to a rejoinder in kind.[1]

It cannot be proved that the defection of so many important officers destroyed the possibility that the army would fight. If a regular purge had been made, as Feversham proposed, and sergeants promoted to fill all vacancies in the commissioned ranks, if Catholic or French officers had been

---

1 Among the pictures which Marlborough collected at Holywell is one (now in Earl Spencer's possession) of Marshal Schomberg. It was painted specially for Marlborough, and it seems unlikely that he would have been at such pains to perpetuate in his own home the memory of a man who had offered him so blatant an insult on such a decisive occasion.

301

placed in the key commands, and if the King himself had led his soldiers to battle, it is probable that a most fierce and bloody event would have followed. But Churchill's desertion, followed as it was by that of his own relations and closest servants, broke the King's spirit. When he saw that he could not even keep the Churchill who had been till now his intimate, faithful servant for nearly a quarter of a century, he despaired. He collapsed morally, and from that moment thought only of sending his wife and child to France and following them as soon as possible. It is this fact, and the personal elements that entered into it, that have made Churchill's desertion of James at Salisbury, although compulsory and inevitable, the most poignant and challengeable action of his life.

And now revolt broke out all over the country. Danby was in arms in Yorkshire; Devonshire in Derby; Delamere in Cheshire. Lord Bath delivered Plymouth to William. Byng, a Rear-Admiral representing the captains under Dartmouth's command, arrived at his headquarters to inform him that the fleet and Portsmouth were at his disposal. City after city rose in rebellion. There was an eager rush of notabilities to greet the rising sun. By one universal, spontaneous convulsion the English nation repudiated James.

It was high time for the wives to do their part. Anne and Sarah had no mind to await the return of the indignant King. James sent orders to search both Churchill's houses, and to arrest Sarah. The Princess prevailed upon the Queen to delay the execution of this last order till the morning, and in the night the two women fled from the Cockpit. There are two theories upon this reasonable step: the first natural panic, and the second long-prepared design. Sarah in her account represents the Princess in a state of terror. She would rather "jump out of the window than face her father." Under her orders Sarah therefore made the best arrangements possible for immediate flight. "All was unconcerted." But this is not convincing. Anne knew that she herself was in no personal danger; her fears were for her beloved Mrs Freeman, who would certainly have borne the brunt of the royal anger. It had not been definitely settled whether when the crisis came Anne should leave the palace and seek protection in the City or whether she should try to join her husband in William's camp. The means of flight had been foreseen, and six weeks earlier a wooden staircase had been constructed from Anne's apartments to those of Sarah, which afforded an unguarded exit from the Cockpit. The Bishop of London was dwelling close at hand in conceal-ment, and Lord Dorset, whose romantic nature was attracted by such a service, was in constant touch with him. When the orders for Sarah's arrest were followed by sure news that Prince George had quitted King James, the two ladies were able to escape. In the dead of night they descended the wooden staircase, found the Bishop and Lord Dorset awaiting them, waded through the mud of Pall Mall, in which Anne lost her shoe, to Charing Cross, and thence were carried in a coach to the Bishop of London's residence in Aldersgate. After a brief halt they set out at daybreak for Dorset's beauti-ful Copt Hall, in the heart of Epping Forest. When their flight was discovered, Lady Clarendon and Anne's waiting-woman raised so loud an outcry that the Princess had been carried off, probably to be murdered by Papists, that the Queen and her household had no small difficulty in pacifying their own Guards. All search for the fugitives was vain, and when the unhappy King reached Whitehall in the afternoon, he could but exclaim in despair, "God help me! Even my children have forsaken me!"[1]

From Copt Hall the Princess and Sarah proceeded without delay to Nottingham. The Bishop, who had discarded his clerical attire, escorted them, armed with sword and pistols, a veritable embodiment of the Church militant here on earth. At Nottingham Devonshire was already in arms at the head of the nobility and gentlefolk of Derbyshire organized into about a thousand horse. The Princess was received with royal honours and rapture by the rebels, and warmly welcomed by

1 See *inter alia* Samuel Pepys' account in Dartmouth Papers, *H.M.C.*, xi, Appendix V, p. 214; Clarke, pp. 226–227; *Conduct*, pp. 17–18; Lediard, pp. 53–54; Clarendon, *Correspondence and Diary*, ii, 207.

the townsfolk. A Court was improvised and a banquet held. In default of servants the dragoon volunteers waited upon the guests, and one of them, Colley Cibber, the poet and playwright, has left us an impression of Sarah which is so vivid and agreeable that it demands inclusion.

We had not been many days at Nottingham, before we heard that the prince of Denmark, with some other great persons, were gone off from the king to the prince of Orange; and that the princess Anne, fearing that the king her father's resentment might fall upon her for her consort's revolt, had withdrawn herself in the night from London, and was then within half a day's journey of Nottingham; on which very morning we were suddenly alarmed with the news, that two thousand of the king's dragoons were in close pursuit to bring her back prisoner to London. But this alarm it seems was all stratagem and was but a part of that general terror which was thrown into many other places about the kingdom on the same time, with design to animate and unite the people in their common defence; it being then given out, that the Irish were everywhere at our heels, to cut off all the Protestants within the reach of their fury. In this alarm our troops scrambled to arms in as much order as their consternation would admit of; when, having advanced some few miles on the London road, they met the princess in a coach, attended only by the Lady Churchill (now duchess dowager of Marlborough), and the lady Fitzharding, whom they conducted into Nottingham through the acclamations of the people. The same night all the noblemen, and the other persons of distinction then in arms, had the honour to sup at her royal highness's table, which was then furnished (as all her necessary accommodations were) by the care and at the charge of the Lord Devonshire.

At this entertainment, of which I was a spectator, something very particular surprised me; the noble guests at the table happening to be more in number than attendants out of liveries could be found for, I, being well known in the lord Devonshire's family, was desired by his lordship's maitre d'hotel to assist at it. The post assigned me was to observe what the lady Churchill might call for. Being so near the table, you may naturally ask me what I might have heard to have passed in conversation at it; which I should certainly tell you, had I attended to above two words that were uttered there, and those were "Some wine and water."

These I remember came distinguished and observed to my ear because they came from the fair guest whom I took such pleasure to wait on. Except at that single sound all my senses were collected into my eyes, which during the whole entertainment wanted no better amusement than stealing now and then the delight of gazing on the fair object so near me. If so clear an emanation of beauty, such a commanding aspect of grace, struck me into a regard that had something softer than the most profound respect in it, I cannot see why I may not without offence remember it; such beauty, like the sun, must sometimes lose its power to choose, and shine into equal warmth the peasant and the courtier. . . . However presumptuous or impertinent these thoughts might have appeared at my first entertaining them, why may I not hope that my having kept them decently secret for full fifty years, may be now a good round plea for their pardon?[1]

We cannot think that Macaulay would have had any difficulty in blaming Churchill, whatever he did. As a Whig historian he is, of course, ardent for the Revolution. Of James he says:

During three years the King had been proof to all argument and to all entreaty. Every Minister who had dared to raise his voice in favour of the civil and ecclesiastical Constitution of the realm had been disgraced. A Parliament eminently loyal had ventured to protest gently and respectfully against a violation of the fundamental laws of England, and had been sternly reprimanded, prorogued, and dissolved. Judge after Judge had been stripped of the ermine for declining to give decisions opposed to the whole common and statute law. The most respectable Cavaliers had been excluded from all share in the government of their counties for refusing to betray the public liberties. Scores of clergymen had been deprived of their livelihood for observing their oaths. Prelates, to whose steadfast fidelity the King owed the crown which he wore, had on their knees besought him not to command them to violate the laws of God and of their land. Their modest petition had been treated as a seditious libel. They had been browbeaten, threatened, imprisoned, prosecuted and had narrowly escaped utter ruin. Then at length the nation, finding that right was borne down by might, and that even supplication was regarded as a crime, began to think of trying the chances of war.[2]

1 *An Apology for the Life of Mr Colley Cibber* (1740), pp. 57–59.
2 *History*, ii, 469–470.

Yet when Churchill obeyed this imperious call and took the action which enabled a good cause to triumph without the shedding of English blood, Macaulay denounces him with all the pungent rhetoric and elaborate scorn of which he is master. Now all rebellion is treason. To be guilty of treason is to be a traitor. Nineteen-twentieths of England, we are assured, were at this time traitors. Apparently this almost universal crime was only infamous in one man. For all the others Macaulay makes ample excuses; nay, they are glorified. The bishops, begged by the harassed sovereign for succour and accorded their every request, refused even to make a pronouncement against the invader. Fine spirit among the bishops! A regiment, asked to proclaim its readiness to fight for the enforcement of the Tests, threw down its arms. Patriotic feeling among the troops! Bishop Compton, taxed by James with having signed the invitation to William, avoided the lie direct by an ingenious subterfuge. "Sir," he said, "I am quite confident that there is not one of my brethren who is not as guiltless as myself in this matter." Questioned again the next day when all the others had denied, he said, "I gave your Majesty my answer yesterday." "The equivocation," says Macaulay, "was ingenious." He had "parried the question with an adroitness which a Jesuit might have envied." How clever!

Danby seized York. He spread a rumour that the Papists (of whom scarcely any existed in the neighbourhood) were up and were slaying the Protestants, and then rode to the rescue of the city at the head of a hundred horsemen crying, "No Popery! A free Parliament! The Protestant religion!" On this wave he disarmed the garrison and placed the governor under arrest. But what was this? Rebellion, treason, lying propaganda; sharp practice by any computation? No, says Macaulay, "Danby acted with rare dexterity." To ride into a peaceful city after having terrified the inhabitants with the shameful falsehood that their lives were in danger, and then to disarm the faithful officers and guardians of the King's peace, is described as "rare dexterity." The peers, who by scores had been conspiring, intriguing, and preparing

LITTLE ROCK PUBLIC LIBRARY

for active rebellion against James for six months past, had all sworn the Oath of Allegiance on taking their seats in the Upper House. But here Macaulay shows us how civic duty rightly overrides mere ceremonial obligations. He invites us to admire all these perjured nobles. They struck for England in a good cause without being hampered by the pedantry of scruple. The Lord-Lieutenants were the King's personal representatives, and special obligations of fidelity rested upon them. Yet how manly, how enlightened, how public-spirited they were in such large numbers to desert and abandon King James, once it was quite clear how the event was going! The oath of a Privy Councillor is more solemn and explicit even than the oath of a Lord-Lieutenant. Macaulay places his tinsel chaplets on the brows of every Privy Councillor who worked for James's undoing and expulsion.

From this universal commendation there is but one exception. In Churchill all resistance to James was shameful. Because he did not immediately go to James and, falling on both knees, declare, "I am opposed to Your Majesty, I am therefore a traitor, put me to death," he is a scoundrel—nay, more; he is the only scoundrel in England! What in all others was the hard but sacred duty of sustaining civil and religious liberty without regard to personal or party ties, in Churchill becomes the most infamous trick of the seventeenth century. What in all others was the broad heave of the British shoulders against insufferable burdens and injury, in him is the extremity of personal dishonour. What in all the rest is rightful, salutary action in a great crisis, in Churchill is "a dark conspiracy." But for Churchill's action, England would have been drenched with English blood—yet he alone is the villain. The event is glorious: the instrument dishonoured. The end was indispensable to British freedom: the means, we are assured, were disgraceful to Churchill's character. The relief and joy of the nation that an inevitable revolution was accomplished without the agony of civil war have resounded through the ages; and with them echo the censures upon the one man whose action, and whose only possible action, brought so great a blessing.

307

The King, having assembled such peers and Privy Councillors as were still in London, was advised by them to enter into negotiations with the Prince of Orange and to accord an amnesty to all who had joined him. He nominated Halifax, Nottingham, and Godolphin as his Commissioners to treat with William. He did not know that Halifax and Nottingham had both been privy to William's design. Neither did Halifax know that the King had no intention to treat, and was only using the negotiations as the means of gaining time to send his wife and child abroad and to follow them himself. William, on his part, was in no hurry, and more than a week passed before the necessary safe-conducts were granted to the Commissioners, and they were conducted to his headquarters, which had now reached Hungerford. Meanwhile James had sent his infant heir to Portsmouth with orders to Dartmouth to send him at once to France. Dartmouth, for all his loyalty, refused to obey this fatal command, which he declared would render him "guilty of treason to Your Majesty and the known laws of the kingdom." "Pardon me therefore, Sir," he wrote from Spithead on December 3,

if on my bended knees, I beg of you to apply yourself to other counsels; for the doing this looks like nothing less than despair to the degree of not only giving your enemies encouragement, but distrust of your friends and people, who I do not despair but will yet stand by you, in the defence and right of your lawful successor. . . . Pray, Sir, consider further on this weighty point: For can the Prince's being sent to France, have other prospect than the entailing a perpetual war upon your nation and posterity; and giving France always a temptation to molest, invade, nay hazard the conquest of England, which I hope in God never to see. . . .[1]

But James was not to be deterred. The baby Prince was brought back from Portsmouth, and on the night of December 9 the Queen, escorted only by Count Lauzun and Riva, an Italian gentleman, escaped, with her child, to Gravesend and thence to France. As soon as the King knew that his wife and son were safely off he prepared to follow them.

[1] Dalrymple, ii, Part II, 246.

LITTLE ROCK PUBLIC LIBRARY

THE REVOLUTION

Elaborate arrangements having been made to deceive the Court and the Council, the King stole from the palace an hour or two after midnight on December 11, crossed the river, and rode hard for the coast. He endeavoured to plunge his realm into anarchy. He threw the Great Seal into the Thames; and sent orders to Feversham to disband the Army, and to Dartmouth to sail with what ships he could for Irish ports. Dartmouth, stricken to the heart by his master's desertion of his post, placed the fleet under the orders of William. But Feversham, with reckless wickedness, scattered the soldiers, unpaid but not disarmed, upon the population. General consternation ensued. The King's Commissioners saw they had been befooled. The wildest rumours of impending Irish massacres spread through the land. The London mob sacked the foreign embassies, and every one seized arms in defence of hearth and home. A wild panic and terror, long remembered as "Irish Night," swept the capital. Undoubtedly a complete collapse of civil government would have occurred but for the resolute action of the Council, which was still sitting in London. With difficulty they suppressed the storm, and, acknowledging William's authority, besought him to hasten his marches to London.

But the very next day, while the Council was sitting, a poor countryman arrived at the door with an appealing message from the King. James had actually got on board a ship, but, missing the tide, was caught, mauled, grabbed, and dragged ashore by the Faversham fishermen and townsfolk, who took him for a Jesuit in flight. What followed is briefly and well told by Ailesbury, who gives unconsciously a picture which historians seem to have missed. Ailesbury had striven hard to dissuade James from his flight, and when the news that the fugitive had been intercepted at the coast was brought to the decapitated Council, he broke the prolonged silence by proposing that his Majesty should be invited to return forthwith to his post. Charged with this task, he set out by coach and a-horse to retrieve his master out of the hands of the mob at Sheerness. He was haughtily received by the royal captive. His high jack-boots prevented him from falling on

309

his knees when entering the presence, and he could only bob his knee. Whereat James, unshaven, ill-fed, rounded up and put in the pound like an errant bull by the local townsfolk and seamen, but unshakably sure of his royal rights, remarked, "Ha! It was all Kings when I left London." To this reception at the end of his loyal and difficult journey through the turbulent, panic-stricken towns of Kent and by roadways infested with revolt and disorder Ailesbury—so he tells us—used some extremely plain language, to which his sovereign was graciously pleased to hearken. He then proceeded to collect some victuals, bake the best bread possible in the circumstances, and ask the King whether he would not dine in state. His Majesty signified his pleasure; the local dignitaries and some of the populace were admitted wonder-struck to the miserable dwelling, and the faithful Gentleman of the Bedchamber, jack-boots notwithstanding, managed (by holding on to the table) to serve him on the knee; thus restoring public confidence and decorum. At intervals throughout the day fragments of the disrupted royal household arrived in Romney. The barber, with the valets and clothes, arrived in the afternoon; the cooks a little later. The Board of Green Cloth was on the spot by dusk; the royal saddle-horses came in during the night, and a troop of Life Guards were reported approaching the next morning. Thus the Court was reconstituted, though in a somewhat skeleton state.

Ailesbury stayed by his master thenceforward. He arranged for a hundred troopers of the Life Guards to be drawn up in single file to encourage him with their acclamations. He persuaded James to drive through the City of London, where the people, perplexed and dumbfounded by the awful event of his flight, received him with relief and almost enthusiasm. He accompanied James from Whitehall when, at William's order, he was escorted by the Dutch Guard down the river to Rochester. He shared with him the peril of the "hideous shooting of the bridge" on the swift, outflowing tide. Once this danger was overcome, the royal party picnicked agreeably in the boats, the King passing food and wine to the Dutch captain of the convoying flotilla.

310

Ailesbury abode with the King at Rochester, and again endeavoured to prevent his leaving the island. William, who had been profoundly inconvenienced by his return and longed for his fresh departure, caused hints to reach him that his life was in danger. James, no physical coward—indeed, as we have seen, a proved veteran by sea and land—was cowed to his marrow by the overwhelming tide of adverse opinion and the wholesale desertion and repudiation of almost all on whom he had counted. After some days of painful suspense the unhappy man escaped to the river by the back door, which the Prince of Orange had taken pains to leave unguarded, and this time succeeded in leaving English soil for ever. We are told in his so-called memoirs that he expected he would be sent to the Tower, "which no King ever quitted except for his grave," and he felt it his sacred duty to preserve his royal person from such outrageous possibilities.

But though the downfall and flight of this impolitic grandson of Henry of Navarre were at the time ignominious, his dignity has been restored to him by history. Heredity, fatalism, the besetting Stuart infatuation of obstinacy, his stern religious faith, his convinced patriotism according to his lights, all combined to lead him to disaster. He was doomed alike by his upbringing, his office, and his nature. His fixed domestic ideas made an effective foreign policy impossible. His Catholic convictions left him a stubborn anomaly upon a Protestant throne. He was at once a capable administrator and a suicidal politician; a man virtuous in principle and gross in practice; a personage equally respectable and obnoxious. Yet he carried with him into lifelong exile an air of royalty and honour which still clings to his memory.

On the afternoon of December 23 William learned that the King had fled, and felt himself in one form or another undisputed master of England. He lost no time in taking the step for the sake of which he had come across the water. The French Ambassador was given twenty-four hours to be gone from the island, and England was committed to the general coalition against France.